WORLD WATCHER

On Manufacturing War

DIANA JOHNSTONE

Clarity Press, Inc.

Clarity Press, Inc.
2625 Piedmont Rd. NE, Ste. 56
Atlanta, GA 30324, USA
https://www.claritypress.com

Praise for *World Watcher*

"As a young journalist in the early 1990s I discovered the work of Diana Johnstone in the publication *In These Times.* Here was the European correspondent I was looking for. Having lived eight years in Europe in the 1980s, I was bitterly disappointed in the dispatches from Europe in the *New York Times* and *Washington Post.* Johnstone was a reporter who didn't push the U.S. agenda, as those papers did, but took an independent view of American behavior (and European subservience) abroad. That will banish you to the margins. Fortunately that meant publishing much of her extraordinary work in the pages of *Consortium News,* which I edit. From her groundbreaking reporting on the wars that broke up Yugoslavia, to the Russophobia that fueled Russiagate and NATO's war in Ukraine against Moscow, Diana Johnstone is a treasure of American journalism who has left a legacy of reporting, the likes of which we may never see again, that corrects the record of decades of American malfeasance in Europe. You will not see the history of the past half century the same after reading the articles in this book."

JOE LAURIA, editor-in-chief, *Consortium News,* former *Boston Globe, Sunday Times of London* and *Wall Street Journal* correspondent

"Diana Johnstone is a brilliant longtime observer and journalist who seeks to understand, at the deepest level, what is happening in our world's geopolitics—and is particularly critical of U.S. policy and influence since WWII. I highly recommend this to a new generation wanting to understand our times and destiny."

OLIVER STONE

"Diana Johnstone has written another excellent book. *World Watcher: On Manufacturing War* is essential to understanding our time."

PAUL CRAIG ROBERTS

"Few writers have illuminated the inner workings of power and social movements with more clarity and insight than Diana Johnstone. A brilliant and gifted writer, her work has long been essential reading. *World Watcher* showcases her mastery of complex topics and penetrating analysis into the roots of our imperial decay and assault on what is left of our open societies."

CHRIS HEDGES

More Praise

"Diana Johnston's new book is a tour d'horizon over the labyrinth of lies and narratives that impact our consciousness and instill in us a justified fear of apocalypse. As opinions are manufactured, so too are false heroes, the excuses for aggression, the caricatures of purported enemies, Trotskyist illusions, pandemic dystopias, etc. Johnstone challenges the reader with her lucid analysis of the Gaza genocide, the power of the Israel Lobby, the decadence of the European Union, the ICC cover-up of imperialist crimes, Washington's addiction to war. She asks questions that are shunned by the mainstream media, gives answers that may shock you."

ALFRED DE ZAYAS, Independent UN Expert and
author, *Building a Just World Order*

"Diana Johnstone is without question among the most distinguished journalists of her generation. She is that rare professional who achieves the high, thinly populated ground wherein journalists meet public intellectuals, historians, philosophers, and littérateurs. *World Watcher* ranges widely and wisely. I love this book for its sure-footed variety. Johnstone's mind and pen move with ease and always with worthy insight from the Russian Revolution to European politics—her pieces on Germany and Yugoslavia are especially pithy—through to 9/11, terrorism, 'conspiracy theories,' and Joe Biden's excesses. This is a not-to-be-missed display of the exceptional breadth of Johnstone's work and the depth of her thinking over many decades."

PATRICK LAWRENCE, *The Floutist*

Table of Contents

PART I: Political Ideas | 1

1. The West and the Russian Revolution: A Century
   of Counter-Revolution 3
   APRIL 2017

2. In Defense of Conspiracy Theory 14
   SEPTEMBER 2006

3. ICC: Imperialist Crimes Cover-up 21
   JUNE 2011

4. Antifa In Theory and In Practice 25
   OCTOBER 2017

5. Trotskyist Delusions: Obsessed with Stalin, They See
   Betrayed Revolutions Everywhere. 30
   MAY 2018

6. The Lynching of the Charismatic Geek 35
   NOVEMBER 2019

7. The Great Pretext … for Dystopia 38
   A review of *Covid-19: The Great Reset,* by
   Klaus Schwab and Thierry Malleret
   NOVEMBER 2020

PART II: Yugoslavia | 47

1. Seeing Yugoslavia Through a Dark Glass 49
   AUGUST 1998

2. Alija Izetbegovic: Islamic Hero of the Western World 72
   JULY 1999

3. NATO's Humanitarian Trigger. 83
   MARCH 1999

4. The Lie of a Good War. 88
    JUNE 2004

5. NATO's Kosovo Colony 95
    FEBRUARY 2008

6. Richard Holbrooke, Opportunist Extraordinary. 105
    DECEMBER 2010

7. Srebrenica Revisited 109
    OCTOBER 2005

PART III: The Near East | 123

1. Libya War: The Key Question 125
    DECEMBER 2011

2. Turning the Cradle of Civilization into its Graveyard 132
    SEPTEMBER 2015

3. The Political Vulnerability and Impunity of the
    Israel Lobby 137
    MARCH 2018

4. Foul Murder of Another Nation's Hero 144
    JANUARY 2020

5. Gaza Genocide Meets French Devotion to Israel 146
    SEPTEMBER 2024

PART IV: U.S. Politics | 157

1. The Bad Losers and What They Fear Losing. 159
    DECEMBER 2016

2. Trump was elected by Russia? Mass Dementia in the
    Western Establishment. 165
    JULY 2018

3. The 2020 Election: Bourgeois Democracy Meets
    Global Governance 170
    AUGUST 2020

4. Biden Exploits his Capitol Gains. 178
    JANUARY 2021

PART V: European Politics | 183

1. Greece: Down and Out on the European Animal Farm . . . 185
   MARCH 2010

2. The Winners-Take-All Regime of Emmanuel Macron . . . 189
   APRIL 2017

3. Disobedient Hungary: From the Soviet to the
   European Union 197
   SEPTEMBER 2018

4. Brexit: England Came and Went 202
   JANUARY 2020

5. France Stuck in the Extreme Center 206
   APRIL 2022

PART VI: Perpetuating War in Europe | 215

1. Washington's Iron Curtain in Ukraine 217
   JUNE 2014

2. To Understand or Not to Understand Putin 225
   MAY 2014

3. The West Displays its Insecurity Complex 229
   FEBRUARY 2020

4. Revanchism: Replaying the End of World War II as
   World War III 235
   SEPTEMBER 2022

5. Omerta in the NATO Gangster War 245
   SEPTEMBER 2022

6. Germans Down, Russians Out 249
   MARCH 2023

7. Bear Baiting: U.S. Foreign Policy is a Cruel Sport 257
   FEBRUARY 2023

8. D-Day 2024: A Reversal of Alliances 262
   JUNE 2024

9. For Washington, War Never Ends 270
   MARCH 2022

— PART I —
POLITICAL IDEAS

The West and the Russian Revolution: A Century of Counter-Revolution*

APRIL 2017

Lenin foresaw that revolution in Russia would trigger communist revolution in Germany and from there throughout the Western industrialized world. This was the Bolshevik leader's major error of appreciation. In reality, the Bolshevik Revolution was the start of a century of counter-revolution in the West. Lenin and his fellow Russian exiles imagined revolution as a way of incorporating Russia into the advanced but henceforth socialist West. Instead, they alienated it as never before. A revolution intended to bring an era of world peace ushered in an era of bitter conflict and war.

Isolated in a backward nation, Bolshevik leaders held onto power by repressive measures that largely defined the Soviet Union in the eyes of the West, blacking out any recognition of the revolution's positive achievements.

There was always a misunderstanding on all sides of what the revolution really was and really did. Theoretically, in Marxist terms, the proletariat, on the basis of its objective material interests, would lead a fundamental social revolution, leading to a classless society. The classic model was the bourgeois revolution that overthrew the nobility. This comparison was wishful thinking, if only because the so-called bourgeoisie throughout civilized history had always been a partner in the ruling class. Despite the momentary success of the soviets (councils), power was never taken by the proletariat but by intellectuals acting in

---

*Original version: *Monthly Review,* April 14, 2017. https://monthlyreview.org/2017/07/01/the-western-left-and-the-russian-revolution/

its name, mobilizing the working class to achieve rapid industrialization. The extensive appropriations and debt defaults involved in creating a national economy enraged Western capitalists and shareholders, but their implacable hostility was linked also to the fear generated by communist ideology, which was far from descriptive of the Soviet reality. The ideological superstructure is a vastly greater political motivating factor than the conscious self-interest of capitalists. As a matter of fact, there were always capitalists who did business with the Soviet Union, quite oblivious to the taboos propagated by the ideological superstructure. Capitalism is a system, not an <ideology. It can live with various ideologies.

More than the reality, ideology generated enthusiasm and hostility.

Portrayed in the West as a sort of hell on earth, the image of Communist Russia functioned for a century to idealize the West, excuse its faults and provide a pretext for its crimes of aggression. A persistent aspect of the counter-revolution was the identification of "freedom" with capitalism.

For a century, the counter-revolution has arguably been the most determining ideological factor in Western politics, as it has shifted drastically from one form to another. One hundred years after the Russian Revolution, the victory of the counter-revolution is complete. But Western powers still need their inherited antithesis, in changing form, as self-justification.

Quite varying forms of counter-revolutionary ideology can be enumerated.

1. Conservative Reaction

Simple conservative reaction, nostalgic for the prerevolutionary past, such as predominated in the reaction against the French Revolution, was relatively insignificant in a period when the established order had been shaken to the core by the slaughter of World War I. In Russia itself, it was defeated in the civil war. The influence of the conservative aristocratic emigration was mitigated by fatalism and lingering Russian patriotism, and had less political influence on the West than disappointed revolutionaries, whose anger over a confiscated future had more resonance in the West than Tsarist nostalgia.

In the West, the Catholic Church played a significant role in the conservative counter-revolution, and was the leading ideological factor behind Franco and Salazar. The Spanish civil war was the sole occasion where the Soviet Union actively intervened against the counterrevolution in the West. It is significant that this intervention took place in defense of an existing government, that is, with a respect for the status quo that is characteristic of Moscow foreign policy to this day.

In the United States, the reaction against the Bolshevik revolution was a continuation of the violent repression of worker struggles, in the late nineteenth century, which had taken on a particularly nationalist coloration with the persecution of socialists during the First World War, many of them of German origin, stigmatized as "agents of the Kaiser." In his war message, President Woodrow Wilson specifically cast suspicion on the loyalty of the "millions of men and women of German birth" living in the United States. Socialist leader Eugene Debs was sentenced to ten years in prison for opposing U.S. participation in the war.

In the subsequent Red Scare, the Palmer raids targeted Russian and other recent immigrants. The second anniversary of the Bolshevik revolution on November 7, 1919 was the occasion for violent raids against the Union of Russian Workers. In a nation with such a large proportion of immigrant labor, the reaction readily identified communists as "agents of a foreign power." Social radicalism could be denounced as a threat to a vague "Americanism," a notion that the repression helped to forge. The fact that Bolsheviks actually took State power in a great nation and thereupon founded the Third International, pledged to carry out revolution everywhere, inevitably led hostile governments to condemn communism as a form of "treason" on behalf of a foreign power.

In Europe, the conservative reaction was rooted in long traditions, with very contrasting attitudes, including a bourgeoisie and a working class both largely conscious of their respective class interests, as well as a certain anti-bourgeois aristocratic attitude which was capable of mixed feelings toward liberal bourgeois domination.

In the United States, anti-communism helped to define and strengthen "Americanism" as a negative nationalism, supported by Christian fear of "atheistic communism" with its supposed origins in European depravity.

In the United States, anti-communism was based heavily on xenophobia and Christianity in the very classes whose interests were not identical with those of the ruling class. This anti-communism based on a vague "Americanism" held over even into the depressed 1930s, when the Communist Party USA actually succeeded in influencing the labor movement and in the struggle for black rights. This narrow nationalism has helped keep class-consciousness a nearly exclusive upper class trait.

2. Fascism: The counter-mobilization of masses in industrial society

The catastrophe of the Great War plunged leading European conservative thinkers, exemplified by Ortega y Gasset, Paul Valéry and Oswald Spengler, into a deep pessimism concerning the future of Western civilization. The counter-revolution in Europe was in part a reaction to this pessimistic fatalism by resolute imposition of a collective strong will.

Contrary to the uncomplicated repression of "alien communism" in the United States, in the name of "traditional values," Fascism was a genuine counter-revolution, a new "religion," according to its founder Benito Mussolini. But Fascism was most directly opposed to Bolshevism because both were militant mass movements led by dogmatic single parties.

The Fascist reaction can be seen as an effort to counter the decline of the West by mobilizing the masses to reinvigorate a capitalism that war had brought into greater symbiosis with the State. While Bolshevism mobilized the masses to build an industrial society practically from scratch, Fascism set out to save capitalism from its own weaknesses. The fear of expropriation incited capitalists to accept Fascism as it organized the masses for efficient capitalist development without class conflict.

For Mussolini, violence was not only utilitarian but philosophical as well, a necessary demonstration of vigor. The use of violence, especially of organized militia, to repress opponents is a fundamental element of Fascism.

Fascism also belonged to the heyday of industrialization and its creation of masses that could be mobilized for direct political action.

Today, the term "fascist" is thrown around freely, as an all-purpose invective. But it is not applicable without these two elements: an ideological appeal to mass mobilization and the use of violence to achieve political ends. It is scarcely appropriate in today's ultra-individualistic society where the only "mass" to be found is in mass media and its rule by image.

While Italian Fascism was largely theatrical, the German National Socialist version of Fascism focused seriously on destroying Bolshevism, the Soviet Union and the Jews, identified as responsible for all Germany's ills. Here too, capitalism was fostered but submitted to State control. Thanks to the success of the Nazi blitzkrieg against Western nations, the Wehrmacht's invasion of the Soviet Union eventually forced the liberal Western propaganda campaign into a temporary truce with the communist enemy, as the West was obliged to ally with the Red Army in self-defense. Ironically, this interlude led to a new phase of hostility after the war, under the term "totalitarianism," which equated Stalin with Hitler and communism with fascism, leading to a more virulent form of anti-communism than before.

3. Trotskyism and the Permanent Counter-Revolution

In the West, Trotskyism has played a huge ideological role, especially in France and, in different forms, in the United States. The influence of Trotskyism is paradoxical in many ways.

The first paradox is that the followers of Trotsky, the champion of "permanent revolution," ended up being considered less dangerous by Western governments than the "Stalinists," who were condemned by Trotsky for abandoning world revolution in favor of "socialism in one country." In retrospect, one may say that both Stalin and Trotsky were wrong as to what was possible, but Stalin was the more realistic of the two. Despite their relative ideological conservatism, the "Stalinist" parties of the Third International had more success abroad than their Trotskyist rivals, both in promoting national liberation struggles in the Third World and in obtaining social benefits in the West.

With their doctrine of permanent revolution, Trotskyist groups eagerly supported Third World revolutions, despite their links to the "failed" Russian revolution, until they too "failed." Most Trotkyist groups have fallen for the sectarian self-righteousness that has contributed to transforming the current "left" into powerless moralizers.

The "Failed Revolution" Narrative

Many leftists and self-styled revolutionaries in the West lacked all realism about the conditions of "revolution" in Russia or Vietnam. Although led by Communist Parties, neither was exactly a socialist revolution for different reasons.

A century later, it is still hard to view the Russian Revolution outside the ideological framework of either its champions or its adversaries. The fact that the revolution did not turn out to be the first step toward establishment of a true socialist society with freedom and equality does not mean that it was "betrayed." Rather, history had its own dynamic and the dynamic betrayed the revolution. The failure to live up to ideal expectations simply means that the revolution turned out to be something else, which indeed had socialist aspects, but was neither communism nor "the dictatorship of the proletariat." The Russian revolution was led by intellectuals all the way, and the revolution they carried out was primarily the industrial revolution. An industrial revolution led by intellectuals naturally led to extraordinary advances in public education and science, but had the corresponding faults of ideological rigidity and bureaucracy. In an undisciplined peasant country, modernization was forced by repression, and the reigning dogmatism tended to attribute incompetence to deliberate sabotage—just as enemies of the revolution attributed incompetence to evil intent (e.g., the Ukrainian nationalist myth of the "Holodomor").

The leadership's paranoid tendencies were aggravated by the unremitting hostility of Western governments, contributing to what Jean Bricmont calls "the barricade effect"[1], the tendency to become still more defensive, closed and suspicious, as well as repressive of internal dissent, identified with the foreign enemy.

It has become dogma to denigrate Western Communists ("Stalinists") for their blind faith in the Soviet revolution. They are widely dismissed as useless idiots who contributed to upholding a tyrannical system of oppression, and the example of such blind faith is held up as "proof" that opposition to "the system" (whatever it is) can only lead to disaster. The lesson drawn is social conformism.

But both its enthusiastic admirers and its deadly enemies nursed a mistaken impression of what the Russian Revolution really was. The errors of appreciation of its enemies do not encounter the same condemnation as those of its ardent supporters.

Fear in the West was exacerbated by misinterpretation of the notion of "world revolution" in terms of military conquest. The facts indicated the exact opposite. The first international steps of the Bolshevik regime were to give up territory in the haste to make peace. The Bolsheviks never planned to export revolution by force. Rather, at first, they nursed the expectation that the West would come to them, thanks to the revolutionary action of the Western working class. Western leaders and opinion-makers preferred to interpret revolutionary rhetoric as the harbinger of physical attack, by violent subversion or even invasion. This confusion was exacerbated by illusions on all sides. In the United States, much

---

1 Jean Bricmont, *Humanitarian Imperialism: Using Human Rights to Sell War,* English Ed. (Monthly Review Press, 2007).

was made of the expression "overthrow of the government by force and violence" which never had the remotest relevance to reality.

The revolution took place in a vast, economically backward nation emerging from a lost war. The Bolshevik revolution was a major social experiment in a country that needed one. Mass education, social welfare measures, advancement of women were accomplishments that should be appreciated even by today's uncertain standards. A realistic observer, such as Bertrand Russell, could distinguish the positive from the negative and offer constructive criticism. But the West split between uncritical devotees (an isolated minority) and official demonization of Bolshevism as inherently evil and, moreover, a threat to the West of a military as well as an ideological nature.[2]

If it could not be a model for Western socialism, the Soviet Union did indeed serve as a model for Third World countries, especially in East Asia. For intellectuals like Ho Chi Minh, the search for the secret of Western power led eventually to Marxism and the Soviet Union. And indeed, in Vietnam communism was a form of Westernization at the same time that it was a recovery of the nation's independence—something the West was unable to grasp.

In regard to reunited Vietnam, as in regard to the Soviet Union, enthusiasts who had become perfectionists turned into adversaries of the revolution when it failed to meet their expectations. Later, under the banner of Human Rights, they transferred this hostility subsequently not only to Vietnam but in general to Third World governments that had emerged from liberation struggles, often with communist support or pretensions.

Especially in France, the critical stance toward "the Revolution that failed" has never ceased to appeal to intellectuals for whom it preserved their ideal from the hard test of reality. It continues to nourish sectarian condemnation of rival leftists and notably of "dictators" denounced by the United States, at times leading to unnatural de facto alliance between former would-be communist revolutionaries and U.S. military aggression.

The Trotskyist stance, criticizing the revolution for not being revolutionary enough, provided a radical leftist basis for the human rights ideology that has become the religion of the West. This ultra-left attitude contributed to the drastic reversal of positions within the left following

---

2 *The Practice and Theory of Bolshevism* (1920), 3rd edition (Spokesman Books, 1995).

the end of the Vietnam liberation war, which had been enthusiastically supported by left forces throughout the world, notably in the West.

The French public relations campaign in support of Vietnamese "boat people" can be seen as a marker in this transition. The Khmer rouge class revenge massacres aroused a reaction against Third World revolutions, but nobody could accuse Pol Pot of not being revolutionary enough; and moreover, it was communist Vietnam that defeated the Khmer Rouge. The exemplary struggle was that of Vietnam, it had become the ideal, and moreover, the victory of Hanoi led to "re-education" rather than the massive blood bath predicted by the imperialists. It was the "boat people" plight that initiated the Western "disappointment" with Vietnam.

In France, a significant number of May '68 "revolutionaries" re-educated themselves as they pursued successful careers in the media and academia, spreading their disillusioned rancor against the revolutions they once celebrated through the nation's public discourse.

One ironic effect of the Trotskyist critique has not been to promote the permanent revolution, but rather to promote the permanent counter-revolution, in one form or another.

By far the strangest and most exotic example of this metamorphosis is provided by a fairly small but extraordinarily influential American cohort of prewar Trotskyists whose hostility toward Stalinism reached fever-pitch in reaction to alleged mistreatment of Jews in the Soviet Union, after their revolutionary ideal shifted to Israel. After successfully campaigning to get the United States to punish the USSR for restricting educated Jewish emigration to Israel, these activists transformed themselves into the "neoconservatives" who today dominate U.S. foreign policy.[3] All that remains of Trotskyism is devotion to the idea of "permanent

---

3   "Most neoconservative defense intellectuals have their roots on the left, not the right. They are products of the influential Jewish-American sector of the Trotskyist movement of the 1930s and 1940s, which morphed into anticommunist liberalism between the 1950s and 1970s and finally into a kind of militaristic and imperial right with no precedents in American culture or political history. Their admiration for the Israeli Likud party's tactics, including preventive warfare such as Israel's 1981 raid on Iraq's Osirak nuclear reactor, is mixed with odd bursts of ideological enthusiasm for 'democracy.' They call their revolutionary ideology 'Wilsonianism' (after President Woodrow Wilson), but it is really Trotsky's theory of the permanent revolution mingled with the far-right Likud strain of Zionism. Genuine American Wilsonians believe in self-determination for people such as the Palestinians."—Michael Lind, "How Neoconservatives Conquered Washington—and Launched a War," *Antiwar.com,* April 10, 2003. http://www.antiwar.com/orig/lind1.html

revolution"—the permanent revolution of neoliberalism under the banner of Human Rights. In short, the permanent counter-revolution.

4. Human Rights Against Revolution

After the failure of its war in Vietnam, and the related normalization of relations with China by the Nixon administration, the United States engaged in a major ideological shift. In the early 1970s, the United States used the Conference on Security and Cooperation in Europe to redefine its enemy. Under the cover of détente with Moscow, this East-West conference agreed on measures supposedly designed to promote lasting peace. The Helsinki Final Act signed in 1975 endorsed the inviolability of frontiers, territorial integrity of States and non-intervention in internal affairs of other States (measures designed to reassure Moscow, still fearful of German revanchism). However, that last principle was subtly challenged by Washington's new favorite "value": respect for human rights. While seemingly confirming the status quo, this led to a new phase of indirect U.S. interference in the internal affairs of others, no longer in the name of anticommunism but rather as defense of human rights. In 1978, the United States founded the Helsinki Watch group to monitor respect for human rights in Soviet bloc countries. Ten years later Helsinki Watch evolved into Human Rights Watch, whose watchfulness continues to focus on countries where the United States is likely to favor regime change.

This was a major turnaround. From now on, instead of accusing Moscow of sponsoring "subversion" of Western democracies, the United States itself instead turned to subversion of governments accused of "violating human rights."

In practice, NATO intervention in Yugoslavia twenty years later proved that the "human rights" principle could be and was used to destroy territorial integrity of existing States.

5. Social Democracy: The Dependent Rival

The relationship between Soviet communism and Western social democracy is particularly paradoxical. In the post-World War II period of Western recovery and prosperity, Social Democrats had cause for great satisfaction at the improvement of workers' conditions, which they attributed largely to themselves. It was a commonplace among European social democrats to wish for the collapse of the Soviet Union, which gave a bad reputation to "socialism." Without the Soviet Union, they maintained, the march toward real socialism in the West could accelerate and triumph.

Precisely the opposite occurred. The collapse of the Soviet Union has led to the erosion of Western social democracy and the triumph, material and ideological, of the most ruthless reign of finance capitalism and its partner, militarism.

So it becomes clear in retrospect that, favored by the boom of postwar reconstruction, Europe's triumphant social democracy was also a minor element in the counter-revolution, in that it served to woo the working class away from more revolutionary parties inspired by the Bolshevik revolution.

The Counter-Revolution Survives the Revolution

Meanwhile, on the pretext of "defense" against an imaginary "Communist threat," the United States' economic substructure as well as its ideological superstructure were totally subjected to the demands of the ubiquitous Military Industrial Complex. Communism was the pretext that allowed U.S. financial capitalism to feed indefinitely off the government-insured profits of a gluttonous arms industry. This capitalist counter-revolution grew into such an independent monstrosity that it no longer needed its original enemy: anything would do. It can be used to redesign the Middle East for the benefit of Israel, on the grounds of fighting terrorism, or to destroy whole countries on the grounds of the "Responsibility to Protect." Identifying "violations of human rights" as the enemy is a more all-purpose pretext than anticommunism, as thanks to human frailty it can be applied against practically any country in the world, with the help of complacent mass media ready to arouse public indignation over the latest timely outrage.

The cause of Human Rights has been central in morally disarming the left and turning its attention from the struggle for economic equality to individual freedoms. It goes without saying that any social revolution will violate the established "rights" of the dominant classes, and thus Human Rights is a permanently counter-revolutionary doctrine.

At present we are in a phase where the counter-revolution is heavily armed against a revolution that shows little sign of ever existing.

The irony of the Human Rights doctrine is particularly evident in the anti-Russian propaganda of recent years. The collapse of the Soviet

Union has led to a revival of a certain degree of traditional conservatism in Russia, including respect for religion and family values. The United States counter-revolution has thus gone full circle. The "enemy" today is what "anti-communism" claimed to defend yesterday.

Today one can say that the Revolution has been defeated, but the Counter-Revolution has gone insane. It is reduced to a will to destroy any possible eventual adversary, while inventing pretexts as it goes along. It has become institutionalized paranoia, a mortal danger to human civilization.

The Moral of History

The moral of history is to get beyond moralizing in the effort to understand what really happened and what went wrong. Moral condemnation should be saved for the present, where it might do some good, rather than lavished on an irretrievable past.

In Defense of
Conspiracy Theory[*]

SEPTEMBER 2006

The September 11, 2001, attacks on the Twin Towers and the Pentagon were secretly planned by someone and therefore were certainly in some sense a "conspiracy." The term "conspiracy theory" is used exclusively to refer to suggestions that elements in the Bush administration engineered the 9/11 attacks as a pretext to make war against the Muslim world. This has engendered bitter controversy on the left (since the right simply ignores or dismisses such notions).

The spreading popularity of the 9/11 conspiracy hypothesis is a political phenomenon of some significance. I wish to examine both the causes and the effects of this belief, as well as the substance of the hypothesis itself.

The Bush Administration as
Suspect Number One

The so-called "conspiracy theory" is an almost natural result of the distrust and hatred of the Bush administration and of the "neo-conservatives" who laid out a program of U.S. military hegemony in their Project for a New American Century (PNAC). Their misdeeds are so great that in purely moral terms, they seem capable of anything. This is the factor that supplies the emotional and moral readiness to believe the worst.

However, the fact that they may well be morally capable of every conceivable crime does not mean that they are necessarily capable in purely practical terms. The test of the conspiracy hypothesis is not the

---

* Original version: *CounterPunch,* September 15, 2006. https://www. counterpunch.org/2006/09/15/in-defense-of-conspiracy/

character of the alleged conspirators, but the plausibility of the conspiracy in both practical and political terms.

I should note at the outset that I have an open mind about conspiracy theories in general. History is replete with conspiracies. No hypothesis should be rejected automatically because it involves a conspiracy. But each hypothesis must be judged on its own merits, in terms of solid evidence and plausibility, as well as in comparison with conflicting hypotheses. A scientific attitude requires special scepticism in regard to theories one would like, for various personal or ideological reasons, to believe. The wish to pin the supreme crime on the criminal Bush administration is an initial reason to be sceptical.

Who profits from the crime?

The Bush administration has shamelessly exploited 9/11 to instil paranoid fear in the American public in order to justify repressive measures at home and an aggressive war policy abroad. The event seems to have served as the "Pearl Harbor" posited by certain neo-cons as necessary to bring the U.S. public around to their agenda. So the Bush administration can rightly be said to have profited from the crime.

But so did Osama bin Laden, who has become a hero to millions. So did numerous other Islamic extremists, who were inspired by the impact of that event. The plain fact is that the September 11 attacks were greeted rapturously in much of the Arab-Muslim world. They have inspired emulation.

If both sides profited, one profited opportunistically and the other actually designed the attacks to fit its purpose [1]. So the attacks should be examined to see which set of aims it was designed to serve.

The targets and the message

The al Qaeda hypothesis: Osama bin Laden is quoted as saying that the United States was targeted for having sent its troops to violate the land of the holy Mosques and for supporting the Zionist entity. The choice of 9/11 targets contained an eloquent message that was perfectly understood in most of the world. The World Trade Center stood for America's economic power in the world, and the Pentagon its military power. Assuming the targets were chosen by bin Laden and his associates, they were meant to show that this overwhelming power was in reality vulnerable, in a call to Muslims everywhere to fight back against it.

The Bushite conspiracy hypothesis: "The terrorists hate us because we are free, they want to destroy our freedom."

This ignores entirely the symbolism of the targets.

Now, let us suppose that Bushite plotters designed the attacks so that Bush could use them to claim that "they want to destroy us because of our freedom." The choice of targets should support that claim. Suppose one of the planes had crashed into the Statue of Liberty; that would really carry the message that "they want to destroy our freedom." For ordinary Americans, it would be just as shocking as the World Trade Center, indeed more so, while costing a lot less in lives and property.

It should be clear that the choice of targets was perfectly suited to express violent opposition to United States economic and military power (and perhaps political power if, as claimed without proof, the fourth plane was heading for the White House), not primarily the American people and their freedom. The nearly three thousand victims were not the target, but were, as the Americans and Israelis say of their bombing runs, "collateral damage."

W's goat story

Was George W. Bush supposed to be part of the plot? Or was he left out of the planning by his handlers? Either way, an entourage clever enough to pull off the 9/11 spectacle should have been clever enough to manipulate the President to get him to play his important role in the scenario. If the whole thing was a set-up, he should have been made to leap into action, rush to the defense of the nation and show himself heroically on the front lines of this new "war." Instead, looking totally bewildered, he went on reading a goat story, then vanished from sight allowing Mayor Giuliani to hog the limelight. I fail to understand why anyone can interpret that pathetic performance as indication of an "inside job."

The Arab pilots

In any case, whatever the financial or ideological role of Osama bin Laden, focusing on the mysterious cave dweller distracts attention from the actual perpetrators. According to the official version, these were not cave dwellers, but well-educated young men, mostly from Saudi Arabia. To deliver such a strong message to the "evil Empire," they were ready to give up their lives—and the lives of others. This is standard operating practice for warriors and makes them heroes in the eyes of those who sympathize with their cause. Considering the hatred that the United States—alongside Israel—has aroused in the Arab world, there is really nothing so amazing about the fact that a certain number of young Arabs would be willing to sacrifice themselves for such a spectacular act. Of course, we are no longer living in those archaic times when it was possible to respect the courage of even the worst enemy. Today we are living in Manichean times—our dualism matches theirs, and enemies can only be "pure evil." Otherwise, we in the West might do well to drop the obsession with bin Laden and consider what moved those men to do what they did.

One of the conspiracy theories suggests that the planes were actually directed into the Twin Towers by U.S. military guidance systems. It is said that the Towers were too difficult a target for amateur pilots. This does not seem plausible to me: the Towers look like sitting ducks, and the vertical aim could be approximate—unlike an airport runway where both vertical and horizontal precision are necessary.

Demolition

When the towers went down, it reminded viewers of deliberate building demolitions. That doesn't prove anything. There are experts who explain why it must have been demolition, and experts who explain why the collapse was due to the structure of the buildings (especially their vertical design). The layman has no way to judge between these expert explanations—but neither do experts, since scientists cannot be absolutely sure of the cause of a single event that cannot be repeated experimentarily. So we are back to the question of plausibility and motivation.

As to plausibility, supposing the airliner attacks were really engineered by the Bushites, why add demolition? Since somebody would have to place explosives in the two towers, this would enlarge the circle of persons involved in the plot, making exposure more likely. And what is the dividend from demolition to make it worth the additional risk of disclosure?

And why demolish yet another tower? How does that strengthen what is supposed to be the effect of the attacks: to frighten the American people and justify war?

The absence of jet fighter intervention

It is claimed that the Air Force was held back from stopping the operation. But what could U.S. Air Force jets have done in this case? Shoot down loaded airliners over Manhattan—at a time when the hypothesis would have been hijacking rather than suicide attacks on the Twin Towers? It seems more than likely that there was no standard operating defense against such an operation.

The Pentagon

The argument, popularized by Thierry Meyssan, that the Pentagon was struck by a missile rather than by American Airlines flight 77, rests wholly on photographic evidence, or to be more precise, the absence of photographic evidence clearly showing the wreckage of the airliner embedded in the Pentagon. Because the Pentagon is flat, and outside the main Washington urban area, it is not the object of tourists taking amateur photos, especially not early in the morning. Once again, experts are called upon to explain why the projectile striking the Pentagon, could, or could not, have been an airliner. The fact that the appearance of a crash site is ambiguous is scarcely conclusive evidence of anything. And once again, the layman cannot easily judge these conflicting physical interpretations but can quite well use common sense to question motives and plausibility.

Most superficially, there is the issue of eye witnesses. Thierry Meyssan maintained that the only people who claim to have seen an airliner crash into the Pentagon are not credible because employed by the Government. Does that suggest that all government employees were complicit? Moreover, there were numerous non-governmental eye witnesses, mostly commuters on the highways which surround the otherwise rather bare area where the Pentagon is located. Many have described how they were first surprised to see the airliner flying in too low to reach nearby Reagan National Airport.

But on the other hand, how many eye witnesses say they saw a missile strike the Pentagon? Even more to the point, how many eye witnesses saw or heard a missile *being fired* at the Pentagon, if at short range, or traveling in that direction, if at long range?

But the real argument against the Pentagon hypothesis is the list of 58 passengers and crew on flight 77, who have never been seen again. It makes absolutely no sense to get rid of an entire 747 airliner full of people, in order to make way for a missile to do the job attributed to the airliner. What is the point? It is claimed that an airliner couldn't hit the Pentagon, so a missile was required. But the Pentagon is a very large target, visible in an open space. It is sturdier than the Twin Towers, having been built to withstand military attack, so destroying it was harder, but hitting it was not such an extraordinary feat.

U.S. military officers are trained to follow orders, perhaps strange ones, but they tend to be sincerely patriotic. It is not really credible that U.S. military personnel would follow orders to carry out such a ghastly mission—murder a civil airliner full of passengers, shoot a missile into the Pentagon—without somebody among them blowing the whistle. The United States is not a place where people keep secrets. "Let it all hang out" is the national attitude. In addition to patriotism, any one of the alleged conspirators could have been certain of millions of dollars in royalties for telling the story.

Defending conspiracy theory

Personally, as mentioned above, I am quite open to reasonable hypotheses of conspiracy. In the case of the John F. Kennedy assassination, for example, I find the theory that it was organized by a conspiracy of anti-Castro fanatics and gangsters plausible both in terms of feasibility and in terms of motive. But it remains to be proven.

I feel that the extreme version of the 9/11 conspiracy, complete with voluntary demolition of three buildings and a missile striking the Pentagon, gives a bad name to conspiracy theory in general.

Even in the case of 9/11, there is what I would call a "soft" version of the conspiracy theory that deserves investigation, and that is the possible role of secret agents who may have infiltrated the al Qaeda plot enough to know what was afoot but let it happen. Such an hypothesis involves only a few passive "conspirators," who, especially if they were from Israeli Mossad, would have had a patriotic motive: to bring the United States fully to the side of Israel in the "war against terror." There are clear statements from Israeli leaders welcoming this development. And there is the strange incident of the "dancing Israelis" who watched the planes hit the Twin Towers from a distant parking lot.

A full inquiry into this question is difficult for obvious political reasons. So perhaps it is easier, politically, to advance the far more complex and implausible version of an all-out U.S. administration role in staging the 9/11 attacks than to pinpoint a smaller, more plausible, but politically more sensitive target.

Against dualistic simplicity

We are confronted with two opposed versions of moral dualism. Either evil Arabs gratuitously attacked innocent Americans, or else all evil acts are committed by the villains in Washington, and the Arabs are innocent of everything. However, it might be more realistic to acknowledge that Arabs in general are innocent victims of U.S. and Israeli aggression, and, on the other hand, that some of them (for that very reason) want to strike back at the United States by any means possible. Israelis abuse Palestinians with a clear conscience because they have convinced themselves that all Jews are under perpetual threat of a new Holocaust. This chronic fear leads them to commit crimes. After 9/11, Americans are encouraged to suffer from a similar fear and to strike back indiscriminately. Cycles of fear and revenge can lead to a state of war of all against all, in which it is absolutely necessary for the sake of survival to keep a cool head and try to understand why people do the terrible things they do, in order to seek ways to break these cycles.

What does the ICC stand for?
The Imperialist Crimes
Cover-up[*]

JUNE 2011

Last May 16, Luis Moreno Ocampo, chief prosecutor at the International Criminal Court (ICC) in The Hague, officially sought an arrest warrant for Libyan leader Moammer Gaddafi for "crimes against humanity." Also accused were the leader's son Seif al-Islam Gaddafi and Libyan intelligence chief Abdullah Senussi.

U.S. jurist David Scheffer told Agence France Presse: "NATO will doubtless appreciate the ICC investigation and indictment of top Libyan leaders, including Gaddafi."

Well, yes. And nobody is better placed to know what NATO appreciates than David Scheffer.

The day before, Tripoli had made yet another offer of a truce, calling for an end to NATO bombing and for peace negotiations with the armed rebels based in Benghazi. NATO's response took the form of the ICC indictment. When NATO bombs a country to unseat a leader, the targeted leader must be treated like a common criminal. His place cannot be at the negotiating table, but behind bars. An international indictment handily transforms NATO's military aggression into a police action to arrest "an indicted war criminal"—an expression that evacuates the presumption of "innocent until proven guilty."

This is a familiar pattern.

On March 24, 1999, NATO began bombing Yugoslavia in support of armed Albanian rebels in Kosovo. Two months later, in mid-May, as the

---

* Original version: *CounterPunch,* June 2, 2011. https://www.counterpunch.org/2011/06/02/the-imperialist-crime-cover-up/

bombing intensified against Serbia's infrastructure, the chief prosecutor at the International Criminal Tribunal for Yugoslavia (ICTY) in The Hague, Louise Arbour, issued an indictment against Yugoslav president Slobodan Milosevic for crimes against humanity. All but one of the alleged "crimes against humanity" took place in Kosovo during the chaos caused precisely by the NATO bombing.

On March 31, 2011, NATO began bombing Libya, and this time the International Criminal Court was even faster. And the charges were even less substantial. Ocampo said that there was evidence that Gaddafi personally ordered attacks on "innocent Libyan civilians."

In Libya as in the Kosovo war, the accusations are those made by armed rebels supported by NATO, with no discernable trace of independent neutral investigation.

In the spring of 1999, David Scheffer, who was then U.S. Secretary of State Madeleine Albright's Ambassador at large for War Crimes, visited Louise Arbour and provided her with NATO reports on which to base her indictments. Indeed, Scheffer had earlier helped set up the ICTY as instructed by Ms Albright. The May 1999 accusations served their main immediate purpose: to block negotiations and to justify NATO's continued bombing. As Madeleine Albright put it, "We are not negotiating with Milosevic... The indictments, I think, clarify the situation because they really show that we are doing the right thing in terms of responding to the kinds of crimes against humanity that Milosevic has perpetrated."[1]

To sum up, in both cases an "international criminal tribunal/court" intervenes in the midst of a NATO bombing to accuse the leader of the country being bombed of "crimes against humanity" based on flimsy evidence provided by NATO itself or by its rebel clients.

Thus the International Criminal Court turns out to be a continuation of the ICTY, that is, an instrument not of international justice but the judicial arm of Western intervention in weaker countries. The ICC could well stand for Imperialist Crimes Cover-up.

It certainly does not deserve its official title, since it studiously ignores truly "international" crimes, such as U.S. and NATO aggression or the many massacres of civilians that result. Rather, so far the only alleged crimes it has undertaken to prosecute have all been the result of *internal* conflicts taking place in countries on the African continent. In short, the ICC so far acts mainly as a way of putting political pressure

---

1 See Michael Mandel, *How America Gets Away With Murder* (PlutoPress, 2004), pp. 141–145.

on, or justifying military action against, weak governments the Western powers want to replace with leaders of their choice.

Concerning the Gaddafi indictment, Scheffer is quoted by AFP as saying that the move might increase pressure on Gaddafi to think about finding refuge in a country that has not agreed to ICC jurisdiction. This is a senseless remark, since Libya itself has not agreed to ICC jurisdiction. Nor has Sudan, which has not prevented the ICC from going after its president, Omar Al Bashir, even though the ICC is supposed to apply only to countries that have recognized its jurisdiction. But non-recognition of ICC jurisdiction proves to be of no protection for weak countries.

Just as NATO and the ICC continue to pursue Gaddafi on the pretext that he is "killing his own people," in Afghanistan NATO armed forces continue to kill people who are not their own, with impunity.

The ICC has developed into one of the most blatant illustrations of double standards. The United States manipulates the ICC without recognizing its jurisdiction, and having further protected itself by bilateral agreements with a long list of countries that provide immunity for United States citizens as well as by Congressional laws to protect U.S. citizens from the ICC.

Other NATO countries have recognized ICC jurisdiction, but there is no sign that they will ever be troubled by the international court.

Last Sunday, two notoriously nonconformist French lawyers, Jacques Vergès and former foreign minister Roland Dumas, announced that they intended to bring a lawsuit against President Nicolas Sarkozy for "crimes against humanity" in Libya. At a press conference in Tripoli, Dumas deplored that the NATO mission to protect civilians was killing them, and said he was ready to defend Gaddafi at the ICC. Meanwhile, the two lawyers intend to represent the families of victims of NATO bombing in litigation against Sarkozy in French courts. "We are going to break through the wall of silence," announced Vergès.

There is more solid evidence of the civilian victims of NATO bombing, including the three baby grandchildren of Moammer Gaddafi, than of the "crimes against humanity" attributed by Ocampo to the Libyan leader. But the French public has been mesmerized by the propaganda portraying Gaddafi as a bloodthirsty ogre whose only desire is to "kill his own people." Since most people in the West know absolutely nothing about Libya, anything goes.

On Monday, as France and Britain prepared to send in combat helicopters to support the armed rebels and hunt down Gaddafi, NATO secretary general Anders Fogh Rasmussen announced that

Gaddafi's "reign of terror is coming to an end." The real "rain of ter-ror" is the rain of NATO bombs falling on defenseless Tripoli, with the clear intention of terrorizing Libyans into surrendering to the NATO-backed rebels. And there is no sign of it ever coming to an end.

Antifa In Theory and In Practice*

OCTOBER 2017

*"Fascists are divided into two categories:
the fascists and the anti-fascists."*

—Ennio Flaiano, Italian writer and co-author of
Federico Fellini's greatest film scripts

In recent weeks, a totally disoriented left has been widely exhorted to unify around a masked vanguard calling itself Antifa, for anti-fascist. Hooded and dressed in black, Antifa is essentially a variation of the Black Bloc, familiar for introducing violence into peaceful demonstrations in many countries. Imported from Europe, the label Antifa sounds more political. It also serves the purpose of stigmatizing those it attacks as "fascists."

Despite its imported European name, Antifa is basically just another example of America's steady descent into violence.

Historical Pretensions

Antifa first came to prominence from its role in reversing Berkeley's proud "free speech" tradition by preventing right wing personalities from speaking there. But its moment of glory was its clash with right-wingers in Charlottesville on August 12, largely because Trump commented that there were "good people on both sides." With exuberant Schadenfreude, commentators grabbed the opportunity to condemn the despised President for his "moral equivalence," thereby bestowing a moral blessing on Antifa.

---

* Original version: *CounterPunch,* October 9, 2017. https://www. counterpunch.org/2017/10/09/antifa-in-theory-and-in-practice/

Charlottesville served as a successful book launching for *Antifa: the Antifascist Handbook,* whose author, young academic Mark Bray, is an Antifa in both theory and practice. The book is "really taking off very fast," rejoiced the publisher, Melville House. It instantly won acclaim from leading mainstream media such as the *New York Times, The Guardian* and NBC, not hitherto known for rushing to review leftwing books, least of all those by revolutionary anarchists.

The Washington Post welcomed Bray as spokesman for "insurgent activist movements" and observed that: "The book's most enlightening contribution is on the history of anti-fascist efforts over the past century, but its most relevant for today is its justification for stifling speech and clobbering white supremacists."

Bray's "enlightening contribution" is to a tell a flattering version of the Antifa story to a generation whose dualistic, Holocaust-centered view of history has largely deprived them of both the factual and the analytical tools to judge multidimensional events such as the growth of fascism. Bray presents today's Antifa as though it were the glorious legitimate heir to every noble cause since abolitionism. But there were no anti-fascists before fascism, and the label "Antifa" by no means applies to all the many adversaries of fascism.

The implicit claim to carry on the tradition of the International Brigades who fought in Spain against Franco is nothing other than a form of innocence by association. Since we must revere the heroes of the Spanish Civil War, some of that esteem is supposed to rub off on their self-designated heirs. Unfortunately, there are no veterans of the Abraham Lincoln Brigade still alive to point to the difference between a vast organized defense against invading fascist armies and skirmishes on the Berkeley campus. As for the Anarchists of Catalonia, the patent on anarchism ran out a long time ago, and anyone is free to market his own generic.

The original Antifascist movement was an effort by the Communist International to cease hostilities with Europe's Socialist Parties in order to build a common front against the triumphant movements led by Mussolini and Hitler.

Since Fascism thrived, and Antifa was never a serious adversary, its apologists thrive on the "nipped in the bud" claim: "if only" Antifascists had beat up the fascist movements early enough, the latter would have been nipped in the bud. Since reason and debate failed to stop the rise of fascism, they argue, we must use street violence—which, by the way, failed even more decisively.

This is totally ahistorical. Fascism exalted violence, and violence was its preferred testing ground. Both Communists and Fascists were fighting in the streets and the atmosphere of violence helped fascism thrive as a bulwark against Bolshevism, gaining the crucial support of leading capitalists and militarists in their countries, which brought them to power.

Since historic fascism no longer exists, Bray's Antifa have broadened their notion of "fascism" to include anything that violates the current Identity Politics canon: from "patriarchy" (a pre-fascist attitude to put it mildly) to "transphobia" (decidedly a post-fascist problem).

The masked militants of Antifa seem to be more inspired by Batman than by Marx or even by Bakunin.

Storm Troopers of the Neoliberal War Party

Since Mark Bray offers European credentials for current U.S. Antifa, it is appropriate to observe what Antifa amounts to in Europe today.

In Europe, the tendency takes two forms. Black Bloc activists regularly invade various leftist demonstrations in order to smash windows and fight the police. These testosterone exhibits are of minor political significance, other than provoking public calls to strengthen police forces. They are widely suspected of being influenced by police infiltration.

As an example, last September 23, several dozen black-clad masked ruffians, tearing down posters and throwing stones, attempted to storm the platform where the flamboyant Jean-Luc Mélenchon was to address a mass meeting of *La France Insoumise,* today the leading leftist party in France. Their unspoken message seemed to be that nobody is revolutionary enough for them. Occasionally, they do actually spot a random skinhead to beat up. This establishes their credentials as "anti-fascist."

They use these credentials to arrogate to themselves the right to slander others in a sort of informal self-appointed inquisition, expelling from the virtuous left whoever deviates from their canon and thereby tends toward "fascism." High on the list of mortal sins is criticism of the European Union, which is associated with "nationalism" which is associated with "fascism" which is associated with "anti-Semitism," hinting at a penchant for genocide. This guilt by association of ideas goes along with guilt by association of persons.

The term "red-brown" is used to smear anyone with generally leftist views—that is, "red"—with the fascist color "brown." This smear can be based on having the same opinion as someone on the right, speaking on the same platform with someone on the right, being published alongside someone on the right, being seen at an anti-war demonstration also attended by someone on the right, and so on. This is particularly useful for the War Party, since these days, many conservatives are more opposed to war than leftists who have bought into the "humanitarian war" mantra.

Consciously or unconsciously, self-appointed radical revolutionaries can serve as the most useful thought police for the neoliberal war party.

Silencing Necessary Debate

The scarcity of fascists has been compensated by identifying criticism of immigration as fascism. Opposition to mass immigration has increasingly been stigmatized as racism by much of the European left. However, criticism of immigration as a policy is not the same as the attitude toward immigrants as people.

It should be possible to discuss the policy without being accused of personal animosity toward immigrants. After all, trade union leaders have traditionally opposed mass immigration, not out of racism, but because it can be a deliberate capitalist strategy to bring down wages.

In reality, immigration is a complex subject, with many aspects that can lead to reasonable compromise. But to polarize the issue misses the chances for compromise. By making mass immigration the litmus test of whether or not one is a good person, Antifa intimidation impedes reasonable discussion. Without discussion, without readiness to listen to all viewpoints, the issue will simply divide the population into two camps, for and against. And who will win such a confrontation?

Surveys show that mass immigration is increasingly unpopular in all European countries. A left whose principal cause is open borders will become increasingly unpopular.

Wild Goose Chase

In the United States, the worst thing about Antifa is the effort to lead the disoriented American left into a wild goose chase, tracking down imaginary "fascists" instead of getting together openly to work out a coherent positive program. The United States has more than its share of weird individuals, of gratuitous aggression, of crazy ideas, and tracking down these marginal characters, whether alone or in groups, is a huge distraction. The truly dangerous people in the United States are safely ensconced in Wall Street, in Washington Think Tanks, in the executive suites of the sprawling military industry, not to mention the editorial offices of some of the mainstream media currently adopting a benevolent attitude toward "anti-fascists" simply because they are useful in focusing on the mavericks instead of themselves.

The facile use of the term "fascist" gets in the way of thoughtful identification and definition of the real enemy of humanity today. In the contemporary chaos, the greatest and most dangerous upheavals in the world all stem from the same source, which is hard to name, but which we might give the provisional simplified label of Globalized Imperialism. This amounts to a multifaceted project to reshape the world to satisfy the demands of financial capitalism, the military industrial complex, United States ideological vanity and the megalomania of leaders of lesser "Western" powers, notably Israel. It could be called simply "imperialism," except that it is much vaster and more destructive than the historic imperialism of previous centuries. It is also much more disguised. And since it bears no clear label such as "fascism," it is difficult to denounce in simple terms.

The fixation on preventing a political movement that arose over 80 years ago, under very different circumstances, obstructs recognition of the perils of today. Fighting the previous war leads to defeat.

Trotskyist Delusions[*]

Obsessed with Stalin, the disciples of Leon Bronstein
see betrayed revolutions everywhere.

MAY 2018

I first encountered Trotskyists in Minnesota half a century ago during the movement against the Vietnam War. I appreciated their skill in organizing anti-war demonstrations and their courage in daring to call themselves "communists" in the United States of America—a profession of faith that did not groom them for the successful careers enjoyed by their intellectual counterparts in France. So I started my political activism with sympathy toward the movement. In those days it was in clear opposition to U.S. imperialism, but that has changed.

The first thing one learns about Trotskyism is that it is split into rival tendencies. Some remain consistent critics of imperialist war, notably those who write for the World Socialist Web Site (WSWS).

Others, however, have translated the Trotskyist slogan of "permanent revolution" into the hope that every minority uprising in the world must be a sign of the long-awaited world revolution—especially those that catch the approving eye of mainstream media. More often than deploring U.S. intervention, they join in reproaching Washington for not intervening sooner on behalf of the alleged revolution.

A recent article in the International Socialist Review (issue #108, March 1, 2018) entitled "Revolution and counterrevolution in Syria" indicates so thoroughly how Trotskyism goes wrong that it is worthy of a critique. Since the author, Tony McKenna, writes well and with evident conviction, this is a strong not a weak example of the Trotskyist mindset.

McKenna starts out with a passionate denunciation of the regime of Bashar al Assad, which, he says, responded to a group of children who

---

[*] Original version: *Consortium News,* May 4, 2018. https://consortiumnews.com/2018/05/04/trotskyist-delusions-obsessed-with-stalin-they-see-betrayed-revolutions-everywhere/

simply wrote some graffiti on a wall by "beating them, burning them, pulling their fingernails out." The source of this grisly information is not given. There could be no eye witnesses to such sadism, and the very extremism sounds very much like war propaganda—Germans carving up Belgian babies.

But this raises the issue of sources. It is certain that there are many sources of accusations against the Assad regime, on which McKenna liberally draws, indicating that he is writing not from personal observation, any more than I am. Clearly, he is strongly disposed to believe the worst, and even to embroider it somewhat. He accepts and develops without the shadow of a doubt the theory that Assad himself is responsible for spoiling the good revolution by releasing Islamic prisoners who went on to poison it with their extremism. The notion that Assad himself infected the rebellion with Islamic fanaticism is at best a hypothesis concerning not facts but *intentions,* which are invisible. But it is presented as unchallengeable evidence of Assad's perverse wickedness.

This interpretation of events happens to dovetail neatly with the current Western doctrine on Syria, so that it is impossible to tell them apart. In both versions, the West is no more than a passive onlooker, whereas Assad enjoys the backing of Iran and Russia.

"Much has been made of Western imperial support for the rebels in the early years of the revolution. This has, in fact, been an ideological lynchpin of first the Iranian and then the Russian military interventions as they took the side of the Assad government. Such interventions were framed in the spirit of anticolonial rhetoric in which Iran and Russia purported to come to the aid of a beleaguered state very much at the mercy of a rapacious Western imperialism that was seeking to carve the country up according to the appetites of the U.S. government and the International Monetary Fund," according to McKenna.

Whose "ideological lynchpin"? Not that of Russia, certainly, whose line in the early stages of its intervention was not to denounce Western imperialism but to appeal to the West and especially to the United States to join in the fight against Islamic extremism.

Neither Russia nor Iran "framed their interventions in the spirit of anticolonial rhetoric" but in terms of the fight against Islamic extremism with Wahhabi roots.

In reality, a much more pertinent "framing" of Western intervention, taboo in the mainstream and even in Moscow, is that Western support for armed rebels in Syria was being carried out to help Israel destroy its regional enemies. The Middle East nations attacked by the West—Iraq,

Libya and Syria—all just happen to be, or to have been, the last strong-holds of secular Arab nationalism and support for Palestinian rights. There are a few alternative hypotheses as to Western motives—oil pipe-lines, imperialist atavism, desire to arouse Islamic extremism in order to weaken Russia (the Brzezinski gambit)—but none are as coherent as the organic alliance between Israel and the United States, and its NATO sidekicks.

It is remarkable that McKenna's long article (some 12 thousand words) about the war in Syria mentions Israel only once (aside from a footnote citing Israeli national news as a source). And this mention actu-ally equates Israelis and Palestinians as co-victims of Assad propaganda: the Syrian government "used the mass media to slander the protestors, to present the revolution as the chaos orchestrated by subversive interna-tional interests (the Israelis and the Palestinians were both implicated in the role of foreign infiltrators)."

No other mention of Israel, which occupies Syrian territory (the Golan Heights) and bombs Syria whenever it wants to.

Only one, innocuous mention of Israel! But this article by a Trotskyist mentions Stalin, Stalinists, Stalinism no less than *twenty-two times!*

And what about Saudi Arabia, Israel's de facto ally in the effort to destroy Syria in order to weaken Iran? Two mentions, both implicitly denying that notorious fact. The only negative mention is blaming the Saudi family enterprise for investing billions in the Syrian economy in its neoliberal phase. But far from blaming Saudi Arabia for supporting Islamic groups, McKenna portrays the House of Saud as a victim of ISIS hostility.

Clearly, the Trotskyist delusion is to see the Russian Revolution everywhere, forever being repressed by a new Stalin. Assad is likened to Stalin several times.

This article is more about the Trotskyist case against Stalin than it is about Syria.

This repetitive obsession does not lead to a clear grasp of events which are *not* the Russian revolution. And even on this pet subject, something is wrong.

The Trotskyists keep yearning for a new revolution, just like the Bolshevik revolution. Yes, but the Bolshevik revolution ended in Stalinism. Doesn't that tell them something? Isn't it quite possible that their much-desired "revolution" might turn out just as badly in Syria, if not much worse?

Throughout history, revolts, uprisings, rebellions happen all the time, and usually end in repression. Revolution is very rare. It is more a myth than a reality, especially as Trotskyists tend to imagine it: the people all rising up in one great general strike, chasing their oppressors from power and instituting people's democracy. Has this *ever* happened?

For the Trotskyists, this seem to be the natural way things should happen and is stopped only by bad guys who spoil it out of meanness.

In our era, the most successful revolutions have been in Third World countries, where national liberation from Western powers was a powerful emotional engine. Successful revolutions have a program that unifies people and leaders who personify the aspirations of broad sectors of the population. Socialism or communism was above all a rallying cry meaning independence and "modernization"—which is indeed what the Bolshevik revolution turned out to be. If the Bolshevik revolution turned Stalinist, maybe it was in part because a strong repressive leader was the only way to save "the revolution" from its internal and external enemies. There is no evidence that, had he defeated Stalin, Trotsky would have been more tender-hearted.

Countries that are deeply divided ideologically and ethnically, such as Syria, are not likely to be "modernized" without a strong rule.

McKenna acknowledges that the beginning of the Assad regime somewhat redeemed its repressive nature by modernization and social reforms. This modernization benefited from Russian aid and trade, which was lost when the Soviet Union collapsed. Yes, there was a Soviet bloc which despite its failure to carry out world revolution as Trotsky advocated, did support the progressive development of newly independent countries.

If Bashar's father Hafez al Assad had some revolutionary legitimacy in McKenna's eyes, there is no excuse for Bashar.

"In the context of a global neoliberalism, where governments across the board were enacting the most pronounced forms of deregulation and overseeing the carving up of state industries by private capital, the Assad government responded to the heightening contradictions in the Syrian economy by following suit—by showing the ability to march to the tempo of foreign investment while evincing a willingness to cut subsidies for workers and farmers."

The neoliberal turn impoverished people in the countryside, therefore creating a situation that justified "revolution."

This is rather amazing, if one thinks about it. Without the alternative Soviet bloc, virtually the whole world has been obliged to conform to anti-social neoliberal policies. Syria included. Does this make Bashar al Assad so much more a villain than every other leader conforming to U.S.-led globalization?

McKenna concludes by quoting Louis Proyect: "If we line up on the wrong side of the barricades in a struggle between the rural poor and oligarchs in Syria, how can we possibly begin to provide a class-struggle leadership in the USA, Britain, or any other advanced capitalist country?"

One could turn that around. Shouldn't such a Marxist revolutionary be saying: "if we can't defeat the oligarchs in the West, who are responsible for the neoliberal policies imposed on the rest of the world, how can we possibly begin to provide class-struggle leadership in Syria?"

The trouble with Trotskyists is that they are always "supporting" other people's more or less imaginary revolutions. They are always telling others what to do. They know it all. The practical result of this verbal agitation is simply to align this brand of Trotskyism with U.S imperialism. The obsession with permanent revolution ends up providing an ideological alibi for permanent war.

For the sake of world peace and progress, both the United States and its inadvertent Trotskyist apologists should go home and mind their own business.

The Lynching of the Charismatic Geek*

NOVEMBER 2019

Once upon a time, there was a very bright little boy who grew up moving around Australia, never really taking roots. As an adolescent he found his own world in cyberspace, which offered a field for his insatiable curiosity. As he learned about that great world out there and its secrets, he developed his very own rigorous ethic: his vocation was to search for true facts and share them with the public. His moral compass developed free of conformist social codes. Truth was truth, deception was wrong, lies on the part of the powerful should be exposed.

The original sin of Julian Assange was the same as that of Galileo Galilei. Galileo sinned by revealing to the people things the elite already knew or at least surmised, but wished to keep secret from the masses, in order not to shake the people's faith in the official truth. Assange did the same thing with the formation of Wikileaks. The official version of reality was challenged. All lies should be exposed. By far the most sensitive targets of his wide-ranging reality revelations were the lies, the hypocrisy, the inhuman brutality of the United States in its wars of global hegemony. To Assange, these things were simply wrong.

At first, Wikileaks attracted a great deal of popular attention and even acclaim. Julian Assange became famous. He was a geek, but he didn't look like a geek. Tall, handsome, striking with his nearly white hair, Julian was something strange: a charismatic geek.

He arrived in Sweden with near superstar status. Swedish women contrived to get him into their beds. They bragged about having sex with Julian: he was a trophy lover. But the charismatic geek didn't know the social codes of the peculiar Swedish forms of virtuous promiscuity.

---

* As published by *Global Research*, November 4, 2019. https://www. globalresearch.ca/lynching-charismatic-geek/5693868

This lacuna was exploited by his enemies in extravagantly unpredictable ways.

Julian Assange tried to straighten out what seemed to be a serious misunderstanding before leaving Sweden. But the Swedish side failed to make matters clear and he left for London.

In London, he was quickly taken up by the radical chic branch of the British upper class, the champagne and caviar humanitarians. The naïve charismatic geek who didn't know the social codes no doubt thought he was among friends. He didn't belong to any political or social movement in the UK, he depended on the beautiful people who for a time found him an interesting outsider, one of their latest causes.

Julian Assange may have been socially naïve, but he very acutely perceived what the imperial powers were working up against him. The totally unjustifiable demand for extradition to Sweden for questioning—unjustifiable because they had declined to question him while he was there and then declined to question him in the UK—appeared to Julian to be an obvious device to enable Sweden to extradite him to the United States, given the total obedience of post-Olof Palme Sweden to the wishes of Washington. Others didn't see this so clearly, except for the excellent President of Ecuador at the time, Rafael Correa. Correa offered Assange asylum in the tiny Ecuadorian embassy in London. Assange, unconventional, negligent of the codes, but with a clear view of the danger stalking him, jumped the bail set up for him and moved into the embassy.

This was the beginning of his alienation from the caviar humanitarians. At first the smart set defended him. Such glamorous personalities as Jemima Khan and Amal Amamuddin (not yet Clooney) initially defended him and then lost interest. He was not of their world. He did not know how to compromise, he was a geek after all, less and less charismatic as he faded in the shadows of the embassy of Ecuador. It's all very well to denounce lies and tell the truth, but one mustn't overdo it. It's delightful to have a cause when you have a solid social and financial background to fall back on, and when you know how to play the game so as to be in and out at the same time. Julian had none of those social graces. He was honest, intent, stubborn. He was incapable of hypocrisy, even in his own interest. He would not abjure, as Galileo did.

Such stubborn honesty on the part of someone who has nothing—no influential family, no fortune, no social status, no political party, nothing but his stubborn devotion to truth—is unbearable in a society based on lies. The media who profited from his scoops became the most zealous in denouncing him. No wonder: his honesty was a living reproach to the scribblers who had sold out all down the line, who get ahead by adding new touches to the mendacious "common narrative" required by the masters of their careers.

Lies were spread. Someone so honest must have hidden vices. He must be as bad as we are, or worse. The mob gathers. This man who knows the truth but not the social codes is an insult to us all, a freak, a monster, who must be destroyed.

The lynch mob is enormous. The media, politicians, even the judicial authorities. There are no loud shouts for blood but silent cruelty as the Anglo-American ruling Establishment shamelessly contrives to halt the last breath of the outsider who dared expose them for what they are.

The Great Pretext...
for Dystopia*

NOVEMBER 2020

A review of *Covid-19: The Great Reset,*
by Klaus Schwab and Thierry Malleret

By titling their recently published World Economic Forum treatise *Covid-19: The Great Reset,* the authors link the pandemic to their futuristic proposals in ways bound to be met with a chorus of "Aha!"s. In the current atmosphere of confusion and distrust, the glee with which Schwab and Malleret greet the pandemic as harbinger of their proposed socioeconomic upheaval suggests that if Covid-19 hadn't come along by accident, they would have created it (had they been able).

In fact, World Economic Forum founder Klaus Schwab was already energetically hyping the Great Reset, using climate change as the triggering crisis, before the latest coronavirus outbreak provided him with an even more immediate pretext for touting his plans to remake the world.

The authors start right in by proclaiming that "the world as we knew it in the early months of 2020 is no more," that radical changes will shape a "new normal." We ourselves will be transformed. "Many of our beliefs and assumptions about what the world could or should look like will be shattered in the process."

Throughout the book, the authors seem to gloat over the presumed effects of widespread "fear" of the virus, which is supposed to condition people to desire the radical changes they envisage. They employ technocratic psychobabble to announce that the pandemic is already

---

*Published in *Consortium News,* November 24, 2020. https://consortiumnews.com/2020/11/24/diana-johnstone-the-great-pretext-for-dystopia/

transforming the human mentality to conform to the new reality they consider inevitable.

"Our lingering and possibly lasting fear of being infected with a virus … will thus speed the relentless march of automation…" Really?

"The pandemic may increase our anxiety about sitting in an enclosed space with complete strangers, and many people may decide that staying home to watch the latest movie or opera is the wisest option."

"There are other first round effects that are much easier to anticipate. Cleanliness is one of them. The pandemic will certainly heighten our focus on hygiene. A new obsession with cleanliness will particularly entail the creation of new forms of packaging. We will be encouraged not to touch the products we buy. Simple pleasures like smelling a melon or squeezing a fruit will be frowned upon and may even become a thing of the past."

This is the voice of would-be Global Governance. From on high, experts decide what the masses ought to want, and twist the alleged popular wishes to fit the profit-making schemes they are peddling. Their schemes center on digital innovation, massive automation using "artificial intelligence," finally even "improving" human beings by endowing them artificially with some of the attributes of robots: such as problem-solving devoid of ethical distractions.

Engineer-economist Klaus Schwab, born in Ravensburg, Germany, in 1938, founded his World Economic Forum in 1971, attracting massive sponsorship from international corporations. It meets once a year in Davos, Switzerland—last time in January 2020 and next year in May, delayed because of covid.

A Powerful Lobby

What is it, exactly? I would describe the WEF as a combination capitalist consulting firm and gigantic lobby. The futuristic predictions are designed to guide investors into profitable areas in what Schwab calls "the Fourth Industrial Revolution (4IR)" and then, as the areas are defined, to put pressure on governments to support such investments by way of subsidies, tax breaks, procurements, regulations and legislation. In short, the WEF is *the* lobby for new technologies, digital everything, artificial intelligence, transhumanism.

It is powerful today because it is operating in an environment of State Capitalism, where the role of the State (especially in the United States, less so in Europe) has been largely reduced to responding positively to the demands of such lobbies, especially the financial sector.

Immunized by campaign donations from the obscure wishes of ordinary people, most of today's politicians practically need the guidance of lobbies such as the WEF to tell them what to do.

In the twentieth century, notably in the New Deal, the government was under pressure from conflicting interests. The economic success of the armaments industry during World War II gave birth to a Military-Industrial Complex which has become a permanent structural factor in the U.S. economy. It is the dominant role of the MIC and its resulting lobbies that have definitively transformed the nation into State Capitalism rather than a Republic. The proof of this transformation is the unanimity with which Congress never balks at approving grotesquely inflated military budgets. The MIC has spawned media and Think Tanks which ceaselessly indoctrinate the public in the existential need to keep pouring the nation's wealth into weapons of war. Insofar as voters do not agree, they can find no means of political expression with elections monopolized by two pro-MIC parties.

The WEF can be seen as analogous to the MIC. It intends to engage governments and opinion manufacturers in the promotion of a "4IR" which will dominate the civilian economy and civilian life itself. The pandemic is a temporary pretext; the need to "protect the environment" will be the more sustainable pretext. Just as the MIC is presented as absolutely necessary to "protect our freedoms," the 4IR will be hailed as absolutely necessary to "save the environment"—and in both cases, many of the measures advocated will have the opposite effect.

So far, the techno-tyranny of Schwab's 4IR has not quite won its place in U.S. State Capitalism. But its prospects are looking good. Silicon Valley contributed heavily to the Joe Biden campaign, and Biden hastened to appoint its moguls to his transition team.

But the real danger of all power going to the Reset lies not with what is there but with what is not there: any serious political opposition.

Can Democracy Be Restored?

The Great Reset has a boulevard open to it for the simple reason that there is nothing in its way. No widespread awareness of the issues, no effective popular political organization, nothing. Schwab's dystopia is frightening simply for that reason.

The 2020 presidential election has just illustrated the almost total depoliticization of the American people. That may sound odd considering the violent partisan emotions displayed. But it was all much ado about nothing. There were no real issues debated, no serious political questions raised either about war or about the directions of future economic development. The vicious quarrels were about persons, not policy. Bumbling Trump was accused of being "Hitler," and Wall Street-beholden Democrat warhawks were described by Trumpists as "socialists." Lies, insults and confusion prevailed.

A revival of democracy could stem from organized, concentrated study of the issues raised by the Davos planners, in order to arouse an informed public opinion to evaluate which technical innovations are socially acceptable and which are not. Cries of alarm from the margins will not influence the intellectual relationship of forces. What is needed is for people to get together everywhere to study the issues and develop well-reasoned opinions on goals and methods of future development. Unless faced with informed and precise critiques, Silicon Valley and its corporate and financial allies will simply proceed in doing whatever they imagine they can do, whatever the social effects.

Serious evaluation should draw distinctions between potentially beneficial and unwelcome innovations, to prevent popular notions from being used to gain acceptance of every "technological advance," however ominous.

Redefining Issues

The political distinctions between left and right, between Republican and Democrat, have grown more impassioned just as they reveal themselves to be incoherent, distorted and irrelevant, based more on ideological bias than on facts. New and more fruitful political alignments could be built through confrontation with specific concrete issues.

We could take the proposals of the Great Reset one by one and examine them in both pragmatic and ethical terms.

1. Thanks to the pandemic, there has been a great increase in the use of teleconferences, using Skype, Zoom or other new platforms. The WEF welcomes this as a trend. Is it bad for that reason? To be fair, this innovation is positive in enabling many people to attend conferences without the expense, trouble and environmental cost of air travel. It has the negative side of preventing direct human contact. This is a simple issue, where positive points seem to prevail.

2. Should higher education go on line, with professors giving courses to students via internet? This is a vastly more complicated question, which should be thoroughly discussed by educational institutions themselves and the communities they serve, weighing the pros and cons, remembering that those who provide the technology want to sell

it, and care little about the value of human contact in education—not only human contact between student and professor, but often life-determining contacts between students themselves. On-line courses may benefit geographically isolated students, but breaking up the educational community would be a major step toward the destruction of human community altogether.

3. Health and "well-being." Here is where the discussion should heat up considerably. According to Schwab and Malleret: "Three industries in particular will flourish (in the aggregate) in the post-pandemic era: big tech, health and wellness." For the Davos planners, the three merge. Those who think that well-being is largely self-generated, dependent on attitudes, activity and lifestyle choices, miss the point. "The combination of AI [artificial intelligence], the IoT [internet of things] and sensors and wearable technology will produce new insights into personal well-being. They will model how we are and feel [...] precise information on our carbon footprints, our impact on biodiversity, on the toxicity of all the ingredients we consume and the environments or spatial contexts in which we evolve will generate significant progress in terms of our awareness of collective and individual well-being."

Question: do we really want or need all this cybernetic narcissism? Can't we just enjoy life by helping a friend, stroking a cat, reading a book, listening to Bach or watching a sunset? We better make up our minds before they make over our minds.

4. Food. In order not to spoil my healthy appetite, I'll skip over this. The tech wizards would like to phase out farmers, with all their dirty soil and animals, and industrially manufacture enhanced artificial foods created in nice clean labs—out of what exactly?

The Central Issue: Homo Faber

5. What about human work? "In all likelihood, the recession induced by the pandemic will trigger a sharp increase in labor-substitution, meaning that physical labor will be replaced by robots and 'intelligent' machines, which will in turn provoke lasting and structural changes in the labor market." This replacement has already been underway for decades. Along with outsourcing and immigration, it has already weakened the collective power of labor. But clearly, the tech industries are poised to go much, much further and faster in throwing humans out of work.

The covid crisis and social distancing have "suddenly accelerated this process of innovation and technological change. Chatbots, which often use the same voice recognition technology behind Amazon's Alexa, and other software that can replace tasks normally performed by human employees, are being rapidly introduced. These innovations provoked by necessity (i.e. sanitary measures) will soon result in hundreds of thousands, and potentially millions, of job losses."

Cutting labor costs has long been the guiding motive of these innovations, along with the internal dynamic of technology industry to "do whatever it can do." Then socially beneficial pretexts are devised in justification. Like this:

"As consumers may prefer automated services to face-to-face interactions for some time to come, what is currently happening with call centers will inevitably occur in other sectors as well."

"Consumers may prefer…"! Everyone I know complains of the exasperation of trying to reach the bank or insurance company to explain an emergency, and instead to be confronted with a dead voice and a choice of irrelevant numbers to click. Perhaps I am underestimating the degree of hostility toward our fellow humans that now pervades society, but my impression is that there is a vast unexpressed public demand for LESS automated services and MORE contact with real persons who can think outside the algorithm and can actually UNDERSTAND the problem, not simply cough up preprogrammed fixes. There is a potential movement out there. But we hear nothing of it, being persuaded by our media that the greatest problem facing people in their daily lives is to hear someone exhibit confusion over someone else's confused gender.

In this, I maintain, consumer demand would merge with the desperate need of able-minded human beings to earn a living. The technocrats earn theirs handsomely by eliminating the means to earn a living of other people.

Here is one of their great ideas. "In cities as varied as Hangzhou, Washington DC and Tel Aviv, efforts are under way to move from pilot programs to large-scale operations capable of putting an army of delivery robots on the road and in the air." What a great alternative to paying human deliverers a living wage! And incidentally, a guy riding a delivery bicycle is using renewable energy. But all those robots and drones? Batteries, batteries and more batteries, made of what materials, coming from where and manufactured how? By more robots? Where is the energy coming from to replace not only fossil fuels, but also human physical effort?

At the last Davos meeting, Israeli intellectual Yuval Harari issued a dire warning that: "Whereas in the past, humans had to struggle against exploitation, in the twenty-first century the really big struggle will be against irrelevance… Those who fail in the struggle against irrelevance would constitute a new 'useless class'—not from the viewpoint of their friends and family, but useless from the viewpoint of the economic and political system. And this useless class will be separated by an ever-growing gap from the ever more powerful elite."

6. And the military. Our capitalist prophets of doom foresee the semi collapse of civil aviation and the aeronautical industry as people all decide to stay home glued to their screens. But not to worry! "This makes the defense aerospace sector an exception and a relatively safe haven." For capital investment, that is. Instead of vacations on sunny beaches, we can look forward to space wars. It may happen sooner rather than later, because, as the Brookings Institution concludes in a 2018 report on "How artificial intelligence is transforming the world," everything is going faster, including war.

"The big data analytics associated with AI will profoundly affect intelligence analysis, as massive amounts of data are sifted in near real time … thereby providing commanders and their staffs a level of intelligence analysis and productivity heretofore unseen. Command and control will similarly be affected as human commanders delegate certain routine, and in special circumstances, key decisions to AI platforms, reducing dramatically the time associated with the decision and subsequent action."

So, no danger that some soft-hearted officer will hesitate to start World War III because of a sentimental attachment to humanity. When the AI platform sees an opportunity, go for it!

"In the end, warfare is a time competitive process, where the side able to decide the fastest and move most quickly to execution will generally prevail. Indeed, artificially intelligent intelligence systems, tied to AI-assisted command and control systems, can move decision support and decision-making to a speed vastly superior to the speeds of the traditional means of waging war. So fast will be this process especially if coupled to automatic decisions to launch artificially intelligent autonomous weapons systems capable of lethal outcomes, that a new term has been coined specifically to embrace the speed at which war will be waged: hyperwar."

Americans have a choice. Either continue to quarrel over trivialities or wake up, really wake up, to the reality being planned and do something about it.

The future is shaped by investment choices. Not by naughty speech, not even by elections, but by investment choices. For the people to regain power, they must reassert their command over how and for what purposes capital is invested. And if private capital balks, it must be socialized. This is the only revolution—and it is also the only conservatism, the only way to conserve decent human life. It is what real politics is about.

— PART II —
YUGOSLAVIA

Seeing Yugoslavia Through a Dark Glass: Politics, Media and the Ideology of Globalization*

AUGUST 1998

Years of experience in and out of both mainstream and alternative media have made me aware of the power of the dominant ideology to impose certain interpretations on international news. During the Cold War, most world news for American consumption had to be framed as part of the Soviet-U.S. contest. Since then, a new ideological bias frames the news. The way the violent fragmentation of Yugoslavia has been reported is the most stunning example.

I must admit that it took me some time to figure this out, even though I had a long-standing interest and some knowledge of Yugoslavia. I spent time there as a student in 1953, living in a Belgrade dormitory and learning the language. In 1984, in a piece for *In These Times*,[1] I warned that extreme decentralization, conflicting economic interests between the richer and poorer regions, austerity policies imposed by the IMF and the decline of universal ideals were threatening Yugoslavia with "re-Balkanization" in the wake of Tito's death and desanctification. "Local ethnic interests are reasserting themselves," I wrote. "The danger is that these rival local interests may become involved in the rivalries of outside powers. This is how the Balkans in the past were a powder keg of world war." Writing this took no special clairvoyance. The danger of

---

* This article is an expanded version of a talk given on May 25, 1998, at an international conference on media held in Athens, Greece. Original version: *Covert Action Quarterly,* No. 65, Fall 1998.

1 "The Creeping Trend to Re-Balkanization," *In These Times*, October 3-9, 1984, p. 9

Yugoslavia's disintegration was quite obvious to all serious observers well before Slobodan Milošević arrived on the scene.

As the country was torn apart in the early nineties, I was unable to keep up with all that was happening. In those years, my job as press officer for the Greens in the European Parliament left me no time to investigate the situation myself. Aware that there were serious flaws in the way media and politicians were reacting, I wrote an article warning against combatting "nationalism" by taking sides for one nationalism against another, and against judging a complex situation by analogy with totally different times and places.[2] "Every nationalism stimulates others," I noted. "Historical analogies should be drawn with caution and never allowed to obscure the facts." However, there was no stopping the tendency to judge the Balkans, about which most people knew virtually nothing, by analogy with Hitler Germany, about which people at least imagined they knew a lot, and which enabled analysis to be rapidly abandoned in favor of moral certitude and righteous indignation.

However, it was only later, when I was able to devote considerable time to my own research, that I realized the extent of the deception—which is in large part self-deception.

I mention all this to stress that I understand the immense difficulty of gaining a clear view of the complex situation in the Balkans. The history of the region and the interplay of internal political conflicts and external influences would be hard to grasp even without propaganda distortions. Nobody can be blamed for being confused. Moreover, by now, many people have invested so much emotion in a one-sided view of the situation that they are scarcely able to consider alternative interpretations.

It is not necessarily because particular journalists or media are "alternative" that they are free from the dominant interpretation and the dominant world view. In fact, in the case of the Yugoslav tragedy, the irony is that "alternative" or "left" activists and writers have frequently taken the lead in likening the Serbs, the people who most wanted to continue to live in multi-cultural Yugoslavia, to Nazi racists, and in calling for military intervention on behalf of ethnically defined secessionist movements[3]—all supposedly in the name of "multi-cultural Bosnia," a

2 "We Are All Serbo-Croats," *In These Times,* May 3, 1993, p. 14.

3 "Ethnically defined" because, despite the argument accepted by the international community that it was the Republics that could invoke the right to secede, all the political arguments surrounding recognition of independent Slovenia and Croatia dwelt on the right of Slovenes and Croats as such to self-determination.

country which, unlike Yugoslavia, would have to be built from scratch by outsiders.

The Serbs and Yugoslavia

Like other Christian peoples in the Ottoman Empire, the Serbs were heavily taxed and denied ownership of property or political power reserved for Muslims. In the early years of the nineteenth century, Serb farmers led a revolt that spread to Greece. The century-long struggle put an end to Ottoman rule in Europe.

The Habsburg monarchy found it natural that when one empire receded, another should advance, and sought to gain control over the lands lost to the Ottoman Turks. Although Serbs had rallied to the Habsburgs in earlier wars against the Turks, Serbia soon appeared to Vienna as the main obstacle to its own expansion into the Balkans. By the end of the nineteenth century, Vienna was seeking to fragment the Serb-inhabited lands to prevent the emergence of "Greater Serbia." The Austro-Hungarian Empire took control of Bosnia-Herzegovina and fostered the birth of Albanian nationalism (as converts to Islam, Albanian feudal chieftains enjoyed privileges under the Ottoman Empire and combatted the Christian liberation movements).

Probably because they had been deprived of full citizens' rights under the Ottoman Turks, and because their own society of farmers and traders was relatively egalitarian, Serb political leaders throughout the nineteenth and early twentieth centuries were extremely receptive to the progressive ideals of the French Revolution. While all the other liberated Balkan nations imported German princelings as their new kings, the Serbs promoted their own pig farmers into a dynasty, one of whose members translated John Stuart Mill's "On Liberty" into Serbian during his student days. Nowhere in the Balkans did Western progressive ideas exercise such attraction as in Serbia, no doubt due to the historic circumstances of the country's emergence from four hundred years of subjugation.

Meanwhile, intellectuals in Croatia, a province of the Austro-Hungarian Empire increasingly rankling under subordination to the Hungarian nobility, initiated the Yugoslav movement for cultural, and eventually political, unification of the South Slav peoples, notably the Serbs and Croats, separated by history and religion (the Serbs having been converted to Christianity by the Greek Orthodox Church and the Croats by the Roman Catholic Church) but united by language. The idea of a "Southslavia" was largely inspired by the national unification of neighboring Italy, occurring around the same time.

In 1914, the Austro-Hungarian Empire seized the pretext of the assassination of the Archduke Francis Ferdinand to declare war and crush Serbia once and for all. When Austria-Hungary lost the world war it had thus initiated, leaders in Slovenia and Croatia chose to unite with Serbia in a single kingdom. This decision enabled both Slovenia and Croatia to go from the losing to the winning side in World War I, thereby avoiding war reparations and enlarging their territory, notably on the Adriatic coast, at the expense of Italy. The joint Kingdom was renamed "Yugoslavia" in 1929. The conflicts between Croats and Serbs that plagued what is called "the first Yugoslavia" were described by Rebecca West in her celebrated book, *Black Lamb and Grey Falcon*, first published in 1941.

In April 1941, Serb patriots in Belgrade led a revolt against an accord reached between the Kingdom of Yugoslavia and Nazi Germany. This led to Nazi bombing of Belgrade, a German invasion, creation of an independent fascist state of Croatia (including Bosnia-Herzegovina), and attachment of much of the Serbian province of Kosovo to Albania, then a puppet of Mussolini's Italy. The Croatian Ustashe undertook a policy of genocide against Serbs, Jews and Gypsies within the territory of their "Greater Croatia," while the Germans raised SS divisions among the Muslims of Bosnia and Albania.

In Serbia itself, the German occupants announced that one hundred Serbian hostages would be executed for each German killed by resistance fighters. The threat was carried out. As a result, the royalist Serbian resistance (the first guerrilla resistance to Nazi occupation in Europe) led by Draza Mihailovic adopted a policy of holding off attacks on the Germans in expectation of an Allied invasion. The Partisans, led by Croatian communist Josip Broz Tito, adopted a more active strategy of armed resistance, which made considerable gains in the predominantly Serb border regions of Croatia and Bosnia and won support from Churchill for its effectiveness. A civil war developed between the Mihailovic's "Chetniks" and Tito's Partisans—which was also a civil war between Serbs, since Serbs were the most numerous among the Partisans. These divisions between Serbs—torn between Serbian and Yugoslav identity —have never been totally healed, and help explain the deep confusion among Serbs during the breakup of Yugoslavia.

After World War II, the new Communist Yugoslavia tried to build "brotherhood and unity" on the myth that all the peoples had contributed equally to liberation from fascism. Mihailovic was executed, and school children in post-war Yugoslavia learned more about the "fascist" nature of his Serbian nationalist "Chetniks" than they did about Albanian and Bosnian Muslims who had volunteered for the SS, or even about the killing of Serbs in the Jasenovac death camp run by Ustashe in Western Bosnia.

After the 1948 break with Moscow, the Yugoslav communist leadership emphasized its difference from the Soviet bloc by adopting a policy of "self-management" supposed to lead eventually to the "withering away of the State." Tito repeatedly revised the Constitution to strengthen local authorities, while retaining final decision-making power for himself. When he died in 1980, he thus left behind a hopelessly complicated system that could not work without his arbitration.[4] Serbia in particular was unable to enact vitally necessary reforms because its territory had been divided up, with two "autonomous provinces," Voivodina and Kosovo, able to veto measures taken by Serbia, while Serbia could not intervene in their affairs.

In the 1980s, the rise in interest rates and unfavorable world trade conditions dramatically increased the foreign debt Yugoslavia (like many "third world" countries) had been encouraged to run up thanks to its standing in the West as a socialist country not belonging to the Soviet bloc. The IMF arrived with its familiar austerity measures, which could only be taken by a central government. The leaders of the richer Republics—Slovenia and Croatia—did not want to pay for the poorer ones. By a break from the weakened central government, the question would arise of privatization of State and social property, and local communist leaders in Slovenia and Croatia could expect to get a greater share for themselves within the context of division of Yugoslavia into separate little states.[5]

At this stage, a gradual, negotiated dismantling of Yugoslavia into smaller States was not impossible. It would have entailed reaching agreement on division of assets and liabilities, and numerous adjustments to take into account conflicting interests. If pursued openly, however, it might have encountered popular opposition—after all, very many people, perhaps a majority, enjoyed being citizens of a large country with an

---

4 See Svetozar Stojanovic, "The Destruction of Yugoslavia," *Fordham International Law Journal* 19, no. 2 (December 1995), pp. 341–343.

5 For an excellent and detailed account of the economic and constitutional factors leading to the breakup of Yugoslavia, see Susan Woodward, *Balkan Tragedy* (Brookings Institution, 1995).

enviable international reputation. What would have been the result of a national referendum on the question of preservation of Yugoslavia?

None was ever held. The first multiparty elections in postwar Yugoslavia were held in 1990, not nationwide in all of Yugoslavia, but separately by each Republic—a method which in itself reinforced separatist power elites. Sure of the active sympathy of Germany, Austria and the Vatican, leaders in Slovenia and Croatia prepared the *fait accompli* of unilateral, unnegotiated secession, proclaimed in 1991. Such secession was illegal, under Yugoslav and international law, and was certain to precipitate civil war. The key role of German (and Vatican) support was to provide rapid international recognition of the new independent Republics, in order to transform Yugoslavia into an "aggressor" on its own territory.[6]

Political Motives

The political motives that launched the anti-Serb propaganda campaign are obvious enough. Claiming that it was impossible to stay in Yugoslavia because the Serbs were so oppressive was the pretext for the nationalist leaders in Slovenia and Croatia to set up their own little statelets which, thanks to early and strong German support, could "jump the queue" and get into the richmen's European club ahead of the rest of Yugoslavia.

The terrible paradox is that very many people, in the sincere desire to oppose racism and aggression, have in fact contributed to demonizing an entire people, the Serbs, thereby legitimizing both ethnic separatism

---

6 Recognition of the internal administrative borders between the Republics as "inviolable" international borders was in effect a legal trick, contrary to international law, which turned the Yugoslav army into an "aggressor" within the boundaries its soldiers had sworn to defend, and which transformed the Serbs within Croatia and Bosnia, who opposed secession from their country, Yugoslavia, into secessionists. This recognition flagrantly violated the principles of the 1975 Final Act (known as the Helsinki Accords) of the Conference on, now Organization for, Security and Cooperation in Europe (CSCE), notably the territorial integrity of States and nonintervention in internal affairs. Truncated Yugoslavia was thereupon expelled from the OSCE in 1992, sparing its other members from having to hear Belgrade's point of view. Indeed, the sanctions against Yugoslavia covered culture and sports, thus eliminating for several crucial years any opportunity for Serbian Yugoslavs to take part in international forums and events where the one-sided view of "the Serbs" presented by their adversaries might have been challenged.

and the new role of NATO as occupying power in the Balkans on behalf of a theoretical "international community."

Already in the 1980s, Croatian and ethnic Albanian separatist lobbies had stepped up their efforts to win support abroad, notably in Germany and the United States,[7] by claiming to be oppressed by Serbs, citing "evidence" that, insofar as it had any basis in truth, referred to the 1920-1941 Yugoslav kingdom, not to the very different post-World War II Yugoslavia.

The current campaign to demonize the Serbs began in July 1991 with a virulent barrage of articles in the German media, led by the influential conservative newspaper, the *Frankfurter Allgemeine Zeitung* (FAZ). In almost daily columns, FAZ editor Johann Georg Reismüller justified the freshly, and illegally, declared "independence" of Slovenia and Croatia by describing "the Yugo-Serbs" as essentially Oriental "militarist Bolsheviks" who have "no place in the European Community." Nineteen months after German reunification, and for the first time since Hitler's defeat in 1945, German media resounded with condemnation of an entire ethnic group reminiscent of the pre-war propaganda against the Jews.[8]

This German propaganda binge was the signal that times had changed seriously. Only a few years earlier, a seemingly broad German peace movement had stressed the need to put an end to "enemy stereotypes"

---

7 In Washington, the campaign on behalf of Albanian separatists in Kosovo was spearheaded by Representative Joe DioGuardi of New York, who after losing his Congressional seat has continued his lobbying for the cause. An early and influential convert to the cause was Senator Robert Dole. In Germany, the project for the political unification of all Croatian nationalists, both communist and Ustashe, with the aim of seceding and establishing "Greater Croatia," was followed closely and sympathetically by the Bundesnachrichtendienst (BND), West Germany's CIA, which hoped to gain its own sphere of influence on the Adriatic from the breakup of Yugoslavia. The nationalist unification, which eventually brought former communist general Franjo Tudjman to power in Zagreb with the support of the Ustashe diaspora, got seriously underway after Tito's death in 1980, during the years when Bonn's current foreign minister, Klaus Kinkel, was heading the BND. See Erich Schmidt-Eenboom, *Der Schattenkrieger: Klaus Kinkel und der BND* (Düsseldorf: ECON Verlag, 1995).

8 This point is developed by Wolfgang Pohrt, "Entscheidung in Jugoslawien," in *Bei Andruck Mord: Die deutsche Propaganda und der Balkankrieg,* edited by Wolfgang Schneider (Hamburg: Konkret, 1997). A sort of climax was reached with the July 8, 1991 cover of the influential weekly *Der Spiegel,* depicting Yugoslavia as a "prison of peoples" with the title "Serb Terror."

(*Feindbilder*). Yet the sudden ferocious emergence of the enemy stereo-type of "the Serbs" did not shock liberal or left Germans, who were soon repeating it themselves. It might seem that the German peace movement had completed its historic mission once its contribution to altering the image of Germany had led Gorbachev to endorse reunification. The least one can say is that the previous efforts at reconciliation with peoples who suffered from Nazi invasion stopped short when it came to the Serbs.

In the Bundestag, German Green leader Joschka Fischer pressed for disavowal of "pacifism" in order to "combat Auschwitz," thereby equat-ing Serbs with Nazis. In a heady mood of self-righteous indignation, German politicians across the board joined in using Germany's past guilt as a reason, not for restraint, as had been the logic up until reunification, but on the contrary, for "bearing their share of the military burden." In the name of human rights, the Federal Republic of Germany abolished its ban on military operations outside the NATO defensive area. Germany could once again be a "normal" military power—thanks to the "Serb threat."

The near unanimity was all the more surprising in that the "enemy stereotype" of the Serb had been dredged up from the most belligerent German nationalism of the past. "*Serbien muss sterbien*" (a play on the word sterben, to die), meaning "Serbia must die" was a famous popular war cry of World War I.[9] Serbs had been singled out for slaughter during the Nazi occupation of Yugoslavia. One would have thought that the younger generation of Germans, seemingly so sensitive to the victims of Germany's aggressive past, would have at least urged caution. Very few did.

On the contrary, what occurred in Germany was a strange sort of mass transfer of Nazi identity, and guilt, to the Serbs. In the case of the Germans, this can be seen as a comforting psychological projection which served to give Germans a fresh and welcome sense of innocence in the face of the new "criminal" people, the Serbs. But the hate cam-paign against Serbs, started in Germany, did not stop there. Elsewhere, the willingness to single out one of the Yugoslav peoples as the villain calls for other explanations.

---

9 The slogan was immortalized in the 1919 play by Austrian playwright Karl Kraus, *Die letzten Tage der Menschheit.*

Media Momentum

From the start, foreign reporters were better treated in Zagreb and in Ljubljana, whose secessionist leaders understood the prime importance of media images in gaining international support, than in Belgrade. The Albanian secessionists in Kosovo or "Kosovars,"[10] the Croatian secessionists and the Bosnian Muslims hired an American public relations firm, Ruder Finn, to advance their causes by demonizing the Serbs.[11] Ruder Finn deliberately targeted certain publics, notably the American Jewish community, with a campaign likening Serbs to Nazis. Feminists were also clearly targeted by the Croatian nationalist campaign directed out of Zagreb to brand Serbs as rapists.[12]

---

10 Albanians in Albania and in Yugoslavia call themselves "Shqiptare" but recently have objected to being called that by others. "Albanians" is an old and accepted term. Especially when addressing international audiences in the context of the separatist cause, Kosovo Albanians prefer to call themselves "Kosovars," which has political implications. Logically, the term should apply to all inhabitants of the province of Kosovo, regardless of ethnic identity, but by appropriating it for themselves alone, the Albanian "Kosovars" imply that Serbs and other non-Albanians are intruders. This is similar to the Muslim party's appropriation of the term "Bosniak," which implies that the Muslim population of Bosnia-Herzegovina is more indigenous that the Serbs and Croats, which makes no sense, since the Bosnian Muslims are simply Serbs and Croats who converted to Islam after the Ottoman conquest.

11 The role of the Washington public relations firm, Ruder Finn, is by now well-known, but seems to have raised few doubts as to the accuracy of the anti-Serb propaganda it successfully diffused. See especially: Jacques Merlino, *Les Vérités yougoslaves ne sont pas toutes bonnes à dire,* (Paris: Albin Michel, 1993; and Peter Brock, "Dateline Yugoslavia: The Partisan Press," *Foreign Policy* no. 93 (Winter 1993–94).

12 No one denies that many rapes occurred during the civil wars in Croatia and Bosnia-Herzegovina, or that rape is a serious violation of human rights. So is war, for that matter. From the start, however, inquiry into rape in Bosnia-Herzegovina focused exclusively on accusation that Serbs were raping Muslim women as part of a deliberate strategy. The most inflated figures, freely extrapolated by multiplying the number of known cases by large factors, were readily accepted by the media and international organizations. No interest was shown in detailed and documented reports of rapes of Serbian women by Muslims or Croats."

The late Nora Beloff, former chief political correspondent of the *London Observer,* described her own search for verification of the rape charges in a letter to *The Daily Telegraph* (January 19, 1993). The British Foreign Office conceded that the rape figures being bandied about were totally uncorroborated, and referred her to the Danish government, then chairing the European Union. Copenhagen agreed that the reports were unsubstantiated but kept repeating

The Yugoslav story was complicated; anti-Serb stories had the advantage of being simple and available, and they provided an easy-to-use moral compass by designating the bad guys.

As the war in Bosnia-Herzegovina got underway in mid-1992, American journalists who repeated unconfirmed stories of Serbian atrocities could count on getting published, with a chance of a Pulitzer prize. Indeed, the 1993 Pulitzer Prize for international reporting was shared between the two authors of the most sensational "Serb atrocity stories" of the year: Roy Gutman of *Newsday* and John Burns of *The New York Times*. In both cases, the prize-winning articles were based on hearsay evidence of dubious credibility. Gutman's articles, mostly based on accounts by Muslim refugees in the Croatian capital, Zagreb, were collected in a book rather misleadingly entitled *A Witness to Genocide*, although in fact he had been a "witness" to nothing of the sort. His allegations that Serbs were running "death camps" were picked up by Ruder Finn and widely diffused, notably to Jewish organizations. Burns' story was no more than an interview with a mentally deranged prisoner in a Sarajevo jail, who confessed to crimes some of which have been since proved never to have been committed.[13]

On the other hand, there was no market for stories by a journalist who discovered that reported Serbian "rape camps" did not exist (German TV reporter Martin Lettmayer[14]), or who included information about Muslim or Croat crimes against Serbs (Belgian journalist Georges Berghezan for one[15]). It became increasingly impossible to challenge the

them. Both said that the EU had taken up the "rape atrocity" issue at its December 1992 Edinburgh summit exclusively on the basis of a German initiative. In turn, Fran Wild, in charge of the Bosnian Desk in the German Foreign Ministry, told Ms. Beloff that the material on Serb rapes came partly from the Izetbegovic government and partly from the Catholic charity Caritas in Croatia. No effort had been made to seek corroboration from more impartial sources.

Despite the absence of solid and comprehensive information, a cottage industry has since developed around the theme. See: Norma von Ragenfeld-Feldman, "The Victimization of Women: Rape and the Reporting of Rape in Bosnia-Herzegovina, 1992–1993," *Dialogue*, no. 21, Paris, March 1997; and Diana Johnstone, "Selective Justice in The Hague," *The Nation*, September 22, 1997, pp. 16–21.

13 See Peter Brock, op. cit. See also, Diana Johnstone, op. cit. *A Witness to Genocide* by Roy Gutman was published by Macmillan, 1993.

14 Martin Lettmayer, "Da wurde einfach geglaubt, ohne nachzufragen," in *Serbien muss sterbien: Wahrheit und Lüge im jugoslawischen Bürgerkrieg*, edited by Klaus Bittermann (Berlin: Tiamat, 1994).

15 Private interview with Georges Berghezan, October 22, 1997.

dominant interpretation in major media. Editors naturally prefer to keep the story simple: one villain, and as much blood as possible. Moreover, after the German government forced the early recognition of Slovenian and Croatian independence, other Western powers lined up opportunistically with the anti-Serb position. The United States soon moved aggressively into the game by picking its own client state—Muslim Bosnia—out of the ruins.

Foreign news has always been much easier to distort than domestic news. Television coverage simply makes the distortion more convincing. TV crews sent into strange places about which they know next to nothing, send back images of violence that give millions of viewers the impression that "everybody knows what is happening." Such an impression is worse than plain ignorance.

Today, worldwide media such as CNN openly put pressure on governments to respond to the "public opinion" which the media themselves create. Christiane Amanpour tells the U.S. and European Union what they should be doing in Bosnia; to what extent this is coordinated with U.S. agencies is hard to tell. Indeed, the whole question of which tail wags the dog is wide open. Do media manipulate government, does government manipulate media, or are influential networks manipulating both?

Many officials of Western governments complain openly or privately of being forced into unwise policy decisions by "the pressure of public opinion," meaning the media. A particularly interesting testimony in this regard is that of Otto von Habsburg, the extremely active and influential octogenarian heir to the defunct Austro-Hungarian Empire, today member of the European Parliament from Bavaria, who has taken a great and one might say paternal interest in the cause of Croatian independence. "If Germany recognized Slovenia and Croatia so rapidly," Habsburg told the Bonn correspondent of the French daily *Figaro*,[16] "even against the will of [then German foreign minister] Hans-Dietrich Genscher who did not want to take that step, it's because the Bonn government was subjected to an almost irresistible pressure of public opinion. In this regard, the German press rendered a very great service, in particular the *Frankfurter Allgemeine Zeitung* and Carl Gustav Ströhm, that great German journalist who works for *Die Welt*."

Still, the virtually universal acceptance of a one-sided view of Yugoslavia's collapse cannot be attributed solely to political designs or

16 Jean-Paul Picaper, *Otto de Habsbourg: Mémoires d'Europe* (Paris: Criterion, 1994), pp. 209–210.

to sensationalist manipulation of the news by major media. It also owes a great deal to the ideological uniformity prevailing among educated liberals who have become the consensual moral conscience in Northwestern Euro-American society since the end of the Cold War.

Down With the State

This ideology is the expression in moralistic terms of the dominant project for reshaping the world since the United States emerged as sole superpower after the defeat of communism and collapse of the Soviet Union. United States foreign policy for over a century has been dictated by a single overriding concern: to open world markets to American capital and American enterprise. Today this project is triumphant as "economic globalization." Throughout the world, government policies are judged, approved or condemned decisively not by their populations but by "the markets," meaning the financial markets. Foreign investors, not domestic voters, decide policy. The International Monetary Fund and other such agencies are there to help governments adjust their policies and their societies to market imperatives.

The shift of decision-making power away from elected governments, which is an essential aspect of this particular "economic globalization," is being accompanied by an ideological assault on the nation-state as a political community exercising sovereignty over a defined territory. For all its shortcomings, the nation-state is still the political level most apt to protect citizens' welfare and the environment from the destructive expansion of global markets. Dismissing the nation-state as an anachronism, or condemning it as a mere expression of "nationalist" exclusivism, overlooks and undermines its long-standing legitimacy as the focal point of democratic development, in which citizens can organize to define and defend their interests.

The irony is that many well-intentioned idealists are unwittingly helping to advance this project by eagerly promoting its moralistic cover: a theoretical global democracy that should replace attempts to strengthen democracy at the supposedly obsolete nation-state level.

Within the United States, the link between anti-nation-state ideology and economic globalization is blurred by the double standard of U.S. leaders who do not hesitate to invoke the supremacy of U.S. "national interest" over the very international institutions they promote in order to advance economic globalization. This makes it seem that such international institutions are a serious obstacle to U.S. global power rather than its expression. However, the United States has the overall military and political power to design and control key international institutions (e.g., the IMF, the World Trade Organization, and the International Criminal Tribunal for Former Yugoslavia), as well as to undermine those it dislikes (UNESCO when it was attempting to promote liberation of media from essentially American control) or to flout international law with impunity (notably in its Central American "back yard"). Given the present relationship of forces, weakening less powerful nation-states cannot strengthen international democracy, but simply tighten the grip of transnational capital and the criminal networks that flourish in an environment of lawless acquisition.

There is no real contradiction between asserting the primacy of U.S. interests and blasting the nation-state barriers that might allow some organized defense of the interests of other peoples. But impressed by the apparent contradiction, some American liberals are comforted in their belief that nationalism is the number one enemy of mankind whereas anything that goes against it is progressive.

Indeed, an important asset of the anti-nation-state ideology is its powerful appeal to many liberals and progressives whose internation-alism has been disoriented by the collapse of any discernable socialist alternative to capitalism and by the disarray of liberation struggles in the South of the planet.

In the absence of any clear analysis of the contemporary world, the nation-state is readily identified as the cause of war, oppression and violations of human rights. In short, the only existing context for institu-tionalized democracy is demonized as the mere expression of a negative, exclusive ideology, "nationalism." This contemporary libertarian view overlooks both the persistence of war in the absence of strong States and the historic function of the nation state as framework for the social pact embodied in democratic forms of legislative decision-making.

Condemnation of the nation state in a structuralist rather than his-torical perspective produces mechanical judgments. What is smaller than the nation state, or what transcends the nation state, must be better. On the smaller scale, "identities" of all kinds, or "regions," generally undefined, are automatically considered more promising by much of the current generation. On the larger scale, the hope for democracy is being transferred to the European Union, or to international NGOs, or to theo-retical institutions such as the proposed International Criminal Court. In the enthusiasm for an envisaged global utopia, certain crucial questions are being neglected, notably: Who will pay for all this? How? Who will enforce which decisions? Until such practical matters are cleared up, brave new institutions such as the ICC risk being no more than further instruments of selective intervention against weaker countries. But the illusion persists that structures of international democracy can be built over the heads of States that are not themselves genuinely supportive of such democracy.

The simplistic interpretation of the Yugoslav crisis as Serbian "aggression" against peaceful multi-cultural Europe, is virtually unassailable because it is not only credible according to this ideology but seems to confirm it.

It was this ideology that made it possible for the Croatian, Slovenian and Albanian secessionists and their supporters in Germany and the United States in particular to portray the Yugoslav conflict as the struggle of "oppressed little nations" to free themselves from aggressive Serbian nationalism. In fact, those "little nations" were by no means oppressed in Yugoslavia. Nowhere in the world were and are the cultural rights of national minorities so extensively developed as in Yugoslavia (including the small Yugoslavia made up of Serbia and Montenegro). Politically, not only was Tito himself a Croat and his chief associate, Edvard Kardelj, a Slovene, but a "national key" quota system was rigorously applied to all top posts in the Federal Administration and Armed Forces. The famous "self-management socialism" gave effective control over economic enterprises to Slovenians in Slovenia, Croatians in Croatia and ethnic Albanians in Kosovo. The economic gap between the parts of Yugoslavia which had previously belonged to the Austro-Hungarian Empire, that is, Slovenia, Croatia and Serbia's northern province of Voivodina, on the one hand, and the parts whose development had been retarded by Ottoman rule (central Serbia, the Serbian province of Kosovo, Bosnia-Herzegovina, and Macedonia) continued to widen throughout both the first and second Yugoslavia. The secession movement in Slovenia was a typical "secession of the rich from the poor" (comparable to Umberto Bossi's attempt to detach rich Northern Italy from the rest of the country, in order to avoid paying taxes for the poor South). In Croatia, this motivation was combined with a comeback of Ustashe elements which had gone into exile after World War II.

The nationalist pretext of "oppression" was favored by the economic troubles of the 1980s, which led leaders in each Republic to blame the others, and to overlook the benefits of the larger Federal market for all the Republics. The first and most virulent nationalist movements arose in Croatia and Kosovo, where separatism had been favored by Axis occupation of the Balkans in World War II. It was only in the 1980s that a much milder Serbian nationalist reaction to economic troubles provided the opportunity for all the others to pinpoint the universal scapegoat: Serbian nationalism. Western public opinion, knowing little of Yugoslavia and thinking in terms of analogies with more familiar situations, readily sympathized with Slovenian and Croatian demands for independence. In reality, international law interprets "self-determination" as the right to secede and form an independent State only in certain (mostly colonial) circumstances, none of which applied to Slovenia and Croatia.[17]

All these facts were ignored by international media. Appeals to the dominant anti-State ideology led to frivolous acceptance in the West of the very grave act of accepting the unnegotiated breakup of an existing nation, Yugoslavia, by interpreting ethnic secession as a proper form of "self-determination," which it is not. There is no parallel in recent diplomatic annals for such an irresponsible act, and as a precedent it can only promise endless bloody conflict around the world.

The New World Order

In fact, the breakup of Yugoslavia has served to discredit and further weaken the United Nations, while providing a new role for an expanding NATO. Rather than strengthening international order, it has helped shift the balance of power within the international order toward the dominant nation states, the United States and Germany. If somebody had announced in 1989 that the Berlin Wall has come down, now Germany can unite and send military forces back into Yugoslavia—and what is more in order to enforce a partition of the country along similar lines to those it imposed when it occupied the country in 1941—quite a number of people might have raised objections. However, that is what has happened, and many of the very people who might have been expected to object most strongly to what amounts to the most significant act of historical revisionism since World War II have provided the ideological cover and excuse.

Perhaps dazed by the end of the Cold War, much of what remains of the left in the early nineties abandoned its critical scrutiny of the geostrategic *Realpolitik* underlying great power policies and seemed

---

17 See: Barbara Delcourt and Olivier Corten, *Ex-Yougoslavie: Droit International, Politique et Idéologies,* (Editions Bruylant, Editions de l'Université de Bruxelles, 1997). The authors, specialists in international law at the Free University of Brussels, point out that there was no basis under international law for the secession of the Yugoslav Republics. The principle of "self-determination" was totally inapplicable in those cases.

to believe that the world henceforth was determined by purely moral considerations.

This has much to do with the privatization of "the left" in the past twenty years or so. The United States has led the way in this trend. Mass movements aimed at overall political action have declined, while single-issue movements have managed to continue. The single-issue movements in turn engender non-governmental organizations (NGOs) which, because of the requirements of fund-raising, need to adapt their causes to the mood of the times, in other words, to the dominant ideology, to the media. Massive fund-raising is easiest for victims, using appeals to sentiment rather than to reason. Greenpeace has found that it can raise money more easily for baby seals than for combatting the development of nuclear weapons. This fact of life steers NGO activity in certain directions, away from political analysis toward sentiment. On another level, the NGOs offer idealistic internationalists a rare opportunity to intervene all around the world in matters of human rights and human welfare.

And herein lies a new danger. Just as the "civilizing mission" of bringing Christianity to the heathen provided a justifying pretext for the imperialist conquest of Asia and Africa in the past, today the protection of "human rights" may be the cloak for a new type of imperialist military intervention worldwide.

Certainly, human rights are an essential concern of the left. Moreover, many individuals committed to worthy causes have turned to NGOs as the only available alternative to the decline of mass movements—a decline over which they have no control. Even a small NGO addressing a problem is no doubt better than nothing at all. The point is that great vigilance is needed, in this as in all other endeavors, to avoid letting good intentions be manipulated to serve quite contrary purposes.

In a world now dedicated to brutal economic rivalry, where the rich get richer and the poor get poorer, human rights abuses can only increase. From this vast array of man's inhumanity to man, media and government selectively focus on certain countries and certain types of abuses. The case by case approach also distracts from active criticism of global economic structures that favor the basic human rights abuse of a world split between staggering wealth and dire poverty.

Cuba is not the only country whose "human rights" may be the object of extraordinary concern by governments trying to replace local rulers with more compliant defenders of transnational interests. Such a motivation can by no means be ruled out in the case of the campaign against Serbia.[18] There is urgent need to take care to preserve genuine and legitimate efforts on behalf of human rights from manipulation in the service of other political ends. This is indeed a delicate challenge.

NGOs and NATO, Hand In Hand

In former Yugoslavia, and especially in Bosnia-Herzegovina, Western NGOs have found a justifying role for themselves alongside NATO. They gain funding and prestige from the situation. Local employees of Western NGOs gain political and financial advantages over other local people, and "democracy" is not the people's choice but whatever meets with approval of outside donors. This breeds arrogance among the outside benefactors, and cynicism among local people, who have the choice between opposing the outsiders or seeking to manipulate them. It is an unhealthy situation, and some of the most self-critical are aware of the dangers.[19]

---

18 The matter is complex and far from transparent, but there is some grounds to believe that both the Western hostility to and Serbian voters' support for Slobodan Miloševic and his ruling Serbian Socialist Party, is the fact that his government has been slow to use the same drastic methods of "shock treatment," applied in other former socialist countries, to privatize "social property."

19 From his experience in Zagreb, British sociologist Paul Stubbs has written critically about "Humanitarian Organizations and the Myth of Civil Society" (*ArkZin,* no. 55, Zagreb, January 1996): "Particularly problematic is the assertion that NGO's are 'non-political' or 'neutral' and, hence, more progressive than governments which have vested interests and a political 'axe to grind.' [...] This 'myth of neutrality' might, in fact, hide the interests of a 'globalized new professional middle class' eager to assert its hegemony in the aid and social welfare market place. [...] The creation of a 'globalised new professional middle class' who, regardless of their country of origin, tend to speak a common language and share common assumptions, seems to be a key product of the 'aid industry.' In fact, professional power is reproduced through claims to progressive alliance with social movements and the civil society whereas, in fact, the shift towards NGO's is part of a new residualism in social welfare which, under the auspices of financial institutions such as the World Bank and the International Monetary Fund, challenges the idea that states can meet the welfare needs of all. [...] A small number of Croatian psycho-socially oriented NGOs have attained a level of funding, and a degree of influence, which is far in excess of their level of service, number of beneficiaries, quality of staff, and so on, and places them in marked contrast to those providing services in the governmental sector. One Croatian NGO, linked to a U.S. partner organisation, has, for example, received a grant from USAID for over 2 million U.S. dollars to develop a training programme in trauma work. The organisation, the bulk of whose work [...] is undertaken by psychology and social work students, now has prime office space in Zagreb,

Perhaps the most effectively arrogant NGO in regard to former Yugoslavia is the Vienna office of Human Rights Watch/Helsinki. On September 18, 1997, that organization issued a long statement announcing in advance that the Serbian elections to be held three days later "will be neither free nor fair." This astonishing intervention was followed by a long list of measures that Serbia and Yugoslavia must carry out "or else," and that the international community must take to discipline Serbia and Yugoslavia. These demands indicated an extremely broad interpretation of obligatory standards of "human rights" as applied to Serbia, although not, obviously to everybody else, since they included new media laws drafted "in full consultation with the independent media in Yugoslavia" as well as permission meanwhile to all "unlicensed but currently operating radio and television stations to broadcast without interference."[20]

Human Rights Watch/Helsinki concluded by calling on the Organization for Security and Cooperation in Europe (OSCE) to "deny Yugoslavia readmission to the OSCE until there are concrete improvements in the country's human rights record, including respect for freedom of the press, independence of the judiciary and minority rights, as well as cooperation with the International Criminal Tribunal for the former Yugoslavia."

As for the demand to "respect freedom of the press," one may wonder what measures would satisfy HRW, in light of the fact that press freedom already exists in Serbia to an extent well beyond that in many other countries not being served with such an ultimatum. There exist in Serbia quite a range of media devoted to attacking the government, not only in Serbo-Croatian but also in Albanian. As of June 1998, there were 2,319 print publications and 101 radio and television stations in Yugoslavia, over twice the number that existed in 1992. Belgrade alone has 14 daily newspapers. Six state-supported national dailies have a joint circulation of 180,000, compared to around 350,000 for seven leading opposition dailies.[21]

---

large numbers of computers and other technical equipment, and is able to pay its staff more than double that which they would obtain in the state sector.

20 At the time, some 400 radio and television stations had been operating in Yugoslavia with temporary licenses or none at all. The vast majority are in Serbia, a country of less than ten million inhabitants on a small territory of only 88,361 square kilometers.

21 Figures from "State Media Circulation Slips," on page 3 of the June 8, 1998 issue of *The Belgrade Times,* an English-language weekly. There is no doubt that press diversity in Serbia has profited from the extremely acrimonious contest between government-backed media (which are not as bad or as uniform

Moreover, the judiciary in Serbia is certainly no less independent than in Croatia or Muslim Bosnia, and almost certainly much more so. As for "minority rights," it would be hard to find a country anywhere in the world where they are better protected in both theory and practice than in Yugoslavia.[22]

For those who remember history, the Human Rights Watch/Helsinki ultimatum instantly brings to mind the ultimatum issued by Vienna to Belgrade after the Sarajevo assassination in 1914 as a pretext for the Austrian invasion which touched off World War I. The Serbian government gave in to all but one of the Habsburg demands, but was invaded anyway.[23]

---

as alleged) and opposition media seeking foreign backing. Without this ongoing battle, the government would almost certainly have managed to reduce press pluralism considerably, but it is also fair to point out that the champions of independent media need to keep exaggerating the perils of their situation in order to attract ongoing financial backing from the West, notably from the European Union and the Soros Foundation. Private foreign capital is also present: the relatively mass circulation tabloid *Blic* is German-owned.

22 Serbia is constitutionally defined as the nation of all its citizens, and not "of the Serbs" (in contrast to constitutional provisions of Croatia and Macedonia, for instance). In addition, the 1992 Constitution of the Federal Republic of Yugoslavia (Serbia and Montenegro) as well as the Serbian Constitution guarantee extensive rights to national minorities, notably the right to education in their own mother tongue, the right to information media in their own language and the right to use their own language in proceedings before a tribunal or other authority. These rights are not merely formal, but are effectively respected, as is shown by, for instance, the satisfaction of the 400,000-strong Hungarian minority and the large number of newspapers published by national minorities in Albanian, Hungarian and other languages. Romani (Gypsies) are by all accounts better treated in Yugoslavia than elsewhere in the Balkans. Serbia has a large Muslim population of varied nationalities, including refugees from Bosnia and a native Serb population of converts to Islam in Southeastern Kosovo, known as Goranci, whose religious rights are fully respected, and who have no desire to leave Serbia.

23 After obtaining support from Berlin and the Vatican for war against Serbia, Vienna on July 23, 1914, delivered a 48-hour ultimatum to Belgrade containing a list of ten demands, of which the Serbian government accepted all but one: participation of Austrian officials in suppressing anti-Austrian movements on Serbian territory. This refusal was the official reason for Austria's declaration of war on July 28, 1914, which began World War I. See Ralph Hartmann, *Die ehrlichen Makler* (Berlin: Dietz, 1998), pp. 31–33. Hartmann, who was East German ambassador to Yugoslavia from 1982 to 1988, sees German policy toward Yugoslavia as a relentless revenge against the Serbs for the events of 1914 which led to the destruction of the Austro-Hungarian Empire.

The hostility of this new Vienna power, the International Helsinki Federation for Human Rights, toward Serbia, is evident in all its statements, and in those of its executive director, Aaron Rhodes. In a recent column for the *International Herald Tribune*, he wrote that Albanians in Kosovo "have lived for years under conditions similar to those suffered by Jews in Nazi-controlled parts of Europe just before World War II. They have been ghettoized. They are not free, but politically disenfranchised and deprived of basic civil liberties." The comparison could hardly be more incendiary, but the specific facts to back it up are absent. They are necessarily absent, since the accusation is totally false. Ethnic Albanians in Kosovo have never been "politically disenfranchised," and even Western diplomats have at times urged them to use their right to vote in order to deprive Miloševic of his electoral majority. But nationalist leaders have called for a boycott of Serbian elections since 1981— well before Miloševic came on the scene—and ethnic Albanians who dare take part in legal political life are subject to intimidation and even murder by nationalist Albanian gunmen.[24]

---

24 The March 24, 1998 report of the International Crisis Group entitled "Kosovo Spring" notes that: "In many spheres of life, including politics, education and health-care, the boycott by Kosovars of the Yugoslav state is almost total." In particular, "Kosovars refuse to participate in Serbian or Yugoslav political life. The leading Yugoslav political parties all have offices in Kosovo and claim some Kosovar members, but essentially they are 'Serb-only' institutions. In 1997 several Kosovars accused of collaborating with the enemy [i.e., the Serbian State] were attacked, including Chamijl Gasi, head of the Socialist Party of Serbia in Glagovac, and a deputy in the Yugoslav Assembly's House of Citizens, who was shot and wounded in November. The lack of interest of Serb political parties in wooing Kosovars is understandable. Kosovars have systematically boycotted the Yugoslav and Serbian elections since 1981, considering them events in a foreign country."

The ICG, while scarcely pro-Serb in its conclusions, nevertheless provides information neglected by mainstream media. This is perhaps because the ICG addresses its findings to high-level decision-makers who need to be in possession of a certain number of facts, rather than to the general public.

Gasi was not the only target of Albanian attacks on fellow Albanians in the Glogovac municipal district, situated in the Drenica region which the "Kosovo Liberation Army" (UCK) tried to control in early 1998. Others included forester Mujo Sejdi, 52, killed by machinegun fire near his home on January 12, 1998; postman Mustafa Kurtaj, 26, killed on his way to work by a group firing automatic rifles; factory guard Rusdi Ladrovci, ambushed and killed with automatic weapons apparently after refusing to turn over his official arm to the UCK; among others. On April 10, 1998, men wearing camouflage uniforms and insignia of the Army of Albania fired automatic weapons at a passenger car carrying four ethnic Albanian officials of the Socialist Party of Serbia including

In order to gain international support, inflammatory terms such as "ghetto" and "apartheid" are used by the very Albanian nationalist leaders who have created the separation between populations by enjoining their community to boycott all institutions of the Serbian State in order to create a *de facto* secession. Not only elections and schools, but even the public health service has been boycotted, to the detriment of the health of Kosovo Albanians, especially the children.[25]

Human Rights Watch's blanket condemnation of a government which, like it or not, was elected, in a country whose existence is threatened by foreign-backed secessionist movements, contrasts sharply with

---

Gugna Adem, President of the Suva Reka Municipal Board, who was gravely injured; and Ibro Vait, member of the National Assembly of the Republic of Serbia and President of the SPS district board in the city of Prizren. Numerous such attacks have been reported by the Yugoslav news agency Tanjug, but Western media have shown scant interest in the fate of ethnic Albanians willing to live with Serbs in a multi-ethnic Serbia.

25 In March 1990, during a regular official vaccination program, rumors were spread that Serb health workers had poisoned over 7,000 Albanian children by injecting them with nerve gas. There was never any proof of this, no child was ever shown to suffer from anything more serious than mass hysteria. This was the signal for a boycott of the Serbian public health system. Ethnic Albanian doctors and other health workers left the official institutions to set up a parallel system, so vastly inferior that preventable childhood diseases reached epidemic proportions. In September 1996, WHO and Unicef undertook to assist the main Kosovar parallel health system, named "Mother Theresa" after the world's most famous ethnic Albanian, a native of Macedonia, in vaccinating 300,000 children against polio. The worldwide publicity campaign around this large-scale immunization program failed to point out that the same service had long been available to those children from the official health service of Serbia, systematically boycotted by Albanian parents.

Currently, the parallel Kosovar system employs 239 general practitioners and 140 specialists, compared to around 2,000 physicians employed by the Serbian public health system there. Serbs point out that many ethnic Albanians are sensible enough to turn to the government health system when they are seriously ill. According to official figures, 64% of the official Serbian system's health workers and 80% of its patients in Kosovo are ethnic Albanian.

It is characteristic of the current age of privatization that the "international community" is ready to ignore a functioning government service and even contribute to a politically-inspired effort to bypass and ultimately destroy it. But then, Kosovo Albanian separatists, aware of the taste of the times, like to speak of Kosovo itself as a "non-governmental organization."

These facts are contained in the "Kosovo Spring" report of the International Crisis Group.

the traditional approach of the senior international human rights organization, Amnesty International.

What can be considered the traditional Amnesty International approach consists broadly in trying to encourage governments to enact and
abide by humanitarian legal standards. It does this by calling attention
to particular cases of injustice. It asks precise questions that can be answered precisely. It tries to be fair. It is no doubt significant that Amnesty
International is a grassroots organization, which operates under the mandate of its contributing members, and whose rules preclude domination
by any large donor.

In the case of Yugoslavia, the Human Rights Watch/Helsinki approach differs fundamentally from that of Amnesty International in that
it clearly aims not at calling attention to specific abuses that might be
corrected, but at totally condemning the targeted State. By the excessive
nature of its accusations, it does not ally with reformist forces in the
targeted country so much as it undermines them. Its lack of balance, its
rejection of any effort at remaining neutral between conflicting parties,
encourages disintegrative polarization rather than reconciliation and
mutual understanding. For example, in its reports on Kosovo, Amnesty
International considers reports of abuses from all sides and tries to weigh
their credibility, which is difficult but necessary, since the exaggeration
of human rights abuses against themselves is regularly employed by
Albanian nationalists in Kosovo as a means to win international support for their secessionist cause.[26] Human Rights Watch, in contrast, by
uncritically endorsing the most extreme anti-Serb reports and ignoring
Serbian sources, helps confirm ethnic Albanians in their worst fantasies,
while encouraging them to demand international intervention on their
behalf rather than seek compromise and reconciliation with their Serbian
neighbors. HRW therefore contributes, deliberately or inadvertently, to
a deepening cycle of violence that eventually may justify, or require,
outside intervention.

---

26 The ICG "Kosovo Spring" report noted that the two main Kosovar
human rights groups, Keshelli and the Helsinki Committee, closely linked to
nationalist separatist leaders, "provide statistical data on 'total' human rights
violations, but their accounting system is misleading. For instance, of the 2,263
overall cases of 'human rights violations' in the period from July to September
1997, they cite three murders, three 'discriminations based on language...' and
149 'routine checkings.' By collating minor and major offences under the same
heading, the statistics fail to give a fair representation of the situation. Kosovars
further lose credibility by exaggerating repression when speaking to foreign
visitors."

This is an approach which, like its partner, economic globalization, breaks down the defenses and authority of weaker States. It does not help to enforce democratic institutions at the national level. The only democracy it recognizes is that of the "international community," which is summoned to act according to the recommendations of Human Rights Watch. This "international community," the IC, is in reality no democracy. Its decisions are formally taken at NATO meetings. The IC is not even a "community"; the initials could more accurately stand for "imperialist condominium," a joint exercise of domination by the former imperialist powers, torn apart and weakened by two World Wars, now brought together under U.S. domination with NATO as their military arm. Certainly there are frictions between the members of this condominium, but so long as their rivalries can be played out within the IC, the price will be paid by smaller and weaker countries.

Media attention to conflicts in Yugoslavia is sporadic, dictated by Great Power interests, lobbies, and the institutional ambitions of "non-governmental organizations"—often linked to powerful governments—whose competition with each other for financial support provides motivation for exaggerating the abuses they specialize in denouncing.

Yugoslavia, a country once known for its independent approach to socialism and international relations, economically and politically by far the most liberal country in Eastern Central Europe, has already been torn apart by Western support to secessionist movements. What is left is being further reduced to an ungovernable chaos by a continuation of the same process. The emerging result is not a charming bouquet of independent little ethnic democracies, but rather a new type of joint colonial rule by the international community, enforced by NATO.

Alija Izetbegovic: Islamic Hero of the Western World*

JULY 1999

Analysis of the works:
- Alija Izetbegovic, *"Islamic Declaration,"* 1970.
- Alija Izetbegovic, *Islam Between East and West* (Plainfield, Indiana: American Trust Publications, 1984; third edition, 1993), 302 pages.

O f the local figures who emerged from the wreckage of the former Yugoslavia, the President of Bosnia-Herzegovina, Alija Izetbegovic, is by far the most respected in the world outside, and notably in the United States.[1] While younger men like Haris Silajdzic and Mohamed Sacirbey defended his government to the world with consummate skill and in perfect English, Izetbegovic was a largely silent figure on television screens, the elder statesman whose serious mein expressed both worry and serenity, reflecting the martyrdom of his people. The respect accorded him has rarely taken the form of interest in the ideas on which he based his Party of Democratic Action (SDA), the Muslim political movement in control of the Sarajevo government. In Europe and America, Izetbegovic is seen much more as a symbol than as a political leader with a particular program.

The war in Bosnia-Herzegovina aroused far more passion in the West than the earlier war in Croatia because it brought to the television screens the revelation of a European Islam that offered the ideal model for solving a current problem of vital importance in countries such as

---

* Original version: *Covert Action Quarterly,* July 1999

1 It is indicative of his reputation that in March 1997, Izetbegovic received an award for "democracy development" from the U.S. Center for Democracy in Washington, D.C.

France: assimilation of Muslim immigrant populations. Sarajevo was discovered as a multicultural paradise, an oasis of civilization, populated mainly by gentle blue-eyed Muslims, practicing musical instruments and expressing sentiments of tolerance for their neighbors of other religions. The "lukewarm" Islam seen in Sarajevo seemed totally suitable for integration into any European country.

The fact that Bosnia seemed to offer a potential solution to Western Europe's own "Muslim problem" helps explain the vehement hostility that arose against the Bosnian Serbs, whose utterly peculiar rustic nationalism (the same, commentators noted, that had triggered the carnage of World War I) imbued with religious bigotry was held responsible for an unprovoked brutal assault on this exemplary society. Any "ethnic cleansing" would be outrageous, but here the crime was doubly reprehensible: a "genocide" bent on wiping out Europe's best model of a multi-ethnic society including Muslims.

This interpretation of events helps explain the extreme passion aroused, expressed in the slogan, "Europe lives or dies in Sarajevo." Especially on the liberal left, many intellectuals were, and largely remain, convinced that multicultural Sarajevo represented a test case for the survival of European integration in the broadest sense.[2]

Western media, not least those newspapers and television channels (CNN, Arte) devoting the most coverage to the conflict, readily identified idealized Sarajevo with the Bosnian Muslims, and the Islam of Western dreams with the person of Alija Izetbegovic. Any suggestion that Mr. Izetbegovic might be an "Islamic fundamentalist" could only be dismissed with total incredulity and outrage as blatant Serb propaganda, invented to justify aggression and ethnic cleansing. How could the leader of the Bosnian Muslims be an "Islamic fundamentalist" when the Bosnian Muslims were obviously such a model of modern tolerance?

Acceptance of Izetbegovic as the personification of multi-ethnic Bosnia-Herzegovina obscured the fact that the President not only did not

---

2 In his passionately pro-Bosnian book, *Slaughterhouse: Bosnia and the Failure of the West* (Vintage, New York, 1995), the American writer David Rieff points to the major signficance he and many others saw in the war in Bosnia. He had come to Europe to write about immigration, he explains, to see whether the Old Continent would be able to cope as successfully as the United States with the mass influx of people of different cultures. It was "in search of this 'Americanization' of the European future," with the "conviction that in the twenty-first century we would all be polyglot or we would kill one another off," that he discovered the war in Bosnia, which seemed to support the second, pessimistic hypothesis.

represent the population of Bosnia-Herzegovina in all its variety, he did not even represent all the Muslims.[3]

Politics and Religion

That Izetbegovic could not be considered the uncontested leader of a unanimous Muslim community, much less of "multi-ethnic Bosnia," is clear from his own published writings, the "Islamic Declaration," first distributed in 1970 and republished twenty years later, and *Islam Between East and West*, first published in the United States in 1984.

The "Islamic Declaration" was a manifesto, a sort of "what is to be done?" addressed to Bosnian Muslims discontented with their condition and status. For Izetbegovic, it is clear that Muslims cannot be satisfied in a secular order. "Islamic society without an Islamic government is incomplete and impotent... A Muslim, in general, does not exist as an individual. ...to live and exist as a Muslim, he must create an environment, a community, a social order. ... History does not know of a single truly Islamic movement which was not simultaneously a political movement."[4]

The 1970 Islamic Declaration was written in the context of a global awakening of the Muslim world, "made up of 700 million people possessing enormous natural resources and occupying a geographical area of the first importance." "The time of passivity and peace is gone forever..." The time had come to show the way to "the realization of Islam in all fields of private life of the individual, in the family and in society, by

3 The fact is noted in the influential book by Laura Silber and Allan Little, *Yugoslavia: Death of a Nation,* London, Penguin, 1995; page 211: "Fikret Abdic, a local hero in the far northwestern corner of Bosnia, received 1,010,618 votes, compared to 847,386 for Izetbegovic. [...] In an unexplained deal, Abdic, who did not have enough support within the SDA, traded his rightful position as head of the presidency in exchange for naming his man, Alija Delimustafic, as Interior Minister." Chris Hedges, *New York Times-International Herald Tribune,* 26/4/1996, called the deal "bewildering." Except for such rare references, the popularity of the Bihac businessman who favored cooperation with Serbs and Croats was quickly forgotten by Western media which accepted Izetbegovic as the unchallenged leader of his people.

4 An oddly deceptive introduction to *Islam Between East and West* by one Dr. Balic, a Bosnian Muslim teaching at Frankfurt, states that Izetbegovic had no interest in politics. The purpose of this false assertion was no doubt to deny any grounds for the political prosecution of Izetbegovic and his colleagues. Such a claim is belied not only by the historic facts but by the book itself. The very theme running through everything Izetbegovic has written is the necessarily political nature of Islam.

rebirth of Islamic religious thinking and creation of an Islamic community from Morocco to Indonesia."

Izetbegovic singled out two currents within the Muslim community which stood in the way of the political renewal of Islam: the "conservatives" on the one hand and the "modernists" on the other.

The "conservatives" were identified with "hodjas and shayks" who by confining Islam to a "religion," limited to spiritual concerns, kept it in the hands of the clergy, neglecting its necessary political role in the world, and accommodating a secular regime incompatible with fully developed Islamic life. "More closed to science and more open to mysticism," the "hodjas and shayks" criticized by Izetbegovic are evidently linked to the Sufi tradition of mystical Islam, which in some times and places (notably the Caucasus region and Algeria in the nineteenth century) has been the center of particularly violent resistance to the West, but which took quite tame forms in the western territories of the former Ottoman empire.

As for the "modernists," they are considered by Izetbegovic to be a veritable disaster for Islam throughout the Muslim world. They are often influential in public life, but as they also consider Islam merely a religion that need not or cannot order the external world, they too accommodate secularism and prevent Islam from exerting its proper role in ordering all aspects of life. The "Islamic Declaration" very explicitly rejects the intellectual currents which, notably in Arab countries, have attempted to build modern secular nation-states on the Western model of separation between government and religion. For Muslims, Izetbegovic declares, secularism and nationalism are purely negative.

He illustrates this with the example of Turkey, a Muslim country ruined, in his view, by secularism and nationalism. "Turkey as an Islamic country ruled the world. Turkey as a copy of Europe is a third-rate country like a hundred others around the world."

What Izetbegovic has to say about Turkey is particularly significant, inasmuch as he is himself an heir to a Muslim elite in the Balkans which consistently opposed efforts by Istanbul to reform the Ottoman Empire in ways that would diminish the privileges traditionally monopolized by Muslims. (Under Ottoman rule, only Muslims had the right to own land, to occupy administrative posts, to enter town on horseback, or to wear green, among other things.) When Ottoman power was finally driven out of the Balkans by the Serb, Bulgarian and Greek national liberation movements, all Orthodox Christians, a certain number of south Slav Muslims emigrated to Turkey where even today they may constitute a lobby nostalgic for the good old days, as well as a potential source of support for the growing Islamic political restoration in Turkey itself.

The country which Izetbegovic singled out in his "Declaration" as an example and inspiration, as "our great hope," is Pakistan. "Pakistan constitutes the rehearsal for introduction of Islamic order in contemporary conditions and at the present level of development." These words were written before the Islamic Revolution in Iran, which brought a new source of financial backing to Izetbegovic's project of Islamic revival in Bosnia-Herzegovina. For secular society, however, Pakistan as example is no more reassuring, considering its ongoing backing of armed Islamic groups in neighboring countries, notably Afghanistan.[5]

Izetbegovic's constant message is that the Koran calls for unification of religious faith and politics. There can be no "separation of church and state"—a Christian division totally unacceptable to Muslims. "The first and most important" conclusion to be drawn from the Koran is "the impossibility of any connection between Islam and other non-Islamic systems. There is neither peace nor coexistence between the 'Islamic religion' and non-Islamic social and political institutions."

"Having the right to govern its own world, Islam clearly excludes the right and possibility of putting a foreign ideology into practice on its territory. There is thus no principle of secular government and the State must express and support the moral principles of religion."

Izetbegovic's immediate concern in writing the 1970 "Islamic Declaration" was not in combatting the Communist regime in Yugoslavia, which by recognizing a "Muslim nationality" had greatly facilitated the revival of a Muslim consciousness and community. Rather, he was calling for an awakening of an Islamic consciousness as the first necessary step toward eventual restoration of international Islamic unity and Islamic government wherever Muslims would constitute a majority. This is stated quite clearly.

---

5 It may be pointed out that Izetbegovic's criticism of "conservatives" and "modernists" has nothing to do with the distinction, much noted in the West since the Iranian revolution, between Sunni and Shi'ite Muslims. If he rejects Sufi mysticism, that is a tendency found in both. One passage in the Islamic Declaration explicitly rejects a key Shi'ite tenet, the importance of Ali as direct descendent of the Prophet: "The hereditary califate represents the abandoning of the elective principle clearly asserted as an institution of Islam." However, this is no doubt of limited significance in light of Izetbegovic's clear advocacy of a worldwide unity of the Islamic community, regardless of the Sunni-Shi'ite distinction.

"Emphasis on giving priority to religious and moral renewal doesn't mean that Islamic order can be realized without Islamic government... This position means that we don't start with the conquest of power, but by the conquest of men, and that Islamic regeneration is first of all an upheaval in the field of education, and only afterwards in the political field. We must be preachers first and soldiers later."

At what moment will force accompany these educational means? "The choice of this moment is always a precise question and depends on a number of factors. One can however establish a general rule: the Islamic movement can and must take power as soon as it is normally and numerically strong enough not only to destroy the existing non-Islamic government, but also to construct a new Islamic government. ... Acting too soon is as dangerous as acting too late! Seizing power... without adequate moral and psychological preparation and the indispensable minimum of strong and well-trained cadre means making a coup d'Etat, not an Islamic revolution..." (Earlier, he specifies that: "An Islamic regime can be achieved only in countries where Muslims are a majority.")

The "overthrow of the state" was perhaps nearly as distant and hypothetical for Izetbegovic in Yugoslavia in 1970 as it was for Communist Parties in the non-Communist West in the mid-20th century. The precipitation with which Izetbegovic has in fact become President of a largely Muslim and potentially Islamic state is clearly due to a series of events that even a religious visionary is most unlikely to have foreseen in 1970 or even in 1983—although by then, the Islamic Revolution in Iran had opened new prospects. Notably, a sort of competition between Teheran and Saudi Arabia has provided Islamic movements everywhere with a lucrative rivalry for influence between oil-rich sponsors. Izetbegovic's party has been notably successful in winning important political and material support from all Muslim countries regardless of rivalries between them.

Islam as Political Synthesis of a Dualistic World

Islam Between East and West was published first in English in the United States in 1984, at a time when Izetbegovic was in jail in Yugoslavia for "counter-revolutionary" activities. The book was could not be published in Bosnia-Herzegovina until after he was released in a general amnesty in 1988.

The book is a lengthy attempt to elaborate the ideological underpinnings of the central political argument of the "Islamic Declaration." It is thus part of the intellectual preparation which Izetbegovic considered necessary before proceeding to the next step of establishing Islamic government.

All of Izetbegovic's thinking centers on a single simple formula: Islam is the only synthesis capable of unifying mankind's essentially dualistic existence.

"There are only three integral views of the world: the religious, the materialistic, and the Islamic. They reflect three elemental possibilities (conscience, nature, and man), each of them manifesting itself as Christianity, materialism, and Islam. All ideologies ... can be reduced to one of these three" (p.xxv).

The book proceeds to make these reductions. The method employed is to touch briefly on virtually every subject imaginable, citing a wide range of celebrated or obscure facts and authors, usually out of any clear context, in order to illustrate this simple hypothesis. Thus assertion takes the place of logical argument, repetition the place of definition. Izetbegovic is not at all an analytical thinker, but a classifier. His approach is to attempt to fit everything—all philosophy and science, notably—into his three preconceived categories.

These categories are summarized in the book's appendix as the "table of the opposites," in three columns representing the "religious," the "materialistic" and the "Islamic" views of the world. The "Islamic" is the synthesis of the other two, which unites them, as it unites the dual aspects of man's nature. "Man" as a whole thus belongs in the "Islamic" category.

Samples:

Materialistic	Religious	Islamic
Matter	Spirit	Man
Materialism	Religion	(Islam/Man)
Body	Soul	(Islam/Man)
Science	Christianity	(Islam/Man)
Nature	Art	(Islam/Man)
Intelligence	Morality	(Islam/Man)
Society	Community	(Islam/Man)
Power	Morals	Law-Shari'ah
Violence	Non-violence	Justice-Jihad
Civitas Solis	Civitas Dei	Caliphate
-- etc., etc.		

Izetbegovic devotes many pages to expressing his regard for science and attempting to recount what he takes for those of its findings that seem to support his thesis. A golden age of scientific knowledge is one of the benefits he foresees from Islamic renewal. Nevertheless, his own purely ideological approach is light years away from a modern scientific method.

Arbitrarily, Izetbegovic proclaims that "life is dual." Arbitrarily, he proclaims that only Islam overcomes this dualism. "Man experiences the world dualistically, but monism is in the essence of all human thinking." Mere "religion," by clinging to one side of the dichotomy, cannot satisfy man's need for "monism." He is saved because "Islam cannot be classi-fied as a religion. Islam is more than a religion for it embraces life." This is a totalizing, one might say implicitly totalitarian, claim. "There is only one Islam, but like man, it has both soul and body" (op.cit., p. xxxi). By equating "Islam" with "man," Izetbegovic appropriates "humanism" for Islam, giving the term an exclusive theological meaning very far from common acceptance. "Atheistic humanism is a contradiction because if there is no God, then there is no man either" (p. 39). "Everything must serve man, and man must serve God only. This is the ultimate meaning of humanism" (p. 40). "Man cannot be a Christian" because he cannot be a perfectly spiritual being, and the Koran says that "God does not charge anyone with a burden he cannot carry" (p. 227). In contrast, Islam "suits man because it recognizes the duality of his nature... That is why man is the most obvious argument of Islam." (p. 228)

This dualism recalls the two adversaries to Islamic renewal within the Muslim community cited in the "Islamic Declaration." The "con-servatives" are on the "spiritual" or "religious" side of the dichotomy, while the "progressives" are on the "materialistic" side. Both thereby fail to realize Islam in its fullness.

A passage in the chapter on "Drama and Utopia" (p.161) well illus-trates Izetbegovic's rigorous dualism. "Does evil come from inside, from the dark depths of the human soul, or does it come from outside, from the objective conditions of human life? This question divides all people into two large groups: believers and materialists. For believers all evil and good is in man. ... To assert that evil is outside, that a man is evil because the conditions in which he lives are bad, that changes in these conditions would bring changes in man, to insist that man is a result of outside circumstances, is from the religious point of view the most god-less and the most inhuman idea which has ever appeared in the human mind. Such an opinion degrades man to a thing, to a helpless executor of outside, mechanical, unconscious forces. Evil is in man versus evil is in the social environment. These are two mutually exclusive statements."

The mechanism of the dualistic approach can be seen here. Two extreme propositions are set against each other, and proclaimed to be irreconcilable. Their irreconcilability lies precisely in their extreme formulation, and is thus a truism. This approach automatically excludes all intermediate formulations which might combine elements of the two positions and thus render them reconcilable. This exclusion of the intermediate reasoned positions is necessary in order to arrive at the "problem"—a universe of irreconcilable opposites—which can be solved only by an extra-rational miracle: God. Or, for Izetbegovic, to be precise, submission to God's will, that is, Islam.

Only Islam can bring the virtues of religion into the real world. "Being a priori against the use of violence, Christianity and religion in general could not directly influence anything that might improve man's social position." (p. 192) "Islam started as mysticism and ended as a state. Religion accepted the world of facts and became Islam." (p.194) "Islam knows no specifically 'religious' literature in the European sense of the word, just as it knows no pure secular literature. Every Islamic thinker is a theologian, just as every true Islamic movement is also a political movement." (p. 197)

While the "Islamic Declaration" is concise and clear, the 300 pages of *Islam Between East and West* are replete with dubious science, dubious philosophy, erudite references and logical fallacies, all summoned to illustrate the author's sweeping assertions.[6] In this type of text, abound-

---

6 Example: On page 57, Izetbegovic asserts that: "Religiousness is inversely and crime is directly proportional to the largeness of a city." To support this sweeping statement, he cites, in a footnote, "an inquiry" (unidentified) according to which "12 to 13 percent of the inhabitants of Paris come to the Catholic mass, in Lyon 20.9 percent, and in St. Etienne 28.5 percent. Data about crime would certainly show the inverse gradient." Would they indeed? We have no way of knowing. Izetbegovic simply asserts that this relationship exists, and that it is due to the superior "experienced aesthetics" of the countryside in comparison to the city. Aside from the lack of serious supporting data or the dubious superiority of the "experienced aesthetics" of St.Etienne over Paris, this insistence on the moral influence of urban or rural environment is in blatant contradiction to Izetbegovic's central argument, cited above (from p.161), rejecting the "materialistic" argument that evil comes from external "conditions of human life" as "the most godless and the most inhuman idea which has ever appeared in the human mind." But Izetbegovic is immune to accusations of contradiction, since he can reply that "Islam" synthesizes every proposition and its opposite!

ing in truisms and circular reasoning, it is impossible not to find some statements with which one can agree, and others one cannot accept. In short, it is *pure ideology*, a series of statements that one may accept or reject, but that cannot be proved or disproved.

The Political Impact of Izetbegovic's Ideas

Along with a dozen co-religionists, Izetbegovic was arrested in still-communist Yugoslavia and sentenced to prison in 1983 (all were freed by a general amnesty in 1988) for "counter-revolutionary activities" and seeking to transform Bosnia-Herzegovina into an "ethnically pure Islamic state."[7] The very fact that such charges were brought by a Communist state, and again reiterated by "nationalist" Serbs, has seemingly protected Izetbegovic's writings from critical examination.

From a democratic secular viewpoint, there is nothing, absolutely nothing, in either the "Islamic Declaration" or *Islam Between East and West* to justify arresting Mr. Izetbegovic and putting him in prison for five years. The harm done by jailing people for ideas goes beyond the personal injustice suffered. The fact that Izetbegovic was persecuted for his ideas has tended ever since to make any free criticism of those ideas "taboo," since criticism is readily equated with endorsement of communist persecution. Unfortunately, the fear of taking "the wrong side" in one way or another has stood in the way of free and open debate regarding all the main "subversive" writings that marked the ideological crisis of the Titoist regime, notably the most controversial, those of Izetbegovic, Tudjman and of the Serbian Academy of Sciences and Arts. Without open debate, the prevailing tendency has been to cite such texts (often inaccurately) for polemic purposes rather than to examine them fairly and critically.

The unquestionable right of Mr. Izetbegovic to express his ideas without being sent to prison should not preclude evaluating the impact of those ideas on the recent history of Bosnia-Herzegovina. Those ideas became notorious locally as a result of two trials in the 1980s in which Muslims were accused of fomenting counter-revolution of the basis of the "Islamic Declaration." Later, supporters of the Sarajevo regime dismissed any suggestion that Mr. Izetbegovic might be considered an

---

7 Alexandre Popovic, "Islamic Movements in Yugoslavia," in Andreas Kappeler, Gerhard Simon, Georg Brunner & Edward Allworth, Muslim Communities Reemerge: Historical Perspectives on Nationality, Politics and Opposition in the Former Soviet Union and Yugoslavia, Duke University Press, Durham & London, 1994, p.335.

"Islamic fundamentalist" as grotesque Serbian nationalist propaganda. The question was not examined seriously. Insofar as "fundamentalism" can be defined as basing an entire social and political order on religion, then Mr. Izetbegovic is certainly a "fundamentalist." There is another aspect that deserves study, and that is the extent to which fear of the implications of the "Islamic Declaration," specifically the call for an Islamic state *once Muslims are a majority of the population*, drove large numbers of the Orthodox and Catholic Christians of Bosnia-Herzegovina into the arms of nationalist Serb and Croat parties. This is a legitimate question, that needs to be elucidated as part of the process of clarifying the causes of the conflict and working for reconciliation between communities.[8]

---

8 Such a question is typically dismissed out of hand, for example by Silber & Little, op. cit., p. 208. "Serb and Croat nationalists point to the Islamic Declaration, an esoteric document penned by Izetbegovic, in 1973, as proof that Izetbegovic planned to create a Muslim state. In fact, it was a work of scholarship, not politics, intended to promote philosophical discourse among Muslims. In it, he excluded the 'use of violence in the creation of a Muslim state, because it defiles the beauty of the name of Islam.' A more significant indicator of Izetbegovic's orientation was Islam between East and West, first published in the United States in 1984, and then in Yugoslavia after his release from prison four years later. This book mapped out his vision of an Islamic state in the modern world. In it he charts a course between Islamic values and material progress, arguing that the benefits of secular western civilization are without meaning unless they are accompanied by the spiritual values found predominantly in Islamic societies."

Their comments on Izetbegovic's writings are so far off the mark as to raise the question: have they read them? Or are they quoting the author of the work cited in their two footnotes, Srecko M.Dzaja, Bosnia i Bosnjaci u hrvatskom politickom diskursu, Erasmus, December 1994, p. 33? This seems likely. There is in fact nothing "esoteric" about the "Islamic Declaration," nor can it reasonably be called "a work of scholarship, not politics."

To say that the 1984 book "charts a course between Islamic values and material progress" is a gross misreading. In reality, Izetbegovic presents Islamic values themselves as uniting the material and the spiritual, and this is the course he charts, not a course "between" Islamic values and anything else.

What is clear is that Izetbegovic, like, for instance, the Islamic fundamentalists in Algeria, sets great value on modern technology, and sees no contradiction whatsoever between material progress and Islam. This acceptance of the technological fruits of the enlightenment, accompanied by rejection of the enlightenment's philosophical content, recalls the "revolt of the masses" forecast by Jose Ortega y Gasset. In that connection, it can be noted that contemporary American Christian fundamentalists are also highly receptive to modern technology while rejecting the philosophical heritage of the enlightenment.

NATO's Humanitarian Trigger[*]

MARCH 1999

From James Rubin to Christiane Amanpour, the broad range of government and media opinion is totally united in demanding that NATO bomb Serbia. This is necessary, we are told, in order to "avert a humanitarian catastrophe," and because, "the only language Milosevic understands is force"...which happens to be the language the U.S. wants to speak. Kosovo is presented as the problem, and NATO as the solution. In reality, NATO is the problem, and Kosovo is the solution.

After the collapse of the Soviet Union, NATO needed a new excuse for pumping resources into the military-industrial complex. Thanks to Kosovo, NATO can celebrate its 50th anniversary next month by consacration of its new global mission: to intervene anywhere in the world on humanitarian grounds. The recipe is easy: arm a group of radical secessionists to shoot policemen, describe the inevitable police retaliation as "ethnic cleansing," promise the rebels that NATO will bomb their enemy if the fighting goes on, and then interpret the resulting mayhem as a challenge to NATO's "resolve" which must be met by military action.

Thanks to Kosovo, national sovereignty will be a thing of the past — not of course for Great Powers like the U.S. and China, but for weaker States that really need it. National boundaries will be no obstacle to NATO intervention. Thanks to Kosovo, the U.S. can control eventual Caspian oil pipeline routes between the Black Sea and the Adriatic, and extend the European influence of favored ally Turkey.

Last February 23, James Hooper, executive director of the Balkan Action Council, one of the many think tanks that have sprung up to justify the ongoing transformation of former Yugoslavia into NATO protectorates, gave a speech at the Holocaust Museum in Washington at the invitation of its "Committee of Conscience." The first item on his list of "things to do next" was this: "Accept that the Balkans are a

---

* Published in *DIALOGUE* (Paris), No. 29–30, 1999.

region of strategic interest for the United States, the new Berlin if you will, the testing ground for NATO's resolve and U.S. leadership. [...] The administration should level with the American people and tell them that we are likely to be in the Balkans militarily indefinitely, at least until there is a democratic government in Belgrade."

In the Middle Ages, the Crusaders launched their conquests from the Church pulpits. Today, NATO does so in the Holocaust Museum. War must be sacred.

This sacralization has been largely facilitated by a post-communist left which has taken refuge in moralism and identity politics to the exclusion of any analysis of the economic and geopolitical factors that continue to determine the macropolicies shaping the world.

Jean-Christophe Rufin, former vice president of "Doctors Without Borders" recently pointed to the responsibility of humanitarian non-governmental organizations in justifying military intervention. "They were the first to deplore the passivity of the political response to dramatic events in the Balkans or Africa. Now they have got what they wanted, or so it seems. For in practice, rubbing elbows with NATO could turn out to be extremely dangerous."

Already the call for United Nations soldiers to intervene on humanitarian missions raised suspicions in the Third World that "the humanitarians could be the Trojan horse of a new armed imperialism," Rufin wrote in *Le Monde.* But NATO is something else.

"With NATO, everything has changed. Here we are dealing with a purely military, operational alliance, designed to respond to a threat, that is to an enemy," wrote Rufin. "NATO defines an enemy, threatens it, then eventually strikes and destroys it.

"Setting such a machine in motion requires a detonator. Today it is no longer military. Nor is it political. The evidence is before us: NATO's trigger, today, is... humanitarian. It takes blood, a masssacre, something that will outrage public opinion so that it will welcome a violent reaction."

The consequence, he concluded, is that "the civilian populations have never been so potentially threatened as in Kosovo today. Why? Because those potential victims are the key to international reaction. Let's be clear: the West wants dead bodies. [...] We are waiting for them in Kosovo. We'll get them." Who will kill them is a mystery but previous incidents suggest that "the threat comes from all sides."

In the middle of conflict as in Kosovo, massacres can easily be perpetrated... or "arranged." There are always television crews looking precisely for that "top story."

Recently, Croatian officers have admitted that in 1993 they themselves staged a "Serbian bombing" of the Croatian coastal city of Sibenik for the benefit of Croatian television crews. The former Commander of the 113th Croatian brigade headquarters, Davo Skugor, reacted indignantly. "Why so much fuss?" he complained. "There is no city in Croatia in which such tactical tricks were not used. After all, they are an integral part of strategic planning. That's only one in a series of stratagems we've resorted to during the war."

The fact remains that there really is a very serious Kosovo problem. It has existed for well over a century, habitually exacerbated by outside powers (the Ottoman Empire, the Habsburg Empire, the Axis powers during World War II). The Serbs are essentially a modernized peasant people, who having liberated themselves from arbitrary Turkish Ottoman oppression in the 19th century, are attached to modern state institutions. In contrast, the Albanians in the northern mountains of Albania and Kosovo have never really accepted any law, political or religious, over their own unwritten "Kanun" based on patriarchal obedience to vows, family honor, elaborate obligations, all of which are enforced not by any government but by male family and clan chiefs protecting their honor, eventually in the practice of blood feuds and revenge.

The basic problem of Kosovo is the difficult coexistence on one territory of ethnic communities radically separated by customs, language and historical self-identification. From a humanistic viewpoint, this problem is more fundamental than the problem of State boundaries. Mutual hatred and fear is the fundamental human catastrophe in Kosovo. It has been going on for a long time. It has got much worse in recent years. Why?

Two factors stand out as paradoxically responsible for this worsening — paradoxically, because presented to the world as factors which should have improved the situation.

The first is the establishment in the autonomous Kosovo of the 1970s and 1980s of separate Albanian cultural institutions, notably the Albanian language faculties in Pristina University. This cultural autonomy, demanded by ethnic Albanian leaders, turned out to be a step not to reconciliation between communities but to their total separation. Drawing on a relatively modest store of past scholarship, largely originating in Austria, Germany or Enver Hoxha's Albania, studies in Albanian history and literature amounted above all to glorifications of Albanian identity. Rather than developing the critical spririt, they developed narrow ethnocentricy. Graduates in these fields were prepared above all for the career of nationalist political leader, and it is striking the number of literati among Kosovo Albanian secessionist leaders. Extreme cultural autonomy has created two populations with no common language.

In retrospect, what should have been done was to combine Serbian and Albanian studies, requiring both languages, and developing original comparative studies of history and literature. This would have subjected both Serbian and Albanian national myths to the scrutiny of the other, and worked to correct the nationalist bias in both. Bilingual comparative studies could and should have been a way toward mutual understanding as well as an enrichment of universal culture. Instead, culture in the service of identity politics leads to mutual ignorance and contempt.

The lesson of this grave error should be a warning elsewhere, starting in Macedonia, where Albanian nationalists are clamoring to repeat the Pristina experience in Tetova. Other countries with mixed ethnic populations should take note.

The second factor has been the support from foreign powers, especially the United States, to the Albanian nationalist cause in Kosovo. By uncritically accepting the version of the tangled Kosovo situation presented by the Albanian lobby, American politicians have greatly exacerbated the conflict by encouraging the armed Albanian rebels and pushing the Serbian authorities into extreme efforts to wipe them out.

The "Kosovo Liberation Army" (UCK) has nothing to lose by provoking deadly clashes, once it is clear that the number of dead and the number of refugees will add to the balance of the "humanitarian catastrophe" that can bring NATO and U.S. air power into the conflict on the Albanian side.

The Serbs have nothing to gain by restraint, once it is clear that they will be blamed anyway for whatever happens.

By identifying the Albanians as "victims" per se, and the Serbs as the villains, the United States and its allies have made any fair and reasonable political solution virtually impossible. The Clinton administration in particular builds its policy on the assumption that what the Kosovar Albanians — including the UCK — really want is "democracy," American style. In fact, what they want is power over a particular territory, and among the Albanian nationalists, there is a bitter power struggle going on over who will exercise that power.

Thus an American myth of "U.S.-style democracy and free market economy will solve everything" is added to the Serbian and Albanian myths to form a fictional screen making reality almost impossible to discern, much less improve. Underlying the American myth are Brzezinski-style geostrategic designs for expanding NATO as an instrument to ensure U.S. hegemony over the Eurasian land mass.

Supposing by some miracle the world suddenly turned upside down, and there were outside powers who really cared about the fate of Kosovo and its inhabitants, one could suggest the following:

1. stop one-sided demonization of the Serbs, recognize the genuine qualities, faults and fears on all sides, and work to promote understanding rather than hatred;
2. stop arming and encouraging rebel groups;
3. allow genuine mediation by parties with no geostrategic or political interests at stake in the region.

The Lie of a "Good War"*

JUNE 2004

For U.S. politicians, if all wars are good, some are better than others. Democrats prefer Clinton wars and Republicans prefer Bush wars. But in the end, they almost unanimously come together to support all wars. The differences concern the choice of official rationale.

To suggest subtle criticism of the Republican war against Iraq, while making it clear that they are by no means opposed to war as such, the 2004 Democratic election campaigners can be expected to glorify the Kosovo war. The prominence of General Wesley Clark in the Democratic camp makes that quite clear.

John Kerry's foreign policy adviser Will Marshall of the Progressive Policy Institute, author of "Democratic Realism: The Third Way," points to the exemplary nature of the 1999 "U.S.-led intervention in Kosovo." It was "a policy consciously based on a mix of moral values and security interests with the parallel goals of halting a humanitarian tragedy and ensuring NATO's credibility as an effective force for regional stability."

The "humanitarian" rationale sounds better than the "weapons of mass destruction" or the "links to Al Qaeda" which never existed. But then, the "genocide" from which the NATO war allegedly saved the Albanians of Kosovo never existed either.

But while the WMD deception has been exposed, the founding lie behind the Kosovo war is still widely believed. It effectively distracts from the very existence of what Marshall calls the "parallel goal" of strengthening NATO. Aside from the crippling material damage inflicted on the targeted country, the Kosovo lie has caused even more irreparable damage to relations between the Serb and Albanian inhabitants of Kosovo. The situation in that small province of multiethnic Serbia was the result of a long and complex history of conflict, frequently encouraged

---

* Original version: *CounterPunch*, June 24, 2004. https://www. counterpunch.org/2004/06/24/the-lie-of-a-quot-good-war-quot/

and exploited by outside powers, notably by the support to Albanian nationalism by the Axis powers in World War II. Each community accused the other of plotting "ethnic cleansing" and even "genocide." But there were reasonable people on both sides willing to work out a compromise solution. The constructive role of outsiders would have been to calm the paranoid tendencies in both communities and support constructive initiatives. Indeed, the Kosovo problem could have been easily managed, and eventually solved, had the Great Powers so desired. But as in the past, the Great Powers exploited and aggravated the ethnic conflicts for their own purposes. In total ignorance of the complex history of the region, sheeplike politicians and media echoed and amplified the most extreme nationalist Albanian propaganda. This provided NATO with its pretext to demonstrate "credibility." The Great Powers have in effect told the Albanians that all their worst accusations against the Serbs were true. Even Albanians who must know better (such as Veton Surroi) are intimidated and silenced by the racist nationalists backed by the United States.

The result is disastrous. Empowered by their official status as unique victims of Serb iniquity, the Albanians of Kosovo—and especially the youth, raised on a decade of nationalist myth—can give free rein to their cultivated hatred of the Serbs. Armed Albanian nationalists proceeded to drive the Serbian and gypsy populations out of the province. Those remaining do not dare venture out of their ghettos. Albanians willing to live with the Serbs risk being murdered. Ever since the NATO-led force (KFOR) marched into Kosovo in June 1999, violent persecution of Serbs and Roma has been regularly described as "revenge"—which in the Albanian tradition is considered the summit of virtuous conduct. Describing the murder of elderly women in their homes or children at play as acts of "revenge" is a way of excusing or even approving the violence.

Last March 17, following the false accusation that Serbs were responsible for the accidental drowning of three Albanian children, organized mobs of Albanians, including many teenagers, rampaged through Kosovo destroying 35 Serbian Orthodox Christian churches and monasteries, some of them artistic gems dating from the fourteenth century. Well over a hundred churches had already been attacked with fire and explosives in the past five years. The objective is quite clearly to erase all historic trace of centuries of Serb presence, the better to assert their claim to an ethnically pure Albanian Kosovo.

The self-satisfaction of the "international community" was severely shaken by the March violence. The occasional KFOR units that tried to protect Serb sites found themselves in armed clashes with Albanian mobs. In the wake of the rampages, Finnish politician Harri Holkeri resigned two months before expiration of his one-year renewable mandate as head of the U.N. Mission in Kosovo (UNMIK) supposed to administer the province. He was the fourth to get out of the job as fast as he could. Apparently on the verge of a nervous breakdown, Holkeri lamented to a press conference that UNMIK has no intelligence service of its own, and had received no prior hint of the March pogroms. In short, the mass of international administrators, military occupation forces and non-governmental agencies have no idea what is going on in the province they are theoretically running. Indicating his awareness that the only role left for UNMIK was that of scapegoat, Holkeri warned of "difficult days ahead."

That is a safe prediction.

Trouble ahead

On June 11, the former leader of the Kosovo Liberation Army Hashim Thaci, the protégé of Madeleine Albright and of her press officer James Rubin, denounced UNMIK as a "complete failure" and announced that, if he wins Kosovo's forthcoming elections in October, he will implement his "vision of Kosovo as an independent and sovereign state."

The circumstances suggest that not only Thaci, but any newly elected Kosovo Albanian may do the same. Proclamation of Kosovo's independence on the eve of U.S. presidential elections could be shrewd timing. With Iraq exploding, American leaders need to maintain the myth of the "success" in Kosovo. Getting into open conflict with the Albanians could be politically disastrous.

At the same time, many Europeans saw the anti-Serb pogroms in March as evidence that Kosovo has a long way to go to reach the "standards" of democratic human rights and ethnic harmony which UNMIK is mandated to achieve before any final decision on the province's status.

There are serious reasons not to give in to the Albanian demand for an "independent and sovereign Kosovo."

1. Legality

First of all, there is the minor question of legality: minor, inasmuch as the NATO powers have ignored it from the start. The war itself was totally devoid of any legitimate basis in international law. It was officially concluded in June 1999 by a peace accord incorporated into U.N.

Security Council Resolution 1244, which, among other things, obliged the occupying powers to :

• "ensure conditions for a peaceful and normal life for all inhabitants of Kosovo"—which logically should mean "all," and not solely the Albanians;

• "ensure the safe and free return of all refugees and displaced persons"—by which the U.S. negotiators probably meant the Albanians who had fled during the bombing, but since they promptly returned on their own, without difficulty, this stipulation in reality refers to Serbs, Rom and other non-Albanians forced to flee;

• establish an interim political framework "taking full account of [...]the principles of sovereignty and integrity of the Federal Republic of Yugoslavia"—which amounts to recognition that Kosovo remains part of a larger political entity made up of Serbia and Montenegro;

• permit the return of an agreed number of Yugoslav and Serbian personnel, including border control police and customs agents;

• effect the maintenance of civil law and order and the protection of human rights.

In reality, once the United States got its big military foot in the door, Resolution 1244 was scarcely worth the paper it was written on. The United States had other priorities:

• First, in record time, the Pentagon built an enormous military base, "Camp Bondsteel," on a thousand areas of illegally expropriated farmland strategically located near trans-Balkan transit routes, on the approaches to the Middle East and Caspian Sea oil transport.

• The other obvious U.S. priority was to preserve the clandestine wartime alliance with the "Kosovo Liberation Army," not only against the Serbs, but also, implicitly, against any European allies which might seek influence in post-conquest Kosovo. After a sham "disarmament" disposing of a few obsolete light arms, the KLA was renamed the "Kosovo Protection Force" and put on the U.N. payroll. Certain of its officers proceeded to mount armed actions to extend "greater Albania" to neighboring Macedonia and parts of Southern Serbia next to Kosovo. These operations were launched from the American sector, next to Camp Bondsteel.

• As for the internal organization of Kosovo itself, the U.S. priority is, as usual, privatization of the economy. Privatization in practice starts with dismantling whatever government services existed, on the theory that without government interference, private initiative will flourish.

In a very special sense, this has indeed proved to be the case. Kosovo, already a transit area for the largest amount of heroin smuggled from Turkey to Western Europe, has rapidly become the center of a new trade in women sex slaves. The Albanian mafia is by far the biggest operator in these trades. The "internationals" who have come to "civilize" the province provide a thriving local market for prostitutes. If they ever go home, the Albanian mafia can count on the networks it has developed throughout Western Europe to keep business going

2. The economy

In socialist Yugoslavia, Kosovo was by far the poorest area in Yugoslavia, with the highest rate of chronic unemployment. It still is. But then, it benefited from injection of the largest amount of development funds from the rest of the country. Although the sentiment that their poverty was a result of exploitation contributed to the rise of Kosovo Albanian nationalism, the fact is that Kosovo was always heavily subsidized by the rest of Yugoslavia, and as a result was considerably more developed than neighboring Albania.

Since the NATO occupation, Kosovo lives off other sources of income, mainly the flourishing drugs and sex trades. The "international community" has contributed a patchwork of social services (from UNMIK police to NGO counsellors) that provide a temporary substitute for the expulsion of the local branches of the Serbian government. Camp Bondsteel provides the largest number of legitimate jobs to Albanians and may continue to do so even after the demand for chauffeurs and interpreters dries up as the NGOs go home. Saudi Arabia can be counted on to finance mosque construction. But with a per capita income of about $30 per month, it is hard to see where an "independent Kosovo" could scrape up the tax base to pay for a government, especially since so much of the real income is illicit, outside the reach of tax collectors.

Kosovo is only an extreme case of the "transition" from socialism to the free market, as imposed on Eastern Europe by the "international community." The State and its services were removed by NATO military force, whereas elsewhere the demolition process has been more gradual and less dramatic, the result of pressures from the IMF, the World Bank and the European Union. The mass of unemployed young men have little prospect of earning a living other than by getting in on the crime business. It is hard to see what can prevent "independent Kosovo" from being an uncontrollable crime center.

At the end of World War II, in order to defeat the Fascists and combat the Communists, U.S. intelligence services cynically brought the Mafia back to Sicily. The parallel with Kosovo does not go beyond that. For unlike Kosovo, Sicily is an essentially rich island, with a diversified economy and numerous centuries-old sophisticated urban centers where large sectors of a highly educated population have courageously resisted the corruption and violence of the mafia. This aspect of Sicilian society is insufficiently appreciated abroad, where it is more "romantic" to glorify the gangsters. In comparison, Kosovo Albanian society simply does not possess such material or cultural resources for resisting the power of the new mafias that, while feeding on certain clan traditions, are above all a product of neoliberal globalism.

3. Human rights

The protection of "human rights" was the pretext for the 1999 war. In terms of everyday human relations, the situation is far worse than before. This is not widely recognized for two reasons. One, since the "international community" rather than Milosevic is in charge, media interest in Kosovo has virtually evaporated. Second, the victims of persecution and harassment, the children whose school buses are stoned, the old people who are beaten and whose houses are set on fire, the farmers who do not dare go out to cultivate their fields, the hundreds of thousands of refugees from "ethnic cleansing" ... are Serbs. Or sometimes gypsies. Western media early on identified "the Serbs" as the enemies of "multi-ethnic society" and the perpetrators of "ethnic cleansing." The curious result seems to be that the absence of Serbs is understood as the best guarantee of a multi-ethnic society. This, at any rate, is the logic of the attitude taken by the international community in regard to the Ibar valley region of Kosovo north of Mitrovica.

That area, which forms a sort of point reaching into central Serbia, is the largest remaining part of Kosovo where Serbs retain a traditional majority sufficient to defend themselves from Albanian intimidation. When, as happens from time to time, Albanian militants from the ethnically purified region south of the Ibar attempt to cross the river, they are stopped by Serb guards. In this situation, "international community" spokesmen almost invariably take the line that Serb extremists are standing in the way of "multi-ethnic" Kosovo. The fact is deliberately overlooked that, while a certain number of Albanians are still living in Serb-controlled northern Mitrovica, all Serbs and Rom have been driven out of southern Mitrovica, and that if the Albanian activists were granted free access to the north, the probable result would be further ethnic cleansing of what remains of the Serb population.

For some in the "international community," that would be an ideal solution. Once all non-Albanians have been driven out, the professional humanitarians can declare that Kosovo is "multi-ethnic," and there will be nobody left there to dispute this triumphant assertion.

The overriding concern of the West now is to get out of the Kosovo mess in a way that will allow it to continue to celebrate the Kosovo war as a great humanitarian success. Having left the Balkans in a shambles, the human rights warriors can go on to other victories. The only thing to stop them might be a belated recognition of the truth.

Independence in the Brave New World Order

NATO's Kosovo Colony?*

FEBRUARY 2008

Across this last weekend, the Western propaganda machine was working overtime, celebrating the latest NATO miracle: the transformation of Serbian Kosovo into Albanian Kosova. A shameless land grab by the United States, which used the Kosovo problem to install an enormous military base (Camp Bondsteel) on other people's strategically located land, is transformed by the power of the media into an edifying legend of "national liberation."

For the unhappy few who know the complicated truth about Kosovo, the words of Aldous Huxley seem most appropriate: "You shall know the truth, and the truth shall drive you mad."

Concerning Kosovo, truth is like letters written in the sand as the tsunami of propaganda comes thundering in. The truth is available--for instance in George Szamuely's thoroughly informative piece last Friday on CounterPunch.[1]

Fragments of the truth sometimes even show up in the mainstream media, mostly in letters from readers. But hopeless as it is to try to turn back the tide of officially endorsed legend, let me examine just one drop in this unstoppable sea of propaganda: a column by Roger Cohen entitled "Europe's new state," published in the Valentine's Day edition of the *International Herald Tribune.*

Cohen's op ed piece is fairly typical in the dismissive way it deals with Milosevic, Russia and the Serbs. Cohen writes: "Slobodan Milosevic, the late dictator, set Serbia's murderous nationalist tide in motion on April 24, 1987, when he went to Kosovo to declare that Serbian 'ancestors would be defiled' if ethnic Albanians had their way."

---

* Original version: *CounterPunch,* February 18, 2008. https://www.counterpunch.org/2008/02/18/nato-s-kosovo-colony/

1 https://counterpunch.com/szamuely02152008.html

I don't know where Roger Cohen got that quotation, but it is not to be found in the speech Milosevic made that day in Kosovo. And certainly, Milosevic did not go to Kosovo to declare any such thing, but to consult with local Communist League officials in the town of Kosovo Polje about the province's serious economic and social problems. Aside from the province's chronic poverty, unemployment, and mismanagement of development funds contributed from the rest of Yugoslavia, the main social problem was the constant exodus of Serb and Montenegrin inhabitants under pressure from ethnic Albanians. At the time, this problem was reported in leading Western media.

For instance, as early as July 12, 1982, Marvine Howe reported to the *New York Times* that Serbs were leaving Kosovo by the tens of thousands because of discrimination and intimidation on the part of the ethnic Albanian majority:

> "The [Albanian] nationalists have a two-point platform," according to Beci Hoti, an executive secretary of the Communist Party of Kosovo, "first to establish what they call an ethnically clean Albanian republic and then the merger with Albania to form a greater Albania.
>
> Mr. Hoti, an Albanian, expressed concern over political pressures that were forcing Serbs to leave Kosovo. "What is important now," he said, "is to establish a climate of security and create confidence."

And seven months after Milosevic's visit to Kosovo, David Binder reported in the *New York Times* (November 1, 1987):

> Ethnic Albanians in the Government [of Kosovo] have manipulated public funds and regulations to take over land belonging to Serbs. Slavic Orthodox churches have been attacked, and flags have been torn down. Wells have been poisoned and crops burned. Slavic boys have been knifed, and some young ethnic Albanians have been told by their elders to rape Serbian girls.
>
> The goal of the radical nationals among them, one said in an interview, is an "ethnic Albania that includes

western Macedonia, southern Montenegro, part of southern Serbia, Kosovo and Albania itself."

As Slavs flee the protracted violence, Kosovo is becoming what ethnic Albanian nationalists have been demanding for years, and especially strongly since the bloody rioting by ethnic Albanians in Pristina in 1981—an "ethnically pure" Albanian region.

This was in fact the first instance of "ethnic cleansing" in post-World War II Yugoslavia, as reported in *The New York Times* and other Western media, and the victims were the Serbs. The cult of "memory" has become a contemporary religion, but some memories are more equal than others. In the 1990s, the *New York Times* evidently forgot completely what it had said about Kosovo in the 1980s. Why? Perhaps because meanwhile, the Soviet bloc had collapsed and the unity of independent, non-aligned Yugoslavia was no longer in the strategic interest of the United States.

Back to Milosevic in Kosovo Polje on April 24, 1987. An incident occurred when local police (under an Albanian-dominated Communist League government) attacked Serbs who had gathered to protest lack of legal protection. Milosevic famously told them, spontaneously: "No one should beat you any more!" If this is "extreme nationalism," perhaps there should be more of it.

But nowhere do I find a trace of the statement attributed to Milosevic by Cohen. In his speech to local party delegates that followed, which is on the public record, Milosevic referred to the "regrettable incident" and promised an investigation. He went on to stress that "we should not allow the misfortunes of people to be exploited by nationalists, whom every honest person must combat. We must not divide people between Serbs and Albanians, but rather we should separate, on the one hand, decent people who struggle for brotherhood, unity and ethnic equality, and, on the other hand, counter-revolutionaries and nationalists."

I turn again to Aldous Huxley for comfort: "Facts do not cease to exist because they are ignored."

But Huxley also said: "Great is truth, but still greater, from a practical point of view, is silence about truth. By simply not mentioning certain subjects... totalitarian propagandists have influenced opinion much more effectively than they could have by the most eloquent denunciations."

Last Tuesday in Geneva, Russian Foreign Minister Sergei Lavrov tried to convey to journalists his grave concern about the way the United States was handling the Kosovo problem.

"We are speaking here about the subversion of all the foundations and principles of international law, which have been won and established as a basis of Europe's existence at huge effort, and at the cost of pain, sacrifice and bloodletting," he said.

"Nobody can offer a clear plan of action in the case of a chain re-action [of further declarations of unilateral independence]. It turns out that they [the United States and its NATO allies] are planning to act in a hit or miss fashion on an issue of paramount importance. This is simply inadmissible and irresponsible," the Russian diplomat said. "I sincerely fail to comprehend the principles guiding our American colleagues, and those Europeans who have taken up this position," he added.

Roger Cohen dismisses such considerations in five words: "the Russian bear will growl." Russia, he adds, "will scream. But it's backed the wrong horse." There are no issues here, no principles. Just growling and gambling. "Milosevic rolled the dice of genocidal nationalism and lost," says Cohen.

This is not only a false statement, it is a grotesquely meaningless metaphor. Milosevic tried to suppress an armed secessionist movement, secretly but effectively supported by neighboring Albania, the United States and Germany, which deliberately provoked repression by mur-dering both Serbs and Albanians loyal to the government. Like the Americans in similar circumstances, Milosevic relied too heavily on military superiority rather than on political skill. But even the NATO-sponsored International Criminal Tribunal for Former Yugoslavia in The Hague had to abandon any charges of "genocide" against Milosevic in Kosovo. For the simple reason that there was never a shred of evidence for such a charge.

Milosevic is no longer alive, and Russia is far away. But what about the Serbs who still live in the historic part of Serbia called Kosovo? Cohen takes care of that problem in a few words: "Some of the 120,000 Serbs in Kosovo may hit the road."

As Aldous Huxley pointed out, "The propagandist's purpose is to make one set of people forget that certain other sets of people are human."

Then you can tell them to "hit the road."

The "Unique" Case

Russia has warned that Kosovo independence will set a dangerous precedent, encouraging other ethnic minorities to follow the example of the Albanians and demand secession and an independent State. The

United States has dismissed such concerns by flatly asserting that Kosovo is "unique." Well yes, Kosovo is a unique case, and is the only one recognized by the United States until the next "unique case" comes along. When legal criteria have been thrown out, we just have one "unique case" after another.

The "uniqueness" claimed by the United States is a propaganda construction. It is based on the supposed "uniqueness" of Milosevic's repression of the armed secessionist movement, which was not unique at all. It was standard operating procedure throughout history and the world over, in such circumstances. Deplorable, no doubt, but not unique. It was minor indeed compared to the similar but endless and far bloodier anti-insurgency operations in Colombia, Sri Lanka, and Chechnya, not to mention Northern Ireland, Thailand, the Philippines... And unlike the counter-insurgency operations in Iraq and Afghanistan, which kill incomparably more civilians, it was carried out by the legal, democratically elected government of the country, rather than by a foreign power.

The propaganda "uniqueness" is an abstraction. Like every place on earth, Kosovo is indeed unique. But in ways that have nothing to do with the U.S. pretext for taking it over and turning it into a military outpost of empire.

To know how a place is unique, you have to be interested in it.

I have not visited Kosovo since before the 1999 NATO war. On one occasion, in August 1997, I drove around the province in a failing Skoda, at my own expense, just looking. Driving in Kosovo was a bit risky, partly because of the number of dead dogs in the road, and mostly because of local drivers' habit of passing slower vehicles on hills and curves. In northern Kosovo, just outside the town of Zubin Potok, this habit produced one of its inevitable consequences: a head-on collision with serious casualties, which shut down the two-lane highway for hours while ambulances and police sorted things out.

Unable to proceed toward Pristina, I drove back to Zubin Potok to pass the time on the shaded terrace of a roadside restaurant. I was the only customer, and the lone waiter, a tall, handsome young man named Milomir, gladly accepted my invitation to sit down at my table and chat as I sipped glass after glass of delicious strawberry juice.

Milomir was happy to talk to someone familiar with the French city of Metz, which he had visited as a student and remembered fondly. He loved to read and travel, but in 1991 he got married and now had two small daughters to support. Job prospects were poor, even though he had been to university, so he had no choice but to stay in Zubin Potok. As for Europe, even if he could get a visa (impossible for Serbs anyway), he spoke no language more Western than his mother tongue, Serbo-Croatian. He had studied Russian (he loved the literature) and Albanian as his foreign languages. He learned Albanian in order to be able to communicate with the majority in Kosovo. But such communication was difficult. Milomir was very much in favor of a bilingual society, and thought everyone in Kosovo should learn both Serbian and Albanian, but unfortunately this was not the case. The younger generation of Albanians refused to speak Serbian and learned English instead.

The town of Zubin Potok was located near the dam on the Ibar River built in the late 1970s to create hydraulic power. Coming from Novi Pazar, I had driven along the 35-kilometer-long artificial lake created by the dam, looking in vain for a nice place to stop. It seemed that there must have been villages along the Ibar River before the dam was built, and I asked Milomir about this. Yes, he said, the artificial lake had flooded a score of old villages, of ethnically mixed, but mostly Serb population. The Albanian Communist authorities in Pristina had resettled the Serbs outside of Kosovo, around the town of Kraljevo. There were about 10,000 of them.

This was a minor example of the administrative measures taken to decrease the Serb population during the period, before Milosevic, when Albanians were running the province through the local Communist League.

Milomir was not complaining, but simply answering my questions. He did not go too often (by bus--he had no car) to the nearest large city, Mitrovica, because he was afraid of being beaten by Albanians. This was just a fact of life, at a time when (according to Western media) Albanians in Kosovo were being terrorized by Serbian repression.

While we were chatting, a friend of his came along and the conversation turned to politics. There was a presidential campaign underway. The two young men wanted to know which candidate I thought would be best for Serbia in the eyes of the world. Milomir was tending toward Vuk Draskovic, and his friend was for Vojislav Kostunica. Neither would dream of voting for either Milosevic or Seselj, the nationalist leader of the Radical Party.

Zubin Potok Today

I have no idea what has become of Milomir, his wife, his two daughters, or his friend. Zubin Potok is the western-most municipality in the heavily Serb-populated north of Kosovo. From the internet I learn that the population of Zubin Potok municipality (including surrounding villages) has nearly doubled since I passed through. It now comes to approximately 14,900, including about 3,000 internally displaced Serbs (from other areas of Kosovo where the Albanian majority has driven them out), 220 Serbian refugees from Croatia and 800 Albanians. The local assembly is overwhelmingly dominated by Kostunica's Democratic Party of Serbia, but includes two Kosovo Albanian representatives.

Up until now, schools, hospitals, and other public services, as well as the local economy, have continued to function thanks mainly to subsidies from Belgrade. The Albanian declaration of Kosovo independence will create a crisis by demanding an end to such vital subsidies--which, however, an "independent Kosovo" is unable to replace. Moreover, bands of Albanian nationalists are declaring that Zubin Potok "is Albanian" and must be "liberated from the Serbs." They can be seen on You Tube, using the Statue of Liberty as their symbol, and threatening Serbs in Albanian rap.

The European Union is moving in to provide law and order. But the "order" they claim to be protecting is the one defined by the Albanian nationalists. What does that mean to people like Milomir and his little family?

For Roger Cohen, the answer is easy: "hit the road!"

Serbia, by the way, already has the largest number of refugees in Europe, victims of "ethnic cleansing" in Croatia and Kosovo. And Serbs cannot get visas or refugee status in Western Europe. They have been labeled the "bad guys." Only their enemies can be "victims."

Before and After

Kosovo before the NATO war and occupation was, nevertheless, a multiethnic society. The accusation of "apartheid" was simply Albanian propaganda, as the Albanian nationalist leaders chose to use that heavily-charged term to describe their own boycott of Serbs and Serb institutions. Every police action against an Albanian, for whatever reason, whether for suspicion of armed rebellion or for ordinary crime, was described as a "human rights violation" by the Albanian human rights network financed by the United States government. It was an extraordinary situation that the Serbian and Yugoslav governments allowed an illegal separatist "government of Kosovo," headed by Ibrahim Rugova, to hold shop in the center of Pristina, regularly receiving foreign journalists and regaling them with tales of how oppressed they were by the horrid Serbs.

But the laws were the same for all citizens, there were Albanians in local government and in the police, and if there were cases of police brutality (in what country are there no cases of police brutality?), the Albanians at least had nothing to fear from their Serb neighbors. Even then, it was the Serbs who were afraid of the Albanians. Only outside Kosovo could anyone seriously believe that it was the Albanians who were under threat of 'ethnic cleansing' (much less "genocide"). Such a project was simply, obviously, out of the question. It was the Serbs who were afraid, who spoke of sending their children to safety if they had the means, or who spoke bravely of remaining "no matter what." Later, in March 1999, when NATO began to bomb Kosovo, Albanians fled by the hundreds of thousands, and their temporary flight from the war theater was presented as the justification for the bombing that caused it. The press did not bother to report on the Serbs and others who also fled the bombing at that time.

In Kosovo, in 1987, in Pristina and Pec, I observed a peculiar sort of group behavior that reminds me only of school playgrounds in Maryland in my childhood. A gang of kids get together and by various signs, body language, and a minimum of words, convey to some outsiders that they are excluded and despised. I have seen Albanians act in this way toward stray Serbs, especially old women. This variety of mobbing was not violent in 1987, but turned so after NATO occupied the territory. It was encouraged by the official NATO stamp of approval of Albanian hatred for Serbs, delivered by bombs in the spring of 1999.

Of course, there must have been Serbs who hated Albanians. But in my limited, chance experience, what struck me was the absence of hatred for Albanians among Serbs I met. Fear, yes, but not hatred. A great deal of perplexity. Sister Fotina at the Gracanica monastery had a very Christian explanation. We tried to help the Albanians care for their many children, she said, and yet they turn against us. This must be God's way of punishing us for turning away from Christianity during the time of Communism, she concluded. She blamed her fellow Serbs more than the Albanians.

The divine punishment has not been confined to Christians, however. In the southernmost corner of Kosovo live an ancient population called Gorani (meaning mountain people), who converted to Islam under the Ottoman Empire, like most of the Albanians. But their language is Serbian, and this is unacceptable to the Albanians. Estimates vary, but it is agreed that at least two thirds of the Gorani have left since NATO "liberation." Pressure and intimidation have taken various forms. Albanians have moved into the temporarily vacant homes of Gorani who went to Austria and Germany to earn money for their retirement. The NATO-protected Albanian authorities have found ways to deprive Gorani children of schooling in the Serbian language. In the main Gorani town of Dragash, an Albanian mob attacked the health center and caused health workers to flee. Then, last January 5, a powerful explosion destroyed the bank in Dragash. It was the only Serbian bank still allowed to operate in the south of Kosovo, and served mainly to transfer the pensions that allowed local Gorani to survive.

As usual, the crime went unpunished.

David Binder, who used to report on Yugoslavia for the *New York Times*, before he was excluded for knowing too much, reported last November[2] on a long investigation of conditions in Kosovo commissioned by the German Bundeswehr. The existence of this report is proof that the Western governments, while publicly claiming that Kosovo is "ready for independence," know quite well that this is not true. Among other things, Binder reports:

> The institute authors, Mathias Jopp and Sammi Sandawi, spent six months interviewing 70 experts and mining current literature on Kosovo in preparing the study. In their analysis the political unrest and guerrilla fighting of the 1990s led to basic changes which they call a "turnabout in Kosovo-Albanian social structures." The result is a "civil war society in which those inclined to violence, ill-educated and easily influenced people could make huge social leaps in a rapidly constructed soldateska."
>
> "It is a Mafia society" based on "capture of the state" by criminal elements.
>
> In the authors' definition, Kosovan organized crime "consists of multimillion-Euro organizations with guerrilla experience and espionage expertise." They quote a German intelligence service report of "closest ties between leading political decision makers and the dominant criminal class" and name Ramush Haradinaj, Hashim Thaci and Xhavit Haliti as compromised leaders who are "internally protected by

---

2 The Binder story can be found at http://www.balkanalysis.com/.

parliamentary immunity and abroad by international law."

They scornfully quote the UNMIK chief from 2004–2006, Soeren Jessen Petersen, calling Haradinaj "a close and personal friend." The study sharply criticizes the United States for "abetting the escape of criminals" in Kosovo as well as "preventing European investigators from working."

It notes "secret CIA detention centers" at Camp Bondsteel and assails American military training for Kosovo (Albanian) police by Dyncorp, authorized by the Pentagon.

In an aside, it quotes one unidentified official as saying of the American who is deputy chief of UNMIK, "The main task of Steve Schook is to get drunk once a week with Ramush Haradinaj."

Who Goes and Who Stays

Schook has been fired by UNMIK, but UNMIK, the nominally United Nations mission, is being taken over arbitrarily by the European Union. The EU mission is a sort of colonial government which, alongside NATO, plans to govern the ungovernable Albanian territory. However, already movements of armed Albanian patriots are planning their next "war of liberation" against the Europeans.

So, after the Serbs, the Roma, the Gorani, will the Europeans have to "hit the road"? Only the Americans seem sure of staying. Ensconced in their gigantic Camp Bondsteel, they control the strategic routes from Serbia to Greece, and incidentally offer the mass of unemployed Kosovo Albanians their best-paying employment opportunities, notably by taking menial and dangerous jobs serving U.S. forces in Iraq or Afghanistan.

The reality of this shameless land-grab is available to all. I have written about it, Binder has written about it, Szamuely has written about it, many Germans have written about it. The Russians, the Greeks, the Rumanians, the Slovaks and many others know about it. But in the Brave New World Order, it does not exist. People don't know.

I leave the last word to Aldous Huxley: "Most ignorance is vincible ignorance. We don't know because we don't want to know."

Richard Holbrooke, Opportunist Extraordinary*

DECEMBER 2010

It is usually considered polite to avoid sharp criticism of someone who has just died. But Richard Holbrooke himself set a striking example of the breach of such etiquette. On learning of the death in prison of Slobodan Milosevic, Holbrooke did not hesitate to describe him as a "monster" comparable to Hitler and Stalin.

This was rank ingratitude, considering that Holbrooke owed his greatest career success—the 1995 Dayton Accords that ended the civil war in Bosnia-Herzegovina—almost entirely to Milosevic. This was made quite clear in his memoir *To End a War* (Random House, 1998).

But Holbrooke's greatest skill, made possible by media complicity, was to dress up reality in the costume favorable to himself.

The Dayton Peace Accords were presented as a heroic victory for peace extracted by the brilliant Holbrooke from a reluctant Milosevic, who had to be "bombed to the negotiating table" by the United States. In reality, the U.S. government was fully aware that Milosevic was eager for peace in Bosnia to free Serbia from crippling economic sanctions. It was the Bosnian Muslim leader Alija Izetbegovic who wanted to keep the war going, with U.S. military help. In reality, the U.S. bombed the Serbs in order to get Izetbegovic to the negotiating table. And the agreement reached in the autumn of 1995 was not very different from the agreement reached in March 1992 by the three ethnic groups under European Community auspices, which could have prevented the entire civil war, if it had not been sabotaged by Izetbegovic, who withdrew his agreement with the encouragement of the then U.S. ambassador Warren

---

* Original version: *CounterPunch,* December 15, 2010. https://www. counterpunch.org/2010/12/15/holbrooke-or-milosevic-who-is-the-greater-murderer/

Zimmermann. In short, far from being the great peacemaker in the Balkans, the United States first encouraged the Muslim side to fight for its goal of a centralized Bosnia and then sponsored a weakened federated Bosnia—after nearly four years of bloodshed which left the populations bereft and embittered.

The real purpose of all this, as Holbrooke made quite clear in *To End a War*, was to demonstrate that Europeans could not manage their own vital affairs and that the United States remained the "indispensable nation." His book also made it clear that the Muslim leaders were irritatingly reluctant to end war short of total victory, and that only the readiness of Milosevic to make concessions saved the Dayton talks from failure—allowing Holbrooke to be proclaimed a hero.

The functional role of the Holbrooke's diplomacy was to prove that diplomacy, as carried out by Europeans, was bound to fail. His victory was a defeat for diplomacy. The spectacle of bombing plus Dayton was designed to show that only the threat or application of U.S. military might could end conflicts.

Milosevic had hoped that his concessions would lead to peace and reconciliation with the United States. As it happened, his only reward for handing Holbrooke the victory of his career was to have his country bombed by NATO in 1999 in order to wrest from Serbia the province of Kosovo and prepare Milosevic's own fall from office. Holbrooke played a prominent role in this scenario, suddenly posing shoeless in a tent in the summer of 1998 for a photo op seated among armed Albanian secessionists which up to then had been characterized by the State Department as "terrorists." Shortly thereafter he announced to Milosevic that Serbia would be bombed unless he withdrew security forces from the province, in effect ceding it to the ex-terrorists, transformed by the Holbrooke blessing into freedom fighters.

In his long career from Vietnam to Afghanistan, Holbrooke was active on many fronts. In 1977, after Indonesia invaded East Timor and set about massacring the people of that former Portuguese colony, Holbrooke was dispatched by the United States supposedly to promote "human rights" but in reality to help arm the Suharto dictatorship against the East Timorese. Sometimes the government is armed against rebels, sometimes rebels are armed against the government, but despite appearances of contradiction, what is consistent throughout is the cynical exploitation and exacerbation of tragic local conflicts to extend U.S. imperial power throughout the world.

Holbrooke and Milosevic were born in the same year, 1941. When Milosevic died in 2006, Holbrooke gave a long statement to the BBC without a single syllable of human kindness. "This man wrecked the Balkans," said Holbrooke.

"He was a war criminal who caused four wars, over 300,000 deaths, 2.5 million homeless. Sometimes monsters make the biggest impacts on history—Hitler and Stalin—and such is the case with this gentleman."

Holbrooke presented himself as goodness dealing with evil for a worthy cause. When negotiating with Milosevic, "you're conscious of the fact that you're sitting across the table from a monster whose role in history will be terrible and who has caused so many deaths."

Who was the monster? Nobody, including at the Hague tribunal where he died for lack of medical treatment, has ever actually proved that Milosevic was responsible for the tragic deaths in the wars of Yugoslav disintegration. But Holbrooke was never put on trial for all the deaths in Vietnam, East Timor, Afghanistan, Iraq and, yes, former Yugoslavia, which resulted at least in part from the U.S. policies he carried out.

From his self-proclaimed moral heights, Holbrooke judged the Serbian leader as an opportunist without political convictions, neither communist nor nationalist, but simply "an opportunist who sought power and wealth for himself."

In reality, there has never been any proof that Milosevic sought or obtained wealth for himself, whereas Holbrooke was, among many other things, a vice chairman of Credit Suisse First Boston, managing director of Lehman Brothers, vice chairman of the private equity firm Perseus LLC, and a member of the board of directors of AIG, the American International Group, at a time when, according to Wikipedia, "the firm engaged in wildly speculative credit default insurance schemes that may cost the taxpayer hundreds of billions to prevent AIG from bringing down the entire financial system."

Milosevic was on trial for years without ever being able to present his defense before he died under troubling circumstances. Holbrooke found that outcome perfectly satisfying: "I knew as soon as he reached The Hague that he'd never see daylight again and I think that justice was served in a weird way because he died in his cell, and that was the right thing to do."

There are many other instances of lies and deceptions in Holbrooke's manipulation of Balkan woes, as well as his totally cynical exploitation of the tragedies of Vietnam, East Timor, Iraq and Afghanistan. But still, his importance should not be overstated. Moral monsters do not always make a great impact on history, when they are merely the vain instruments of a bureaucratic military machine running amok.

Using War as an Excuse for More War

Srebrenica Revisited*

OCTOBER 2005

L ast summer, almost the entire political spectrum in the Western world joined in a chorus of self-flagellation on the 10th anniversary of the Srebrenica massacre. The dominant theme was "culpa nostra": "we" let it happen, "we" didn't want to know about it, and "we" mustn't let it happen again.

Dear reader, who are "we" in this case? How in the world could "we" (you and I) have known or done anything about this at the time? And in fact, how much do "we" really know about it now? We know what we read in the newspapers or see on television. But how precise and accurate is that information? How do we know now that we are much better informed than we were before the event?

Such questions are virtually taboo. Srebrenica has become a sacred symbol of collective guilt, and to raise the slightest question is to be instantly condemned as an apologist for frightful crimes, or as a "holocaust denier."

A left that retains any capacity for critical thinking should regard the lavish public breast-beating over "Srebrenica" (the quotation marks indicate the symbol rather than the actual event) with a certain skepticism. If mainstream media commentators and politicians are so extraordinarily moved by "Srebrenica," this is because it has become an incantation to justify whatever future foreign war the U.S. government and media decide to sell under the label of "humanitarian intervention."

---

* Original Version, *CounterPunch*, October 12, 2005. https://www.counterpunch.org/2005/10/12/srebrenica-revisited/

The Uses of a Massacre

Aside from the probable future use of "Srebrenica," there is the way it has already been used. Indeed, it was perhaps being used even before it happened.

From the the U.N. Secretary General's 1999 Report on Srebrenica, it emerges that the idea of a "Srebrenica massacre" was already in the air at a September 1993 meeting in Sarajevo between Bosnian Muslim president Alija Izetbegovic and members of his Muslim party from Srebrenica. On the agenda was a Serb proposal to exchange Srebrenica and Zepa for some territories around Sarajevo as part of a peace settlement.

"The delegation opposed the idea, and the subject was not discussed further. Some surviving members of the Srebrenica delegation have stated that President Izetbegovic also told them he had learned that a NATO intervention in Bosnia and Herzegovina was possible, but could only occur if the Serbs were to break into Srebrenica, killing at least 5,000 of its people."[1]

Izetbegovic later denied this, but he is outnumbered by witnesses. It is clear that Izetbegovic's constant strategy was to portray his Muslim side in the bloody civil war as pure helpless victims, in order to bring U.S. military power in on his side. On his death bed, he readily admitted as much to his ardent admirer Bernard Kouchner, in the presence of U.S. diplomat Richard Holbrooke. Kouchner reminded Izetbegovic of a conversation he had had with French President Mitterrand in which he "spoke of the existence of 'extermination camps' in Bosnia."

> You repeated that in front of the journalists. That provoked considerable emotion throughout the world. [...] They were horrible places, but people were not systematically exterminated. Did you know that?
>
> Yes. I thought that my revelations could precipitate bombings. I saw the reaction of the French and the others—I was mistaken. [...] Yes, I tried, but the assertion was false. There were no extermination camps whatever the horror of those places.[2]

---

1 Report of the Secretary-General Pursuant to General Assembly Resolution 53/35 (1998), Section IV, paragraph C.115.

2 Bernard Kouchner, "Les Guerriers de la Paix," Grasset, Paris, 2004, pp. 372–375.

Like the Bosnian Serbs, the Muslims also herded their adversaries into "horrible" camps at the start of the civil war, on the way to expulsion. Unlike the Bosnian Serbs, the Bosnian Muslims enjoyed the services of high-powered U.S. public relations experts in the Washington-based Ruder Finn agency who knew how to "spin" the Bosnian conflict in order to equate the Serbs with the Nazis--the quickest and easiest way to win public opinion over to the Muslim side. The news media and political figures were showered with press releases and other materials exaggerating Serb atrocities, whereas Muslim atrocities (such as the decapitations of Serb prisoners, fully documented) remained confidential. To the public, this was a one-sided conflict between a Serbian "fascist aggressor" and innocent victims, all unarmed civilians.

The general public did not know that Srebrenica, described as a "safe area," was not in fact simply a haven for refugees, but also a Muslim military base. The general public did not know what Lord Owen knew and recounted in his important 1995 book, *Balkan Odyssey* (p. 143), namely that in April 1993, Serbian president Slobodan Milosevic was extremely anxious to prevent Bosnian Serb forces from overrunning Srebrenica.

> On 16 April I spoke on the telephone to President Milosevic about my anxiety that, despite repeated assurances from Dr. Karadzic that he had no intention of taking Srebrenica, the Bosnian Serb army was now proceeding to do just that. The pocket was greatly reduced in size. I had rarely heard Milosevic so exasperated, but also so worried: he feared that if the Bosnian Serb troops entered Srebrenica there would be a bloodbath because of the tremendous bad blood that existed between the two armies. The Bosnian Serbs held the young Muslim commander in Srebrenica, Naser Oric, responsible for a massacre near Bratunac in December 1992 in which many Serb civilians had been killed. Milosevic believed it would be a great mistake for the Bosnian Serbs to take Srebrenica and promised to tell Karadzic so.

Thus, many months before the July 1995 "Srebrenica massacre," both Izetbegovic and Milosevic were aware of the possibility and of its potential impact-favorable to the Muslim cause, and disastrous for the Serbs.

A few other indisputable facts should not be overlooked:

Shortly before the Bosnian Serb attack on Srebrenica, the Muslim troops stationed in that enclave carried out murderous attacks on nearby Serb villages. These attacks were certain to incite Serb commanders to retaliate against the Srebrenica garrison.

Meanwhile, the Muslim high command in Sarajevo ordered the Srebrenica commanders, Oric and his lieutenants, to withdraw from Srebrenica, leaving thousands of his soldiers without commanders, without orders, and in total confusion when the foreseeable Serb attack occurred. Surviving Srebrenica Muslim officials have bitterly accused the Izetbegovic government of deliberately sacrificing them to the interests of his State.

According to the most thorough study of Srebrenica events, by Cees Wiebes for the Netherlands Institute for War Documentation report, the Bosnian Serb forces set out in July 1995 to reduce the area held by Bosnian Muslim forces on the outskirts of Srebrenica, and only decided to capture the town itself when they unexpectedly found it undefended.

> The VRS [Republika Srpska Army] advance went so well that the evening of July 9 saw an important "turning point" [...] The Bosnian Serbs decided that they would no longer confine themselves to the southern part of the enclave, but would extend the operation and take the town of Srebrenica itself. Karadzic was informed that the results achieved now put the Drina Corps in a position to take the town; he had expressed his satisfaction with this and had agreed to a continuation of the operation to disarm the "Muslim terrorist gangs" and to achieve a full demilitarization of the enclave. In this order, issued by Major General Zdravko Tolimir, it was also stated that Karadzic had determined that the safety of UNPROFOR soldiers and of the population should be ensured. Orders to this effect were to be provided to all participating units. [...] The orders made no mention of a forced relocation of the population. [...] A final instruction, also of significance, was that the population and prisoners of war should be treated in accordance with the Geneva Convention. On July 11 all of Srebrenica fell into the hands of the Bosnian Serbs.

In testimony to a French parliamentary commission inquiry into Srebrenica, General Philippe Morillon, the UNPROFOR officer who first called international attention to the Srebrenica enclave, stated his belief that Bosnian Serb forces had fallen into a "trap" when they decided to capture Srebrenica.

Subsequently, on February 12, 2004, testifying at the International Criminal Tribunal for former Yugoslavia (ICTY) in The Hague, General Morillon stressed that the Muslim commander in Srebrenica, Naser Oric, "engaged in attacks during Orthodox holidays and destroyed villages, massacring all the inhabitants. This created a degree of hatred that was quite extraordinary in the region, and this prompted the region of Bratunac in particular---that is the entire Serb population---to rebel against the very idea that through humanitarian aid one might help the population that was present there."

Asked by the ICTY prosecutor how Oric treated his Serb prisoners, General Morillon, who knew him well, replied that "Naser Oric was a warlord who reigned by terror in his area and over the population itself. I think that he realized that these were the rules of this horrific war, that he could not allow himself to take prisoners. According to my recollection, he didn't even look for an excuse. It was simply a statement: One can't be bothered with prisoners."

Morillon recounted how

> ...the Serbs took me to a village to show me the evacuation of the bodies of the inhabitants that had been thrown into a hole, a village close to Bratunac. And this made me understand the degree to which this infernal situation of blood and vengeance [...] led to a situation when I personally feared that the worst would happen if the Serbs of Bosnia managed to enter the enclaves and Srebrenica.
>
> I feared that the Serbs, the local Serbs, the Serbs of Bratunac, these militiamen, they wanted to take their revenge for everything that they attributed to Naser Oric. It wasn't just Naser Oric that they wanted to revenge, take their revenge on, they wanted to revenge their dead on Orthodox Christmas.

* * *

In short, Srebrenica, whose Serb population had been chased out by Muslim troops at the start of the civil war in 1992, was both a gathering point for civilian Muslim refugees and a Muslim army base. The enclave lived from international humanitarian aid. The Muslim military did not allow civilians to leave, since their presence was what ensured the arrival of humanitarian aid provisions which the military controlled.

When the Bosnian Serb forces captured the town on July 11, 2005, civilians were clamoring to leave the enclave, understandably enough, since there was virtually no normal economic life there. Much has been made of the fact that Serb forces separated the population, providing buses for women, children and the infirm to take them to Tuzla, while detaining the men. In light of all that preceded, the reason for this separation is obvious: the Bosnian Serbs were looking for the perpetrators of raids on Serb villages, in order to take revenge.

However, only a relatively small number of Muslim men were detained at that point, and some of them are known to have survived and eventually been released in exchange for Serb prisoners. When the Serb forces entered the town from the south, thousands of Muslim soldiers, in disarray because of the absence of commanding officers, fled northwards, through wild wooded hills toward Tuzla. It is clear enough that they fled because they feared exactly what everyone aware of the situation dreaded: that Serb soldiers would take vengeance on the men they considered guilty of murdering Serb civilians and prisoners.

Thousands of those men did in fact reach Tuzla, and were quietly redeployed. This was confirmed by international observers. However, Muslim authorities never provided information about these men, preferring to let them be counted among the missing, that is, among the massacred. Another large, unspecified number of these men were ambushed and killed as they fled in scenes of terrible panic. This was, then, a "massacre," such as occurs in war when fleeing troops are ambushed by superior forces.

Counting the victims

So we come to the question of numbers. The question is difficult, both because of the uncertainty that surrounds it, and because merely pointing to this uncertainty is instantly denounced as "revisionism" and lack of respect for the victims. This reproach is not logical. Victims are victims, whether few or many, and respect is not in proportion to their numbers.

The question of numbers is complex and has been dealt with in detail by others, recently by an independent international Srebrenica research group which will soon publish its findings in book form.[3]

Suffice it here to note the following:

1. The sacralization of the estimated number of victims. In many if not most disasters, initial estimates of casualties tend to be inflated, for various reasons, such as multiple reports of the same missing person, and are subsequently corrected downwards. This was the case for the World Trade Center disaster, where initial estimates of up to 10,000 victims were finally brought down to less than 3000, and there are many other examples. In the case of Srebrenica, the figure of 8,000 originated with September 1995 announcements by the International Committee of the Red Cross that it was seeking information about some 3,000 men reportedly detained as well as about some 5,000 who had fled to central Bosnia. Neither the Bosnian Serbs nor the Muslims were ever forthcoming with whatever information they had, and the "8,000" figure has tended ever since to be repeated as an established total of "Muslim men and boys executed by Serb forces." It can be noted that this was always an estimate, the sum of two separate groups, the smaller one of prisoners (whose execution would be a clear war crime) and the larger one of retreating troops (whose "massacre" as they fled would be the usual tragic consequence of bitter civil war). Anyone familiar with the workings of journalism knows that there is a sort of professional inertia which leads reporters to repeat whatever figure they find in previous reports, without verification, and with a marked preference for big numbers. This inertia is all the greater when no truly authoritative figures ever emerge.

The number of bodies exhumed: Despite unprecedented efforts over the past ten years to recover bodies from the area around Srebrenica, less than 3,000 have been exhumed, and these include soldiers and others--Serb as well as Muslim--who died in the vicious combats that took place during three years of war. Only a fraction have been identified.

2. The political desire for the largest possible number. Aside from the journalistic inertia mentioned above, the retention of the unproven high figure of massacre victims in the case of Srebrenica is clearly the result of political will on the part of two governments: the Bosnian Muslim government of Alija Izetbegovic and, more importantly, the government of the United States. From the moment that Madeleine Albright

---

3 "Srebrenica: The Politics of War Crimes," by George Bogdanich, Tim Fenton, Philip Hammond, Edward S. Herman, Michael Mandel, Jonathan Rooper and George Szamuely. See http://www.srebrenica-report.com/politics.htm.

brandished satellite photos of what she claimed was evidence of Serb massacres committed at Srebrenica (evidence that was both secret, as the photos were shown in closed session to the Security Council, and circumstantial, as they showed changes in terrain which might indicate massacres, not the alleged massacres themselves), the U.S. used "Srebrenica" for two clear purposes:

• to draw attention away from the U.S.-backed Croatian offensive which at that very time was driving the Serb population out of the Krajina which, as much as Srebrenica, was supposed to be protected by the United Nations;

• to implicate Bosnian Serb leaders in "genocide" in order to disqualify them from negotiating the future of Bosnia-Herzegovina. (The U.S. preferred to replace them at Dayton by Milosevic, whose eagerness to end the war could be exploited to get concessions the Bosnian Serbs might refuse.)

Exploitation of "Srebrenica" then helped set the stage for the Kosovo war of 1999:

• by blaming the United Nations (whose failure to defend Srebrenica was in reality the inevitable result of the unwillingness of the United States to give full support to U.N. ground forces), NATO emerged as the only agent capable of effective "humanitarian intervention."

• by falsely identifying Milosevic with the Bosnian Serb leadership and by exploiting the notion that Srebrenica killings were part of a vast Serb plan of "genocide" carried out against non-Serbs for purely racist reasons, Madeleine Albright was able to advocate the NATO war against Yugoslavia as necessary to prevent "another Srebrenica" in Kosovo, where the situation was altogether different.

To use "Srebrenica" as an effective instrument in the restructuring of former Yugoslavia, notably by replacing recalcitrant Serb leaders by more pliable politicians, the crime needed to be as big as possible: not a mere war crime (such as the United States itself commits on a serial basis, from Vietnam to Panama to Iraq), but "genocide": "the worst atrocity in Europe since the Holocaust." That arouses the Hitler image, which is always good for the image of the United States as saviour from across the seas, and implies a plan decided at the highest levels, rather than the brutal behavior of enraged soldiers (or paramilitaries, the probable culprits in this case) out of control.

But what plan for genocide includes offering safe passage to women and children? And if this was all part of a Serb plot to eliminate Muslims, what about all the Muslims living peacefully in Serbia itself, including thousands of refugees who fled there from Bosnia? Or the Muslims in the neighboring enclave of Zepa, who were unharmed when the Serbs captured that town a few days after capturing Srebrenica? To get around these common sense obstacles, the ICTY prosecution came up with a sociologist who provided an "expert" opinion: the Srebrenica Muslims lived in a patriarchal society, therefore killing the men was enough to ensure that there would be no more Muslims in Srebrenica. This amounts to shrinking the concept of "genocide" to fit the circumstances.

It was on basis of this definition that in August 2001 the Tribunal found Bosnian Serb General Radislav Krstic guilty of "complicity in genocide." Although he neither ordered, participated in or was even aware of any executions, the judges ruled that he took part in what the ICTY calls a "joint criminal enterprise" simply by capturing Srebrenica, since he must have been aware that genocide was "a natural and foreseeable consequence." This is the ruling that established "genocide" as the official description of events at Srebrenica.

Why such relentless determination to establish Srebrenica as "genocide"? A December 27, 2003, Associated Press dispatch provided an explanation: "On a practical level, if the court determines Srebrenica does not fit the legal definition of genocide, it would be very difficult to make the charge stick against Milosevic," said the U.S. jurist Michael Scharf, one of the designers of the ICTY who has also coached the judges for the trial of Saddam Hussein, and a professor at Case Western Reserve University School of Law.

"And it is crucial that he be convicted of genocide," Scharf said. If Milosevic can't be convicted, "then who can you convict of genocide in the modern age?" he asked.

The legal definition of genocide could also come into play in an Iraqi war-crimes tribunal, which has vowed to follow international legal precedent.

It is striking that from the very start, the effort of the United States and of the Tribunal in The Hague—which it mainly finances, staffs and controls—has been to establish what it calls "command responsibility" for Serb crimes rather than individual guilt of actual perpetrators. The aim is not to identify and punish men who violated the Geneva conventions by executing prisoners, but rather to pin the supreme crime on the top Serb leadership.

The office of the ICTY prosecutor has chosen to rely heavily on a single confessed participant in the Srebrenica massacre. This person is one Drazen Erdemovic, a petty criminal of Croatian nationality who was hospitalized in Serbia in March 1996 after a near-fatal brawl in a bar in Novi Sad. Quite possibly in order to escape further threats from his personal enemies, Erdemovic confessed to Western news media to having taken part in mass murder in Bosnia. He was arrested by Serb authorites who then, at his request, turned him over to the Hague Tribunal.

From then on, the prosecution has used Erdemovic repeatedly as its star witness, using the U.S. procedure of "plea bargaining" by which a confessed criminal gets off lightly by incriminating somebody else the prosecution wants to convict. He has told his story to the judges at his own brief trial, where he was exempted from cross examination thanks to his guilty plea, as well as at a hearing incriminating Karadzic and Mladic (in the absence of any legal defense) and at various trials whenever "Srebrenica" comes up.

His story goes like this: after briefly serving in the Bosnian Muslim army, Erdemovic joined an international mercenary militia unit that seems to have been employed by the Bosnian Serb command for sabotage operations on enemy territory. On July 16, 1995, his unit of eight men executed between 1,000 and 1,200 Muslim men near the village of Pilice, some 40 kilometers north of Srebrenica. From around 10:30 in the morning to 3 o'clock in the afternoon, these eight mercenaries emptied bus load after bus load of prisoners and lined them up to be shot by groups of ten.

Now in fact, it seems that a serious crime was indeed committed in Pilice. Subsequent forensic investigators exhumed 153 bodies. One hundred and fifty-three executions of prisoners of war is a serious crime, and there is material evidence that this crime was committed. But 1,200? According to the manner of execution described by Erdemovic, it would have taken 20 hours to murder so many victims. Yet the judges have never questioned this elementary arithmetic discrepancy, and Erdemovic's word has consistently been accepted as gospel truth by the International Criminal Tribunal in The Hague.[4]

Why this insistence on an implausibly higher number than can be supported by material evidence? Obviously, the Tribunal wants to keep the figures as high as possible in order to sustain the charge of "genocide." The charge of "genocide" is what sharply distinguishes the indictment of Serbs from indictments of Croats or Muslims for similar crimes committed during the Yugoslav disintegration wars.

---

4 Germinal Civikov, "Kalaschnikow und Einzelfeuer: Der Fall Drazen Erdemovic," Freitag, 16 September 2005.

In August 2000 after not quite four and a half years in jail, the self-confessed mass murderer Erdemovic was freed, given a new identity, residence in an unspecified Western country and a "job," so to speak, as occasional paid and "protected" witness for the ICTY.

In contrast, General Krstic was sentenced to 35 years in prison and will be eligible for parole in 20 years.

Clearly, the purpose of the "genocide" charge is not to punish the perpetrators but to incriminate the Bosnian Serb, and the Yugoslav Serb, chain of command right up to the top.

Srebrenica As Myth

The transformation of Srebrenica into myth was illustrated last July by an article in the Italian leftist daily Liberazione (close to the "Communist Refoundation" party) reporting on a semi-documentary film entitled "Srebrenica, luci dall'oblio" ("Srebrenica, lights from oblivion").[5] The title suggests that the film-makers have rescued from oblivion a tragically neglected event, when in fact, rarely in the history of warfare has a massacre been the focus of so much attention.

Here we have the usual self-flagellation: "...what happened in Srebrenica: the massacre of 9,000 civilians, in the most total silence/absence on the part of the world institutions [responsible for] peace..." The author accepts without question the term "genocide" and raises the figure of victims to new heights. "Around 9,000 men between the ages of 14 and 70 were transported by truck to nearby centers where they were massacred and buried in mass graves..." This was "the greatest mass genocide committed since the days of Nazism until today..." What is the point of this exaggeration, this dramatization? Why is Srebrenica so much more terrible than the war that ravaged Vietnam, with countless massacres and devastation of the countryside by deadly chemicals, or the cold-blooded massacre of surrendering Iraqis at the end of the first Gulf War in 1991? But that is a genuinely forgotten massacre--not only forgotten, but never even recognized in the first place, and the "international community" has not sent teams of forensic scientists to find and identify the victims of U.S. weapons.

In all probability the film-makers, aspiring artists and "genocide experts" who consider "Srebrenica" suitable material for touching the emotions of the public believe that they are serving the interests of peace

---

5 Davide Turrini "Il genocidio jugoslavo rivive sullo schermo," Liberazione, 12 July 2005.

and humanity. But I would suggest quite the contrary. The misrepresentation of "Bosnia" as scene of a deliberate "genocide" against Muslims, rather than a civil war with atrocities on all sides, contributes to a spirit of "conflict of civilizations." It has helped recruit volunteers for Islamic terrorist groups.

The political exploitation of Srebrenica has turned the Bosnian war into a morality pantomime between pure good and pure evil, a version of events which the Serbs can never really accept and the Muslims have no desire to give up. This stands in the way of unbiased investigation and serious historical analysis. Reconciliation is in fact ruled out by the moralistic insistence that a stark distinction must be made between "aggressor" and "victim." This stark difference exists between NATO and Yugoslavia, or between the U.S. and Iraq, where an overwhelmingly superior military power deliberately launched an aggressive war against a sovereign country that neither attacked nor threatened it.

But the war in Bosnia-Herzegovina was not of that nature. The war there was the result of an extraordinarily complex legal situation (an unsettled small Federal Republic constitutionally composed of three "nationalities": Serb, Muslim and Croat, itself part of a disintegrating larger Federal Republic) exacerbated by myriad local power plays and the incoherent intervention of Great Powers. Moreover, this occurred in a region where memories of extremely bloody civil war during World War II were still very much alive. To a large extent, the fighting that broke loose in 1992 was a resumption of the vicious cycle of massacres and vengeance that devastated Bosnia-Herzegovina in 1941–44, when the Nazi occupation broke up Yugoslavia and attached Bosnia-Herzegovina to Greater Croatia, which proceeded to eliminate Serbs.

Today it is an unquestioned dogma that recalling atrocies is a "duty of memory" to the victims, something that must be endlessly repeated, lest we forget. But is this really so obvious? The insistence on past atrocities may simply prepare the next wave, which is what has already happened in the Balkans, and more than once. Because in reality, the dead victims cannot profit from such memories. But the memory of victimhood is a moral and political capital of great value for the heirs of victimhood and especially for their self-appointed champions. And in the case of Bosnia, it promises to bring considerable financial gain. If Milosevic, as former president of Serbia, can be convicted of genocide, then the Bosnian Muslims hope to win billions of dollars in reparations that will keep Serbia on its knees for the foreseeable future.

* * *

The obsessive reference to "Srebrenica" has a negative effect far beyond the Balkans.

The "Srebrenica massacre" is part of a dominant culture discourse that goes like this: We people in the advanced democracies have reached a new moral plateau, from which we are both able and have a duty both to judge others and to impose our "values" when necessary. The others, on a lower moral plateau, must be watched carefully, because unlike us, they may commit "genocide." It is remarkable how "genocide" has become fashionable, with more and more "genocide experts" in universities, as if studying genocide made sense as a separate academic discipline. What would all these people do without genocide? I wonder what is behind the contemporary fascination with genocide and serial killers, and I doubt that it is a sign of a healthy social psychology.

In the world today, few people are threatened by "genocide" in the sense of a deliberate Hitler-style project to exterminate a population--which is how most people understand the term. But millions of people are threatened, not by genocidal maniacs, but by genocidal conditions of life: poverty, disease, inadequate water, global climate change. The Srebrenica mourning cult offers nothing positive in regard to these genocidal conditions. Worse, it is instrumentalized openly to justify what is perhaps the worst of all the genocidal conditions: war.

The subliminal message in the official Srebrenica discourse is that because "we" let that happen, "we" mustn't let "it" happen again, ergo, the United States should preventively bomb potential perpetrators of "genocide." Whatever happened in Srebrenica could have best been prevented, not by U.S. or NATO bombing, but by preventing civil war from breaking out in Bosnia Herzegovina to begin with. This prevention was possible if the "international community," meaning the NATO powers, Europe and the United States, had firmly insisted that the Yugoslav crisis of 1990 should be settled by negotiations. But first of all, Germany opposed this, by bullying the European Union into immediate recognition of the secession of Slovenia and Croatia from Yugoslavia, without negotiation. All informed persons knew that this threatened the existence of Bosnia Herzegovina. The European Union proposed a cantonization plan for Bosnia Herzegovina, not very different from the present arrangement, which was accepted by leaders of the Bosnian Muslim, Serb and Croat communities. But shortly thereafter, Muslim president Alija Izetbegovic reneged, after the U.S. ambassador encouraged him to hold out for more. Throughout the subsequent fighting, the U.S. put obstacles in the way of every European peace plan.[6] These years of obstruction enabled the United States to take control of the eventual peace settlement in Dayton, in November 1995.

This rejection of compromise, which plunged Bosnia-Herzegovina into fratricidal war, was supported at the time by a chorus of humanitarians--not least politicians safely ensconced in the European Parliament who voted for "urgent resolutions" about situations of which they were totally ignorant--claiming that Bosnia must be a centralized State for the sake of "multiculturalism." These were the same humanitarians who applauded the breakup of multicultural Yugoslavia--which in fact created the crisis in Bosnia.

Clearly, whoever executes unarmed prisoners commits a very serious crime whether in Bosnia or anywhere else. But when all is said and done, it is an illusion to think that condemning perpetrators of a massacre in Bosnia will ensure that the next civil war somewhere in the world will be carried out in a more chivalrous manner. War is a life and death matter, and inevitably leads people to commit acts they would never commit in peacetime.

The notion that war can be made "clean," played according to rules, should not be the main focus of international law or of peace movements. War first of all needs to be prevented, not policed.

The false interpretation of "Srebrenica" as part of an ongoing Serb project of "genocide" was used to incite the NATO war against Yugoslavia, which devastated a country and left behind a cauldron of hatred and ethnic cleansing in Kosovo. The United States is currently engaged in a far more murderous and destructive war in Iraq. In this context, the Western lamentations that inflate the Srebrenica massacre into "the greatest mass genocide since Nazi times" are a diversion from the real existing genocide, which is not the work of some racist maniac, but the ongoing imposition of a radically unjust socio-economic world order euphemistically called "globalization."

---

6 See David Owen, *Balkan Odyssey* (London: Victor Gollancz, 1995). Lord Owen, who, as co-chairman of the steering committee of the International Conference on the Former Yugoslavia, attempted from August 1992 to June 1995 to negotiate a peace settlement in Bosnia-Herzegovina, concludes (Indigo paperback, p. 400): "From the spring of 1993 to the summer of 1995, in my judgement, the effect of U.S. policy, despite its being called 'containment,' was to prolong the war of the Bosnian Serbs in Bosnia-Herzegovina."

— PART III —
THE NEAR EAST

Libya War: The Key Question*

DECEMBER 2011

These days the humanitarian warriors are riding high, thanks to their proclaimed victory in Libya. The world's only superpower, with moral, military and mercenary support from the democracy-loving emirate of Qatar and the historic imperialist powers, Britain and France, was unsurprisingly able to smash the existing government of a sparsely populated North African state in a mere seven months. The country has been violently "liberated" and left up for grabs. Who gets what pieces of it, among the armed militia, tribes and Islamist jihadists, will be of no more interest to Western media and humanitarians than was the real life of Libya before Qatar's television channel Al Jazeera aroused their crusading zeal back in February with undocumented reports of imminent atrocities.

Libya can sink back into obscurity while the Western champions of its destruction hog the limelight. To spice up their self-congratulations, they accord some derisive attention to the poor fools who failed to jump on the bandwagon.

In the United States, and even more so in France, the war party poopers were few in number and almost totally ignored. But it is as good an occasion as any to isolate them even further.

In his article, "Libya and the Left: Benghazi and After," Michael Bérubé uses the occasion to bunch together the varied critics of the war as "the Manichean left" who, according to him, simply respond with kneejerk opposition to whatever the United States does. He and his kind, in contrast, reflect deeply and come up with profound reasons to bomb Libya.

He starts off:

*Original version: *CounterPunch*, December 1, 2011. https://www.counterpunch.org/2011/12/01/heres-the-key-question-in-the-libyan-war/

In late March of 2011, a massacre was averted—
not just any ordinary massacre, mind you. For had
Qaddafi and his forces managed to crush the Libyan
rebellion in what was then its stronghold, Benghazi,
the aftershocks would have reverberated well beyond
eastern Libya. As Tom Malinowski of Human Rights
Watch wrote, "Qaddafi's victory—alongside Egyptian
president Hosni Mubarak's fall—would have signaled
to other authoritarian governments from Syria to Saudi
Arabia to China that if you negotiate with protesters
you lose, but if you kill them you win."…

The NATO-led attack on Qaddafi's forces therefore did much more than prevent a humanitarian catastrophe in Libya—though it should be acknowledged
that this alone might have been sufficient justification.
It helped keep alive the Arab Spring…

Now all that is perfectly hypothetical.

Whatever massacre might have been averted in March, other massacres took place instead, later on.

That is, if crushing an armed rebellion implies a massacre, a victorious armed rebellion also implies a massacre, so it becomes a choice of
massacres.

And, had the Latin American and African mediation proposals been
taken up, the hypothetical massacre might have been averted by other
means, even if the armed rebellion was defeated—a hypothesis the pro-
war party refused to consider from the outset.

But even more hypothetical is the notion that the failure of the
Libyan rebellion would have fatally damaged "the Arab spring." This is
pure speculation, without a shred of supporting evidence.

Authoritarian governments certainly did not need a lesson to teach
them how to deal with protesters, which ultimately depends on their political and military means. Mubarak lost not because he negotiated with
protesters but because his U.S.-financed Army decided to dump him. In
Bahrain, Saudi Arabia helps kill the protesters. In any case, authoritarian
Arab rulers, not least the Emir of Qatar, hated Gaddafi, who had the habit
of denouncing their hypocrisy to their faces at international meetings.
They could only take heart from his downfall.

These pro-war arguments are in a class with the "weapons of mass
destruction" in Iraq or the threat of "genocide" in Kosovo—hypothetical

dangers used to justify preventive war. "Preventive war" is what allows a military superpower, which is too powerful ever to have to defend itself against foreign attack, to attack other countries anyway. Otherwise, what's the point of this superb military if we can't use it? as Madeleine Albright once put it.

Later on in his article, Bérubé cites his fellow humanitarian warrior Ian Williams, who argued that the litany of objections to intervention in Libya "evades the crucial question: Should the world let Libyan civilians die at the hands of a tyrant?" Or in other words, the "key question" is: "When a group of people who are about to be massacred ask for help, what do you do?"

With this selection of the guilt-tripping "crucial" or "key" question, Bérubé and Williams sweep away all the various legal, ethical and political objections to the NATO attack on Libya.

But nothing has authorized these gentlemen to decide which is the "key question." In reality, their "key question" raises a number of other questions.

First of all: Who is the group of people? Are they really about to be massacred? What is the source of the information? Could the reports be exaggerated? Or could they even be invented, in order to get foreign powers to intervene?

A young French film-maker, Julien Teil, has filmed a remarkable interview in which the secretary general of the Libyan League for Human Rights, Slimane Bouchuiguir, candidly admits that he had "no proof" of the allegations he made before the U.N. Human Rights Commission which led to immediate expulsion of the official Libyan representative and from there to U.N. Resolutions authorizing what turned into the NATO war of regime change. Indeed, no proof has ever been produced of the "bombing of Libyan civilians" denounced by Al Jazeera, the television channel financed by the Emir of Qatar, who has recuperated a large share of Libyan oil business from the "liberation war" in which Qatar participated.

Just imagine how many disgruntled minority groups exist in countries all around the world who would be delighted to have NATO bomb them to power. If all they have to do to achieve this is to find a TV channel that will broadcast their claims that they are "about to be massacred," NATO will be kept busy for the next few decades, to the delight of the humanitarian interventionists.

A salient trait of the latter is their selective gullibility. On the one hand, they automatically dismiss all official statements from "authoritarian" governments as false propaganda. On the other hand, they seem never to have noticed that minorities have an interest in lying about their plight in order to gain outside support. I observed this in Kosovo. For most Albanians, it was a matter of virtuous duty to their national group to say whatever was likely to gain support of foreigners for their cause. Truth was not a major criterion. There was no need to blame them for this but there was no need to believe them, either. Most reporters sent to Kosovo, knowing what would please their editors, based their dispatches on whatever tales were told them by Albanians eager to have NATO wrest Kosovo away from Serbia and give it to them. Which is what happened.

In fact, it is wise to be cautious about what all sides are saying in ethnic or religious conflicts, especially in foreign countries with which one is not intimately familiar. Perhaps people rarely lie in homogeneous Iceland, but in much of the world, lying is a normal way to promote group interests.

The poignant "key question" as to how to answer "a group of people about to be massacred" is a rhetorical trick to shift the problem out of the realm of contradictory reality into the pure sphere of moralistic fiction. It implies that "we" in the West, including the most passive television spectator, possess knowledge and moral authority to judge and act on every conceivable event anywhere in the world. We do not. And the problem is that the intermediary institutions, which should possess the requisite knowledge and moral authority, have been and are being weakened and subverted by the United States in its insatiable pursuit to bite off more than it can chew. Because the United States has military power, it promotes military power as the solution to all problems. Diplomacy and mediation are increasingly neglected and despised. This is not even a deliberate, thought-out policy, but the automatic result of sixty years of military buildup.

The Real Crucial Question

In France, whose president Nicolas Sarkozy launched the anti-Gaddafi crusade, the pro-war unanimity has been greater than in the United States. One of the few prominent French personalities to speak out against it is Rony Brauman, a former president of Médecins sans frontières (Doctors Without Borders) and a critic of the ideology of "humanitarian intervention" promoted by another former MSF leader, Bernard Kouchner. The November 24 issue of Le Monde carried a debate between Brauman and the war's main promoter, Bernard-Henri Lévy, which actually brought out the real crucial question.

The debate began with a few skirmishes about facts. Brauman, who had initially supported the notion of a limited intervention to protect Benghazi, recalled that he had rapidly changed his mind upon realizing that the threats involved were a matter of propaganda, not of observable realities. The aerial attacks on demonstrators in Tripoli were an "invention of Al Jazeera," he observed.

To which Bernard-Henri Lévy replied in his trademark style of brazen-it-out indignant lying. "What!? An invention of Al Jazeera? How can you, Rony Brauman, deny the reality of those fighter planes swooping down to machinegun demonstrators in Tripoli that the entire world has seen?" Never mind that the entire world has seen no such thing. Bernard-Henri Lévy knows that whatever he says will be heard on television and read in the newspapers, no need for proof. "On the one hand, you had a super-powerful army equipped for decades and prepared for a popular uprising. On the other hand, you had unarmed civilians."

Almost none of this was true. Gaddafi, fearing a military coup, had kept his army relatively weak. The Western military equipment has never been used and its purchase, like the arms purchases by most oil-rich states, was more of a favor to Western suppliers than a useful contribution to defense. Moreover, the uprising in Libya, in contrast to protests in the surrounding countries, was notoriously armed.

But aside from the facts of the matter, the crucial issue between the two Frenchmen was a matter of principle: is or is not war a good thing?

Asked whether the Libya war marks the victory of the right of intervention, Brauman replied:

"Yes, undoubtedly... Some rejoice at that victory. As for me, I deplore it for I see there the rehabilitation of war as the way to settle conflicts."

Brauman concluded: "Aside from the frivolity with which the National Transition Council, most of whose members were unknown, was immediately presented by Bernard-Henri Lévy as a secular democratic movement, there is a certain naiveté in wanting to ignore the fact that war creates dynamics favorable to radicals to the detriment of moderates. This war is not over.

"In making the choice of militarizing the revolt, the NTC gave the most violent their opportunity. By supporting that option in the name of democracy, NATO took on a heavy responsibility beyond its means. It is because war is a bad thing in itself that we should not wage it..."

Bernard-Henri Lévy had the last word: "War is not a bad thing in itself! If it makes it possible to avoid a greater violence, it is a necessary evil—that's the whole theory of just war." The idea that this principle exists is "like a sword of Damocles over the heads of tyrants who consider themselves the owners of their people, it is already a formidable progress." Bernard-Henri Lévy is made happy by the thought that since the end of the Libya war, Bashir Al Assad and Mahmoud Ahmadinejad sleep less soundly. In short, he rejoices at the prospect of still more wars.

So there is the crucial, key question: is war a bad thing in itself? Brauman says it is, and the media star known as BHL says it is not, "if it makes it possible to avoid a greater violence." But what violence is greater than war? When much of Europe was still lying in ruins after World War II, the Nuremberg Tribunal issued its Final Judgment proclaiming:

"War is essentially an evil thing. Its consequences are not confined to the belligerent states alone, but affect the whole world. To initiate a war of aggression, therefore, is not only an international crime; it is the *supreme international crime* differing only from other war crimes in that it contains within itself the accumulated evil of the whole."

And indeed, World War II contained within itself "the accumulated evil of the whole": the deaths of 20 million Soviet citizens, Auschwitz, the bombing of Dresden, Hiroshima and Nagasaki, and much, much more.

Sixty years later, it is easy for Americans and Western Europeans, their lives still relatively comfortable, their narcissism flattered by the ideology of "human rights," to contemplate initiating "humanitarian" wars to "save victims"—wars in which they themselves take no more risk than when playing a video game. Kosovo and Libya were the perfect humanitarian wars: no casualties, not even a scratch, for the NATO bombers, and not even the necessity to see the bloodshed on the ground. With the development of drone warfare, such safe war at a distance opens endless prospects for risk-free "humanitarian intervention," which can allow Western celebrities like Bernard-Henri Lévy to strut and pose as passionate champions of hypothetic victims of hypothetical massacres hypothetically prevented by real wars.

The "key question"? There are many important questions raised by the Libya war, and many important and valid reasons to have opposed it and to oppose it still. Like the Kosovo war, it has left a legacy of hatred in the targeted country whose consequences may poison the lives of the people living there for generations. That of course is of no particular interest to people in the West who pay no attention to the human damage wrought by their humanitarian killing. It is only the least visible result of those wars.

For my part, the key issue which motivates my opposition to the Libya war is what it means for the future of the United States and of the world. For well over half a century, the United States has been cannibalized by its military-industrial complex, which has infantilized its moral sense, squandered its wealth and undermined its political integrity. Our political leaders are not genuine leaders but have been reduced to the role of apologists for this monster, which has a bureaucratic momentum of its own—proliferating military bases around the world, seeking out and even creating servile client states, needlessly provoking other powers such as Russia and China. The primary political duty of Americans and their European allies should be to reduce and dismantle this gigantic military machine before it leads us all inadvertently into "the supreme international crime" of no return.

So my principal opposition to this recent war is precisely that, at a time when even some in Washington were hesitant, the "humanitarian interventionists" such as Bernard-Henry Lévy, with their sophistic "R2P" pretense of "protecting innocent civilians," have fed and encouraged this monster by offering it "the low-hanging fruit" of an easy victory in Libya. This has made the struggle to bring a semblance of peace and sanity to the world even more difficult than it was already.

Turning the Cradle of Civilization Into Its Graveyard*

SEPTEMBER 2015

This Monday, September 7, seven Syrian citizens go to court in Paris to pursue their civil suit against French Foreign Minister Laurent Fabius. The five men and two women all lost family members and close friends in massacres by armed rebels supported by Fabius in word and deed. They are asking for one euro of symbolic damages.

In the end the suit will almost surely be thrown out. The September 7 hearing is on an appeal against an earlier ruling that the courts cannot judge acts of the government in this case, even if the complaint is founded. And yet this futile lawsuit makes a crucial point that Western politicians and media would much prefer to ignore.

Western leaders share major responsibility for making much of the world unfit for normal human habitation. And so far, they are getting away with it. The massive refugee crisis swamping Europe is just the beginning of the troubles that these unscrupulous leaders have brought on their own countries.

Laurent Fabius can fairly be called a French neoconservative. His alignment with Israeli policies is seen in the fact that he was the most reluctant of the foreign ministers involved in the Iranian nuclear negotiations to agree to the final settlement.

He has been one of the most gung-ho advocates of regime change in Syria, a country long on the neocon hit list for its Arab nationalism and support for the Palestinian cause.

The Syrian plaintiffs note that:

---

* Original version, *CounterPunch,* September 7, 2015. https://www. counterpunch.org/2015/09/07/turning-the-cradle-of-civilization-into-its-graveyard/

- On May 29, 2012, Fabius declared that France would intervene against the Syrian regime.
- On August 17, 2012, Fabius declared that Syrian President Bashar el Assad "did not deserve to be alive on earth."
- On December 14, 2012, speaking out against the Obama administration decision to designate the Al Nusra Front as a terrorist group, Fabius objected that the Al Nusra Front was "doing a good job on the ground."
- On March 13, 2013, Fabius announced that France and Britain were going to deliver arms to the rebels.

As a group, the plaintiffs maintain that by his declarations, Foreign Minister Fabius stirred up civil war in Syria and encouraged armed rebel attacks against the existing government. Individually, each of the plaintiffs lost family members and close friends in armed attacks and massacres carried out by the al Nusra militia allied rebel groups.

Israel's Ghastly Twin: the "Islamic State"

Under U.S. leadership and Israeli influence, French political leaders have championed "regime change" in Libya and Syria on the tacit assumption that civil war would be better for the people of those countries than living under a "dictatorship." In practice, however, most people can get along better without a vote than without a roof over their heads. Or without their heads.

It is hardly surprising that the carefully filmed and diffused videos of "Islamic State" (IS) disciplinary methods have caused panic among people living in their path of conquest.

War causes people to become refugees. Western media pay close attention to refugees only when they like the "story." Huge attention was paid to Kosovo Albanians fleeing temporarily from the 1999 NATO war against the Serbs, because those refugees could be described as victims of Serbian "ethnic cleansing" and thus as justification of the NATO war itself.

But no such media concern was aroused over the much greater number of refugees who fled from the 2003 United States invasion of Iraq and have never returned. Over a million Iraqi refugees fled into Syria, where they were well received.

The situation in the Middle East is critical. Armed by leftover U.S. military equipment in Iraq, enriched by illicit oil sales, its ranks swollen by young Jihadis from all over the world, the Islamic State threatens the people of Lebanon and Jordan, already struggling to take care of masses of refugees from Palestine, Iraq and now Syria. Fear of the decapitating Islamic fanatics is inciting more and more people to risk everything in order to get to safety in Europe.

The Islamic State is truly the horrible enemy caricature of the "Jewish State," another political entity based on an exclusive religious identity. Like Israel it has no clearly defined borders, but with a vastly larger potential demographic base.

The only force that can stop the Islamic State from expanding its fanatic rule over all of Mesopotamia and beyond is the Syrian State led by Bashar al Assad. The choice is not between Assad and "Western democracy." The choice is between Assad and the Islamic State. But Western leaders have still not fully dropped their demented cry: "Assad must go!"

Refugees, Migrants and Terrorists

The results of this madness are washing up on the shores of the Mediterranean. Images and sentiment have replaced thinking about causes and effects. One photo of a drowned toddler causes a media and political uproar. Are people surprised? Didn't they know that toddlers were being torn to pieces by U.S. bombing of Iraq, by U.S. drones in Afghanistan, Pakistan, Yemen? What about the toddlers obliterated by NATO's war to "free Libya" from its "dictator"?

The current refugee crisis in Europe is the inevitable, foreseeable, predicted result of Western policy in the Middle East and North Africa. Gaddafi's Libya was the wall that kept hundreds of thousands of Africans from migrating illegally to Europe, not only by police methods but even more effectively by offering them development at home and decently paid jobs in Libya. Now Libya is the source both of economic migrants and of refugees from Libya itself, as well as from other lands of des-peration. In order to weaken Sudan, the United States (and Susan Rice in particular) championed creation of the new country of South Sudan, which is not a country at all but the scene of rival massacres driving more and more fugitives toward unwelcoming countries.

The famous photo of little Aylan drowned in the Mediterranean is used very largely to make Europeans feel guilty. The leaders should in-deed feel guilty—and not least the rich egomaniac Bernard-Henri Lévy, who prides himself on having talked the French government of Nicolas Sarkozy into starting war against Libya, where, he claimed, there were no Islamic extremists, but only pro-Westerners yearning for democracy. Thanks to NATO, Islamic extremists have since run roughshod over the whole country.

German Chancellor Angela Merkel has agreed to take in eight hundred thousand Syrian refugees. This is admirable on humanitarian grounds. Germany is economically strong and demographically weak; with its gradually shrinking population, middle class Syrians, many of them terrified Christians, may seem to be a welcome addition to the population. But it deepens political divisions within Germany and in Europe.

This is particularly the case in the new EU countries of Eastern Europe. Starting with Hungary, their leaders are making it clear that those countries are above all concerned with their ethnic identity, and don't want to take in a lot of people who don't speak their language. Unlike countries of Western Europe, the Eastern European tier of ethnic states have no tradition of taking in immigrants and no ideological attachment to the Western human rights ideology. In Eastern Europe, "human rights" sounded good to use against Russia and the Soviet Union, but stops there.

The Greek crisis already put heavy strains on the unity of the European Union. For the first time, many people are questioning the whole idea. The crisis showed that there is no real sense of solidarity between the peoples of Europe; when it comes to the crunch, Germans are Germans and Greeks are Greeks, and "European" is an abstraction. The refugee crisis is showing new cracks in "European unity."

Most of Europe today is suffering from massive unemployment, especially the Southern countries where refugees first land: Greece, Italy, Spain. European Union economic policies, already strangling Greece, do not favor job creation for hundreds of thousands of newcomers. Even professionally qualified refugees will find it difficult or impossible to get around rules protecting their professions in host countries. Most jobs they manage to get will probably be low level and illegal, undercutting wages and working conditions in the host countries.

Moreover, it is impossible in the present mass movement of people to distinguish "refugees" from economic "migrants"—that is, from men simply seeking better work opportunities. The EU today has little to offer them, and resentment of this unsought immigration is certain to improve the political fortunes of the nationalist right.

There is another reason that many European citizens feel less than enthusiastic about welcoming hundreds of thousands of unknown foreigners into their communities. The Islamic State has openly boasted of sending terrorists into Europe among the refugees, with the clear intention of committing violent acts to destabilize the West. Of course, the threat of terrorism is being used cynically by governments to enforce police state measures, but that does not mean that the threat of terrorism is unreal. Unfortunately, it exists—thanks very largely to the policies of those very same Western governments.

The refugee crisis should be seen as the warning signal that the United States and its NATO allies—especially Britain and France—are bringing the world to a state of chaos that is going to keep spreading and that is approaching a point of no return.   It is quick and easy to break things. Putting them back together may be impossible. Civilization itself may be more fragile than it seems.

The Political Vulnerability and Impunity of the Israel Lobby*

MARCH 2018

Marx said that philosophers had only interpreted the world, but the point was to change it.

"Interpreting the world" in strictly Marxist scholastic terms can be an obstacle to trying to change it. This may be why Marx said he was not a "Marxist." The political effort to change the world requires more than theory. It calls for readiness to grasp facts and mass psychological factors that offer handles to educating the public (or "raising class consciousness," as Marxists prefer to say), in order to exploit points of political vulnerability in ruling class projects.

The case of the "pro-Israel lobby" illustrates this.

In Marx's time there was no Israel and no "pro-Israel lobby," and so neither Marx nor Hegel nor even Lenin could have analyzed the phenomenon. But Marx was a journalist as well as a theoretician, and it is not far fetched to say that were Marx alive and active today, he would not ignore the political effects of the pro-Israel lobby.

To use Marxist terms, today the ideological superstructure projected by capitalist relations of production is also very different from what it was a century and a half ago. Religious repression has been replaced by hedonistic distraction. Moral authorities have been replaced by the ubiquitous mass media and entertainment industry, projecting images of an alternative reality clearly designed to influence both the self-images of subservient classes and their vision of a dangerous outside world, in

---

*This paper was written in response to certain persons whose strict "Marxist" interpretation of the world—seeing imperialism as caused solely by capitalist economic interests—can prevent them from fully recognizing important ideological factors of political causality. Published in *Consortium News,* March 22, 2018.

order to prevent massive opposition to social injustice at home and aggressive military enforcement of American global hegemony.

The imperialist project is fundamentally contrary to the interests not only of the working class, but increasingly of the middle class as well, including sectors of small business and capitalist enterprises targeting the domestic market, whether in goods or services. But people are often more influenced by their emotions and their moral sense than by their economic self-interest. The ruling class propaganda machine exploits emotions and moral sensibility, with tales of murderous "dictators" and appeals to defend "human rights" and "democracy" in unfamiliar countries.

The notion that the inherent contradictions in capitalist production will cause the system to collapse had not been confirmed by reality, especially since capitalism thrives on the creative aspect of contradictions. Waiting for these contradictions to destroy capitalism is a very long wait. However, political action can thrive on spotting and exploiting contradictions in the imperialist propaganda narrative. And this is essential for building popular opposition to the U.S.-led global hegemonic project whose endless wars appear increasingly to be leading toward nuclear apocalypse.

One of these contradictions which is a potential weak point in the ideological superstructure justifying wars is the pro-Israel influence on foreign policy in the United States, and also in European NATO countries.

The Role of the Israel Lobby

In the United States, there is no problem using the term "lobby," since lobbyists constitute a considerable portion of the Washington social scene. Legitimately, lobbyists are there to plead for a cause, but increasingly, they add "campaign contributions" to their arguments, to such an extent that almost the entire Congress is working not for just one lobby but for several.

The two most notorious lobbies in terms of financial contributions are the National Rifle Association (NRA) and the American Israel Public Affairs Committee (AIPAC).

The influence of the NRA is both financial and ideological. Its lawyers have managed to persuade the courts of an absurd interpretation of the Second Amendment of the Constitution of the United States, which reads: "A well-regulated Militia being necessary to the security of a free State, the right of the people to keep and bear Arms shall not be infringed." To any sensible person with a minimum understanding of history, it is obvious that the purpose of this amendment was to protect an organized right to bear arms, and not the right of every individual, sane or insane, to wander the streets and school grounds brandishing automatic weapons. The idea back in 1791 was to prevent the Federal Government from imposing military rule on the States, and to nullify a traditional aristocratic privilege. Thanks to the propagandistic work of the lobby and its supporters, "the right to bear arms" as an individual right has become practically a dogma in the United States, which far from protecting individuals from tyranny, allows themselves to kill each other in record numbers and to be gunned down all the more readily by police who "feel threatened" by the slightest gesture of a "suspect"—even for a minor traffic violation. Economically, the NRA lobby benefits the arms manufacturers, but has long been tolerated by the public because of its ideological justification in terms of "individual liberties."

In the United States, both the financial and ideological influence of the Israel lobby is enormous, but on foreign rather than domestic policy. The evidence of this is blatantly obvious and massively documented, and can be illustrated by the repeated standing ovations by the U.S. Congress to Benjamin Netanyahu precisely at a time when he was in open opposition to the President of the United States, Barack Obama.

The military industrial complex dominates the U.S. economy. Its very survival demands wars to justify its existence. U.S. imperial wars require pretexts. This is where Israel comes in.

Many observers have pointed to resemblances between the historic and religious myths of Israel and the United States: settler nations "chosen by God" with the divine right to drive out the indigenous peoples, and with an infinite sense of being morally superior to their neighbors: "the only democracy in the Middle East," or the "exceptional shining city on the hill."

Intellectual advocates of Greater Israel, many of them with double American-Israeli nationality, usually designated as "neo-conservatives," have vigorously and successfully exploited these mythical points of resemblance in order to construct an ideology of "exceptionalism" which provides the superstructure of American globalizing capitalism at its most aggressive. The main vehicle of this influence has been the "think tanks," the privately funded research centers in Washington that create the propaganda echoed by mainstream media and politicians. Take the example of the Brookings Institution, which until about twenty years ago, was considered relatively "liberal" in the American sense, potentially critical of military expansion. But then Brookings accepted a record donation of thirteen million dollars from Israeli-American billionaire Haim Saban and in 2002 responded by establishing the Saban Center for Middle East Studies, which of course promotes the pro-Israel line in Congress and the media. Note that Saban was the primary donor to Hillary Clinton's presidential candidacy, while another Israeli billionaire, Sheldon Adelson, successfully bet on Trump. Their influence is undeniable, all the more since both of them boast about it.

All of this is as far from a "plot" or a "conspiracy" as you can get, since it is all perfectly open. Israeli leaders do not hesitate to brag about their influence on U.S. policy.

The political point is not that Israel "created U.S. imperialism," which of course has its roots in the 19th century wars to wrest control of former Spanish colonies, both in Central America and in the Philippines, all in the name of a glorious "manifest destiny."

The political point about the Israel lobby is that it is potentially a particularly vulnerable element in the propaganda narrative, a point that, if denounced, could contribute to building popular opposition to U.S. imperialism.

Most Americans are no longer pioneers, and their religious convictions are weakening. This development is hidden by the apparent growth in influence of Evangelical Christian sects. This is due primarily to a Republican Party strategy to win over Southern states by catering to the religious views of poorly educated sectors of the populations in the region. The Evangelical narrative of "the Rapture" is certainly considered nonsense by U.S. ruling classes and has absolutely no influence on their policy-making, although it may be exploited to gain support. What does have an influence is the prospect of a big United States and a little Israel hand in hand dictating the world's political and economic order.

But just as the excess of school massacres is producing popular opposition to the gun lobby, the obvious influence of the Israel lobby is beginning to encounter open opposition. And the U.S. imperialist narrative is so tied to Israel that if support for Israel collapsed, it would deal a serious blow to the "superstructure" or propaganda narrative used to sell militarism and war to the American people.

On the eve of massive joint U.S. Israeli military maneuvers this month, U.S. Third Air Force commander Lt. Gen. Richard Clark reassured the Jerusalem Post that U.S. ground troops would be ready to risk their lives for Israel. "We are ready to commit to the defense of Israel and anytime we get involved in a kinetic fight there is always the risk that there will be casualties. But we accept that, as in every conflict we train for and enter, there is always that possibility," Clark told the Post.

Dying for Israel is unlikely to be a wildly popular prospect among Americans, who might wonder why heavily armed, U.S.-subsidized, nuclear-power Israel can't defend itself.

In short, a political campaign denouncing the Israel lobby, which is directly responsible for unanimous pro-Israel votes in Congress, for billions of dollars appropriated to Israel every year, and for dragging the U.S. into Middle East "wars for Israel," would have the best chance of building serious political opposition to a military buildup that threatens to lead to a major clash with Russia. This is an opportunity that should not be missed.

But what obstructs such a campaign, which certainly can't be mounted by mainstream media, but must come from the grass roots?

The left. Or large sectors of a very weakened left.

On the one hand, there are those (self-styled Trotskyists in particular) who like to fancy that every uprising anywhere, for whatever reason, must be the start of a "revolution," and who confound Islamic fanatics with Spanish Republicans and are ready to support all measures taken against "dictators" (who in the Middle East turn out to be exclusively Israel's chosen enemies). And there are also those who cry that one absolutely must not denounce the Israel lobby because anything that sounds like "the Jewish lobby" can only be a revival of the anti-Semitism of the 1930s which led to the Holocaust.

Finally, the role of the lobby is hotly denied by certain more or less dogmatic Marxists, who maintain that imperialism can only be the product of economic interests, such as oil pipelines, and who dismiss ideological factors as trivial.

It is clear that the Israeli lobby is able to exert an extraordinary influence on the quality and direction of U.S. imperialism precisely because, for over a generation, the mere hint of "anti-Semitism" is enough to destroy a person's reputation, career and even friendships. Jews and Zionists are not the same thing, but it is in the interest of Israel to insist that they are, which is a way of shielding Israel—and its lobby—from effective criticism. All that is needed to shut people up is to insist that mentioning the "lobby" is a step toward reopening Auschwitz.

This attitude is not only mistaken, it is precisely what is fostering anti-Jewish feeling.

Denunciation of the Israel lobby has nothing in common with the attacks on the alleged "Judeo-Masonic lobby" and its alleged "plots" back in the 1930s.

In those days, a large number of Jews were engaged in progressive causes, defending the Spanish Republic, fighting for equal rights for African-Americans, playing an important role in labor unions. The 1930s attacks on "Judeo-Bolshevism" or "the Judeo-Masonic plot" came from a reactionary right that attacked Jews *precisely because* they were a key element of the left.

Today, there is nothing progressive about Zionism, with its ethnic claims of Jewish privilege, or about Israel as it wages its endless war of attrition against the Palestinian inhabitants of the land its has arrogated to itself.

Jews themselves are sharply divided. It is true that many have been wooed away from progressive causes by the Zionist illusion. But many remain active as a positive force for equality, social justice and peace.

Israel has no right to speak for "all Jews" or to claim that criticism of Israel is "anti-Semitic." That claim is a form of hostage taking—Zionists hide behind the Jewish martyrs to Nazism.

So long as the left, with its somewhat contrived bad conscience, refuses to insist on that distinction, the identification of Jews with Zionism—originating with the Zionists—is being taken up by two wings of the emerging right—emerging precisely because the left is declining as a result of its lack of intellectual rigor and political courage.

On the one hand, part of the far right, which sees clearly that Israel is a reactionary, racist state, are hastening to proclaim their support for Netanyahu and his policies.

On the other hand, a tour of the Internet shows that a growing number of bloggers accept the identification of Jews with Israel, considering its obvious strong political influence in Congress and the media, as evidence that "Jews rule the world." This idea grows precisely because it is taboo and cannot be debated publicly.

Especially in Europe, for obvious reasons, fear of being labeled "anti-Semitic" is particularly strong, and stands in the way of recognizing the existence of an Israeli "lobby." The very word is taboo because of its irrelevant historic connotations. The United States could not pursue aggressive military policy in the Middle East and against Russia without the existence of NATO and the support of Europeans leaders. This fear in Europe of being identified with past persecution of Jews is an element that preserves NATO and leads the world into catastrophic war.

We are not living in the time of Marx, nor in the 1930s, nor in the 1940s. The manifestations of imperialism have altered considerably and offer their own ideological weak points. The Israel lobby is one of these. It is a serious error to shy away from this attack, either on the grounds that "the lobby" is not a sufficient cause of imperialism, or from fear of being falsely stigmatized as complicit with the crimes of an earlier generation.

To change the world, one must live in the present.

Foul Murder of Another Nation's Hero: An American Disgrace*

JANUARY 2020

The criminal assassination of General Qassem Soleimani was not only an act of war, it was an act of low treachery and crass stupidity. Among the self-justifying lies, leaders of the perpetual war regime in Washington claim that locating the targeted military leader was a brilliant accomplishment of U.S. intelligence.

Not at all! The Lebanese newspaper Al-Binaa reports that the Americans were routinely informed of Soleimani's arrival in Baghdad simply because he was an official visitor, invited as military advisor to the Iraqi government. U.S. forces are responsible for Baghdad airport security. So they had to know since they were responsible… for the security of an official honored guest.

This should give all U.S. allies an uneasy feeling about the implications of American "protection" of their "security."

Of course, leaders of the NATO satellites and their media propaganda machines largely pretend to believe Uncle Sam's big lies: the General had to be killed to "save American lives," the only lives that count, especially when they are in somebody else's country killing people whom Israel doesn't like.

The United States has brazenly murdered the war hero of a sovereign nation whose military action has been devoted to defending his own nation (since the U.S.-instigated Iraq-Iran war of the 1980s) and his region from Saudi-backed Sunni fanatics, in the guise of Daech or al Qaeda. Those fanatics have been openly instrumentalized by Israel

* Originally published in *Global Research*, January 5, 2020.

to further the notorious Oded Yinon plan[1] to break up all Arab states into small units, the better to ensure Israel's domination of the region. It matters to non-Arab Shi'ite Iran because it incites armed Sunni fanatics to attack Shi'ites in Syria and other places.

Civilized peoples are capable of respect for their adversaries. A noble warrior on one side can respect a noble warrior on the other side. But there is no respect for anything human in a bunch of machines directed by morons. When the U.S. murders a military strategist more successful than their own grotesquely over-armed losers, Pentagon apologists pretend that he (and not they) is the bloodthirsty killer spreading chaos throughout the Middle East. If any honest history is written in the future, on the scale of barbarism versus civilization, contemporary U.S presidents will rank somewhere well below Attila the Hun, who at least faced his enemies in battle.

---

1 Look it up on Internet : many references.

Hamas and the Shoah

Gaza Genocide Meets French Devotion to Israel*

FEBRUARY 2024

Israel's loyal supporters in the West combat rising world indignation over the suffering of the Palestinian people by changing the subject. When Gazan families are buried under the rubble of their homes, it's not about the plight of the dispossessed Palestinians, it's about eternal Jewish victims, it's about Islamic terrorism, or it's about us. It's about a threat to our Western values.

That is the line taken by most of the French media and political class.

Or there is recourse to Biblical story-telling, featuring vengeance, ethnic slaughter and prophecy of doom. In Israel, Netanyahu declares a struggle between good and evil: "We are the people of the light, they are the people of darkness and light shall triumph over darkness. Now my role is to lead all Israelis to an overpowering victory... We shall realize the prophecy of Isaiah..."

In the United States of America, the crazed prophecies of the Israeli leader find support from an American variant of Judeo-Christianity, more Judeo than Christian, whose followers are taught to believe that gentle Jesus will zoom back to earth as a murderous Avenger while his faithful float up to heaven.

France and the Shoah

Skeptical France is very far from such fantasies. French support to Israel is longstanding and political, but tinged with semi-religious devotion rooted in recent history.

---

* Original version: *Consortium News,* February 8, 2024.

France is officially, even ostentatiously, a secular nation, considerably de-christianized over the past two hundred years. To a unique extent, over the past half century, this religious void has been filled by the sacred remembrance of the Shoah, as the Holocaust is usually called here.

It all began in 1954 when 27-year-old Jewish journalist named Eliezer Wiesel met the 70-year-old Catholic novelist François Mauriac in Paris. Mauriac was deeply moved by Wiesel's "resurrection" from his experience as a prisoner in Auschwitz, seeing him as a Christ figure. For Mauriac, the sacrifice of the Jews recalled the Crucifixion of Jesus. With help from the prominent French writer, Wiesel transformed his copious Yiddish notes into a French memoir, *La Nuit* (Night), the testimony that transformed him into a major spiritual figure of the post-World War II era.

It was Mauriac, the devout Christian, who saw in Wiesel and his people the parallels with Christianity, which as the Shoah was destined to take on the attributes of a state religion in France as memories of the Nazi occupation were transformed into sacred myth.

An Alliance against Arab Nationalism

When the Nazis invaded France, there were approximately 320,000 Jewish people living in France, including a large number of foreign nationals who had fled from antisemitism in Eastern Europe. Those unfortunate exiles made up the bulk of the 74,000 Jews who were brutally rounded up and deported under German occupation. These deportations are the principal factual basis for what developed into a sense of national responsibility for the Shoah comparable to that of Germany itself.

However, of all Nazi-occupied countries, France is the country where the largest percentage of Jews escaped Nazi deportations. An estimated 75% of Jews survived the occupation without being deported, including around 90% of Jews with French citizenship. The reasons for this are controversial, but one result is that France has the largest Jewish population in Europe today—around half a million, the third largest Jewish population in the world, although far behind Israel or the United States (around seven million each).

In recent years, many Jews have moved to Germany from Russia and from Israel itself (118,000 altogether), making France and Germany the home to more Jews than any other member state of the European Union. They are also the countries where institutionalized repentance for the Shoah is most developed. A difference is that a number of prominent

Jews in Germany are sharply critical of Israel (which may get them in trouble with the law), whereas the French Jewish community is more solidly Zionist. The politically influential Representative Council of Jewish Institutions in France (CRIF), a sort of French AIPAC, fiercely defends Israeli interests.

A significant peculiarity of France is that Europe's largest Jewish population is cohabitating with continental Europe's largest population of Muslim origin, mostly Arab. Although France officially avoids ethnic or racial counting, this population is estimated at around fifteen million. While politically disorganized, this community is assumed—especially by Jewish community leaders—to be hostile to Israel. The potential for conflict between these two communities—one very small and very influential, the other very large and disparate—has for years haunted French political leaders.

France and Arab nationalism

When the Jewish State was just a dream, it was seen by some as a sort of socialist project, based on the kibbutz. (This may explain why the Soviet Union was the first government to recognize the State of Israel.) Building on longstanding friendly relations between French Socialists and Zionism, France was the closest Western ally of the new State of Israel. In 1954, the government of Socialist Prime Minister Guy Mollet agreed to sell Israel whatever military equipment it wanted. France even helped Israel develop nuclear weapons. At that time, Tel Aviv and Paris were allied against Arab nationalism, inasmuch as secular, left-leaning Arab States (Egypt, Syria, Iraq) sympathized with both the Palestinians and the rising national liberation movement in French Algeria.

But this changed under De Gaulle, who conceded Algerian independence in 1962, put an arms embargo on the region in 1967 and sought to build balanced relations with Arab States, as part of an effort to develop friendly, post-colonial relations with the global South.

In June 1967, Israel's lightning victory in the Six Days War was celebrated in the streets of Paris by joyous horn honking. But President De Gaulle had opposed the Israeli expansion and called for a sustainable peace based on evacuation of territories conquered by Israel and mutual recognition by the belligerent states.

In a remarkable press conference on November 27, 1967, De Gaulle expressed ongoing support for the existence of Israel as a *fait accompli* while expressing strong misgivings about the future of Jewish rule over Palestinian territories.

After recalling the shared admiration for the Jewish people and sympathy for their suffering, De Gaulle observed, in respect to the creation of a Jewish state, that:

> "Some even dreaded that the Jews, up to then dispersed, but who remained what they had always been, that is an elite people, self-confident and domineering, when once reunited on the site of their ancient greatness, might come to transform the highly moving wishes expressed for nineteen centuries into an ardent and conquering ambition."

De Gaulle recalled that he had promised that France would defend Israel from any Arab attack, but implored Israel not to use its advantage to attack its Arab neighbors.

> "We know that France's voice was not heard. Israel having attacked, in six days of combat seized the objectives it wished to attain. Now, on the captured territories, it is organizing an occupation which cannot go on without oppression, repression, expulsions, and a resistance to all that which it will call terrorism."

In response to these statements, prominent Jewish intellectuals and community leaders ceased to revere De Gaulle as the leader of the Resistance. Around this time, the Resistance itself as national patriotic myth was rapidly discredited as the public imagination of Nazi Occupation came to center on the Holocaust.

Cinema played a role. In 1969, the documentary film by Marcel Ophuls, "The Sorrow and the Pity," convinced audiences that collaboration rather than Resistance had overwhelmingly dominated occupied France. The film had a strong impact on public opinion, not least on young leftists who in May 1968 led a massive libertarian revolt targeting the two political heirs to the Resistance: the French Communist Party and President Charles De Gaulle.

In the revisionist mood of the time, national pride stemming from the Resistance gave way to national shame over the deportation of Jews. This guilt became a sort of public ritual for audiences who watched Claude Lanzmann's nine-hour long documentary "Shoah," released in 1985. In 1990, France adopted a measure called the Gayssot law which can lead to heavy fines and even imprisonment for any questioning of the official version of the Holocaust.

As I wrote in my book *Circle in the Darkness,* heresy defines religion. A French citizen can deny the existence of Napoleon, or any other historic event, but any questioning of the official version of the Shoah is blasphemy. Thus by sacralizing a unique historic event, the Gayssot law in effect established the Shoah as a state religion. The Shoah is celebrated officially and unofficially, not only in the annual Shoah commemoration but almost constantly in school rooms, trips to Auschwitz, radio and television programs, books and films. It has *de facto* replaced Christianity, which had succumbed to *laïcité* (secularism) over a century ago, as the State religion. It has its martyrs and saints, its holy scripture, its rituals, its pilgrimages, everything that Christianity had except redemption.

The Expanding Role of Political Islam

Meanwhile, France's post-war industrial buildup drew thousands of workers from Algeria.

It wasn't until new laws in the 1970s allowed "family reunion" that regrouping of foreign workers with wives and children began to create large immigrant neighborhoods, especially in the suburbs of Paris and other large cities, with their own ethnically distinct religious practices, food and dress, especially veiled women, clashing visibly with French customs.

The growth of these communities had a strong impact on the political environment. The National Front, a coalition of far right groups led by Jean-Marie Le Pen, called for stopping immigration, and the new left issued from the May '68 movement became their champions. In the early 1980s, in order to accommodate European unification, Socialist President François Mitterrand abandoned the program of nationalizations and social measures for which he had been elected in coalition with the French Communist Party (PCF). The PCF left the coalition and subsequently lost its influential role in assimilating foreign workers into French society, even while opposing unlimited immigration. Having abandoned their economic program, the Socialists adopted human rights and anti-racism as their defining issues, condemning opposition to immigration as racist. Accused of antisemitism, the National Front was condemned as a pariah with no fit place in the Republic. This condemnation was ensured by Le Pen's conviction under the Gayssot law for having stated, in an interview, that gas chambers were "a detail of World War II."

While the left has moved toward an "open border" acceptance of immigration, it has increasingly advocated measures to ban Muslim customs seen to violate the official French doctrine of *laïcité*. French *laïcité* was institutionalized by the 1905 law on the separation of Church and State, which finally deprived the Catholic Church of its traditional role in education. In response to an apparent growth of religious practice among younger Muslims, *laïcité* was revitalized by banning religious identity signaling in public schools, notably by prohibiting school girls from wearing Muslim headscarves to cover their hair. This focus on female dress later produced a ban on wearing the burka in public. While intended to promote cultural assimilation, such measures can also feed Muslim resentment at being a discriminated minority.

Western Schizophrenia toward Islam

In 1979, Western attitudes toward Islam entered their drastically schizophrenic period, decrying the Islamic Revolution in Iran as a political and human rights disaster, while giving full support to Islamic Mujahidin in neighboring Afghanistan. French political exhibitionist Bernard Henri Lévy was a most zealous supporter of Afghan Muslims opposing the Russian incursion which failed to save modernizing progressive forces in Kabul.

It was President Carter's chief strategist Zbigniew Brzezinski who saw the potential of militant Islam to defeat Soviet influence in Central Asia. In the 1990s, the United States secretly backed illegal arming of Mujahidin to fight on the Islamic side in Bosnia, against Serbia, considered in Washington a miniature Russia. For leaders of the enlightened West, the most medieval expressions of Islam were considered a useful tool against the rival enlightenment in the East, based on Marxism.

Israel's initial enemies were linked to secular Arab nationalism: the Popular Liberation Forces (PLF), Fatah and the Popular Front for the Liberation of Palestine (PFLP). In Gaza, the local branch of the Islamic Brotherhood, banned in Egypt and hostile to secular groups, looked harmless, especially since its leader, Sheikh Ahmad Yassin, was a quadriplegic confined to a wheelchair and half blind. Yassin built an Islamic center, called the Mujamma, which gained popularity by a variety of social and charitable activities. The Israeli overlords favored this development as it rivaled the secular resistance groups. Israeli officially recognized the Mujamma in 1979 and the number of mosques in Gaza doubled under Israeli administration.

It was only during the Palestinian uprising in December 1987, known as the First Intifada, that Sheikh Yassin created Hamas, dedicated to Islamic resistance. Close to the people through its cultural and sports activities, the Islamic organization had a popular base that eventually led to electoral success in Gaza against the secular Palestine Liberation Organization (PLO) in 2006.

The complicated U.S. instrumentalization of al Qaeda in Afghanistan, the Islamic revolution in Iran, U.S. support to Saddam Hussein's war against Iran before waging war against Saddam Hussein, led in mysterious ways to the dramatic September 11, 2001 attacks on the World Trade Center in New York and the Pentagon, whose one clear political effect was to cement the U.S.-NATO-Israeli alliance against "Islamic terrorism."

This term has involved confounding different, often mutually hostile, groups with each other as well as falsely associating peaceful Muslims with armed groups. Israeli leaders had always denounced Palestine resisters as terrorists, including those who were Christian. But *Islamic* terrorism was a threat that made it easier to identify Israel as the front line in defense of Western Judeo-Christian civilization.

From then on, the United States and its NATO followers have ravaged the Middle East, using Islamic extremism as official enemy or factual ally, to destroy the three most secular and pro-Palestinian States in the region, Iraq, Libya and Syria, executing Saddam Hussein, murdering Moammer Gaddafi and persisting in illegal occupation and sanctions against Syria aimed at overthrowing Bashir al Assad.

Terrorist Attacks in France

Following the Gaullist tradition, President Jacques Chirac kept France out of the U.S.-led 2003 invasion of Iraq. But subsequent governments aligned with the United States, and Bernard-Henri Lévy ostentatiously goaded France into assaulting Libya. France has paid a heavy price in blowback for its ambiguous encounters with Islam. In the last twelve years, the country has experienced an extraordinary number of authentic Islamic terrorist attacks against civilians by fanatics shouting "Allahu Akbar."

• In March 2012, a man named Mohammed Merah shot dead seven people, including a French rabbi and three young Jewish children in southern France. His stated motives included Palestine and the French ban on the burka.

- On January 7, 2015, two coordinated attacks occurred, causing a major shock to the public. Gunmen entered the offices of the satirical journal Charlie Hebdo and murdered eight well-known cartoonists and two guards, in revenge for having published insulting cartoons of the Prophet. Meanwhile an accomplice killed several people in the course of taking hostages in a kosher grocery.

- The deadliest attack took place in the evening of November 13 the same year, killing 131 people and wounding 413 more when a group of Islamist fanatics attacked a major sports event, sprayed gunfire and grenades into the Bataclan theater during a rock concert and across café terraces in Paris. The Islamic State of Iraq and Syria (ISIS) called the attacks retaliation for French bombing of Syria.

- On Bastille Day 2016, a Tunisian drove a 19-ton cargo truck into a holiday crowd on the Promenade des Anglais in Nice, killing 86 people and injuring 434 before being shot dead by police.

- Twelve days later, an 86-year-old priest was stabbed to death while saying mass in a church in Normandy. ISIS claimed responsibility.

- On October 6, 2020, in the course of a class on freedom of expression, middle school teacher Samuel Paty showed his class Charlie Hebdo cartoons of the Prophet, after permitting Muslim students to leave if they chose. Ten days later, in retribution, the teacher was stabbed and beheaded in the street by 18-year-old Abdullakh Anzorov, an Islamic Chechen refugee accorded political asylum from Russia. This caused an enormous shock in France, not least among the teaching profession.

- On October 13, 2023, a 20-year-old Chechen political refugee shouting Allahu Akbar attacked a school in the northern French city of Arras, stabbing to death French literature teacher Dominique Bernard.

In this context, people in France are particularly sensitive to the term "Islamic terrorism."

When, on October 7, fighters from Gaza succeeded in crossing into Israel, French media and politicians instantly condemned the attack as "Islamic terrorism," implicitly relating it to the long chain of Islamic attacks in France.

Contrary to those attacks, the well organized Hamas fighters carried out a successful military operation, breaching the Israeli wall that imprisons Gaza and overrunning Israeli military bases. This operation had clear objectives, in particular, the taking of hostages to use in exchange for some of the thousands of Palestinian prisoners held by Israel. The hostage-taking was a clear invitation to negotiations, but the Israeli regime loathes any negotiations that could "legitimize" a Palestinian movement.

The government initially banned demonstrations protesting against Israel's massive attacks on the people of Gaza. Peaceful demonstrators were brutalized and fined by police. However, bans have been dropped and pro-Palestinian demonstrations have continued. Opposition to Israel's genocidal retaliation against the people of Gaza is surely strong throughout the French population, especially among the youth, but it has very little political voice and so far, no pollsters are measuring it.

French media echoed wildly exaggerated Israeli reports of Hamas atrocities and the "rise of antisemitism." Newspapers featured growing Jewish fears of being attacked here in France. The Israeli government has deliberately exploited fear of antisemitism to encourage French Jews to move to Israel, but the success of the Hamas incursions risks shaking confidence in Israel as Jews' one safe refuge—cramming half the world's Jewish population into a small space surrounded by enemies.

Left and Right switch positions

In the days following October 7, mainstream media interviewers tested every politician with the demand to condemn Hamas as an "Islamist terrorist organization." Almost all enthusiastically complied, emphasizing their support for "Israel's right to exist" (whatever that might entail). From Communist Party leader Fabien Roussel to Eric Zemmour, founder of a nationalist party to the right of Marine Le Pen's National Rally, French political leaders were unanimous in condemning Hamas' "brutal terrorist attack"—with one exception. That was the country's leading leftwing politician, Jean-Luc Mélenchon.

Mélenchon refused to denounce Hamas as a "terrorist organization." Hamas killings of civilians were "war crimes," like any killing of civilians, he said. The attacks, he tweeted, "prove only one thing: violence only produces and reproduces itself. Horrified, our thoughts and our compassion go to all the distressed populations, victims of it all. A ceasefire should be imposed."

Most parliamentary members of Mélenchon's party *"La France Insoumise"* (LFI, France Unbowed) followed suit, contrary to other sections of the fragmented left. Danièle Obono, an African-born LFI Paris MP was rudely goaded by a hostile TV interviewer into saying that Hamas "is a resistance movement, that's what it calls itself...its objective is the liberation of Palestine... it resists occupation." Within a couple of hours, the Minister of the Interior Gérard Darmanin announced that he was having her charged with "apology for terrorism."

A verbal lynch mob rose up against Mélenchon, a chorus vigorously joined not only by his enemies on the right but also by rivals in smaller parties belonging to the disintegrating leftist electoral coalition NUPES (*Nouvelle Union Populaire, Ecologique et Social*) which he founded. Mélenchon and the LFI are denounced as "Islamo-leftists," flattering terrorists to win over the Muslim vote.

Yonathan Arfi, the president of CRIF, angrily denounced Mélenchon as "an enemy of the Republic." Mélenchon, he raged, "chose not to express solidarity with Israel but to legitimize terrorism by an equivalence between Israel and Hamas."

Meanwhile Serge Klarsfeld, famous as a lifelong Nazi hunter and president of the association Sons and Daughters of Deported Jews of France, rejoiced that Marine Le Pen had completely changed the ideology of her party, the *Rassemblement National,* from that of her father, Jean-Marie Le Pen. Marine Le Pen led her party in a November 12 Paris demonstration against antisemitism while emphasizing her support for Israel. As a result, she has "become respectable," he concluded. Such approval will make it hard to demonize her in future elections as in the past.

Referring to Jean-Luc Mélenchon, Klarsfeld expressed regret that "the far left has abandoned its line of action against antisemitism," while noting that "the extreme left has always had an antisemite tradition."

And thus a long brewing political reversal is being completed, not only in France but across Europe and even America. Israel, whose early supporters were on the left, from the Soviet Union to the French Socialists, is most vigorously championed by the right, whereas more and more people (but rarely politicians) on the left are joining the non-Western world's shock and horror at the genocidal actions of Israel against the Palestinian people.

The War of Civilizations

The most extreme champions of Israel, including numerous commentators and Eric Zemmour, a journalist who founded a nationalist, anti-Muslim party called Reconquest to the right of Marine Le Pen, merge the Israeli-Palestinian conflict into a worldwide war of civilizations. For them, Hamas is just part of an international Islamic war on Western civilization. In this view of things, Israel is the vanguard of Western civilization whose main enemy is antisemitism.

In the midst of this turmoil, President Emmanuel Macron follows the European trends, but with notes of ambiguity confirming his position as perfect centrist. He hesitated before suspending funding to UNRWA, then did so claiming his intention was to obtain a cease-fire. Such uncertainty can only displease both sides of the embittered national division over Gaza.

He stayed away from the politically overcharged November 12 demonstrations against antisemitism, but compensated by leading a February 7 commemoration in Paris of the 42 French and Franco-Israeli victims of the October 7 attacks. The French government chartered a plane to fly in relatives of the victims from Israel. Participants booed and shouted "fascist!" and "terrorists!" at parliamentarians from Mélenchon's party who showed up to pay their respects.

In a cold rain, Macron read out the first names of the 42 victims whose lives, he said, were "shattered by terrorist fury."

"On October 7, at dawn," he said, "the unspeakable resurfaced from the depths of history," producing "the greatest anti-Semitic massacre of our century." So in France, it seems, that what Oct. 7 was really about was not Gaza, nor Israel, and certainly not about the Palestinians, but fundamentally about a resurgence of the impunity wrought by the ever-present Shoah.

— PART IV —
U.S. POLITICS

The Bad Losers
*and What They Fear Losing**

SEPTEMBER 2016

If the 2016 presidential campaign was a national disgrace, the reaction of the losers is an even more disgraceful spectacle. It seems that the political machine backing Hillary Clinton can't stand losing an election.

And why is that?

Because they are determined to impose "exceptional" America's hegemony on the entire world, using military-backed regime changes, and Donald Trump seems poised to spoil their plans. The entire Western establishment, roughly composed of neoconservative ideologues, liberal interventionists, financial powers, NATO, mainstream media and politicians in both the United States and Western Europe, committed to remaking the Middle East to suit Israel and Saudi Arabia and to shattering impertinent Russia, have been thrown into an hysterical panic at the prospect of their joint globalization project being sabotaged by an ignorant intruder.

Donald Trump's expressed desire to improve relations with Russia throws a monkey wrench into the plans endorsed by Hillary Clinton to "make Russia pay" for its bad attitude in the Middle East and elsewhere. If he should do what he has promised, this could be a serious blow to the aggressive NATO buildup on Russia's European borders, not to mention serious losses to the U.S. arms industry planning to sell billions of dollars worth of superfluous weapons to NATO allies on the pretext of the "Russian threat."

The war party's fears may be exaggerated, inasmuch as Trump's appointments indicate that the United States' claim to be the "exceptional," indispensable nation will probably survive the changes in top personnel.

___

* Published in *Consortium News,* September 21, 2016.

159

But the emphasis may be different. And those accustomed to absolute rule cannot tolerate the challenge.

Bad Losers On the Top

Members of the U.S. Congress, the mainstream media, the CIA and even President Obama have made fools of themselves and the nation by claiming that the Clintonite cabal lost because of Vladimir Putin. Insofar as the rest of the world takes this whining seriously, it should further increase Putin's already considerable prestige. If true, the notion that Moscovite hacking could defeat the favorite candidate of the entire U.S. power establishment can only mean that the United States' political structure is so fragile that a few disclosed emails can cause its collapse. A government notorious for snooping into everybody's private communication, as well as for overthrowing one government after another by less subtle means, and whose agents boasted of scaring the Russians into re-electing the abysmally unpopular Boris Yeltsin in 1996,[1] now seems to be crying pathetically, "Mommy, Vlady is playing with my hacking toys!"

Of course, Russians would quite naturally prefer a U.S. president who openly shies away from the possibility of starting a nuclear war with Russia. That doesn't make Russia "an enemy," it is just a sign of good sense. Nor does it mean that Putin is so naïve as to imagine that Moscow could throw the election by a few dirty tricks. The current Russian leaders, unlike their Washington counterparts, tend to take a longer view, rather than imagining that the course of history can be changed by a banana peel.

This whole miserable spectacle is nothing but a continuation of the Russophobia exploited by Hillary Clinton to distract from her own multiple scandals. As the worst loser in American electoral history, she must blame Russia, rather than recognize that there were multiple reasons to vote against her.

The propaganda machine has found a response to unwelcome news: it must be fake. The Washington conspiracy theorists are outdoing themselves this time. The Russian geeks supposedly knew that by revealing a few Democratic National Committee internal messages, they could ensure the election of Donald Trump. What tremendous prescience!

---

1 Michael Kramer, "Rescuing Boris," *TIME,* July 15, 1996. http://content.time.com/time/subscriber/article/0,33009,984833-1,00.html

Obama promises retaliation against Russia for treating the United States the way the United States treats, well, Honduras (and even Russia itself until blocked by Putin). Putin retorted that so far as he knew, the United States was not a banana republic, but a great power able to protect its elections. Washington is loudly denying that. The same mainstream media who brought you Saddam's "weapons of mass destruction" are now bringing you this preposterous conspiracy theory with straight faces.

When intelligence agencies become aware of the activities of rival intelligence agencies, they usually keep the knowledge to themselves, as part of the mutual spook game. Going public with this wild tale shows that the whole point is to persuade the American public that Trump's election is illegitimate, in the hope of defeating him in the electoral college or, if that fails, of crippling his presidency by labeling him a "Putin stooge."

Bad Losers On the Bottom

At least the bad losers on the top know what they are doing and have a purpose. The bad losers on the bottom are expressing emotions without clear objectives. It is false self-dramatization to call for "Resistance" as if the country had been invaded by extraterrestrials. The U.S. electoral system is outmoded and bizarre, but Trump played the game by the rules. He campaigned to win swing States, not a popular majority, and that's what he got.

The problem isn't Trump but a political system which reduces the people's choice to two hated candidates, backed by big bucks.

Whatever they think or feel, the largely youthful anti-Trump protesters in the streets create an image of hedonistic consumer society's spoiled brats who throw tantrums when they don't get what they want. Of course, some are genuinely concerned about friends who are illegal immigrants and fear deportation. It is quite possible to organize in their defense. The protesters may be mostly disappointed Bernie Sanders supporters, but whether they like it or not, their protests amount to a continuation of the dominant themes in Hillary Clinton's negative campaign. She ran on fear. In the absence of any economic program to respond to the needs of millions of voters who showed their preference for Sanders, and of those who turned to Trump simply because of his vague promise to create jobs, her campaign exaggerated the portent of Trump's most politically incorrect statements, creating the illusion that Trump was a violent racist whose only program was to arouse hatred. Still worse, Hillary stigmatized millions of voters as "a basket of deplorables, racist, sexist, homophobic, xenophobic, Islamophobic—you name it." These remarks were made to an LGBT rally, as part of her identity politics campaign to win over a clientele of minorities by stigmatizing the dwindling white majority. The identity politics premise is that ethnic and sexual minorities are oppressed and thus morally superior to the white majority, which is the implied oppressor. It is this tendency to sort people into morally distinct categories that divides Americans against each other, every bit as much—or more—than Trump's hyperbole about Mexican or Islamic immigrants. It has served to convince many devotees of political correctness to regard white working class Americans in the "fly-over" regions as enemy invaders who threaten to send them all to concentration camps.

Terrified of what Trump may do, his opponents tend to ignore what the lame ducks are actually doing. The last gasp Clintonite campaign to blame Hillary's defeat on "fake news," supposedly inspired by The Enemy, Russia, is a facet of the growing drive to censor the Internet—previously for child pornography, or for anti-Semitism, and next on the pretext of combating "fake news," meaning whatever goes contrary to the official line. This threat to freedom of expression is more sinister than eleven-year-old locker-room macho boasts by Trump.

There will and should be strong political opposition to whatever reactionary domestic policies are adopted by the Trump administration. But such opposition should define the issues and work for specific goals, instead of expressing a global rejection that is non-functional.

The hysterical anti-Trump reaction is unable to grasp the implications of the campaign to blame Hillary's defeat on Putin. Do the kids in the street really want war with Russia? I doubt it. But they do not perceive that for all its glaring faults, the Trump presidency provides an opportunity to avoid war with Russia. This is a window of opportunity than will be slammed shut if the Clintonite establishment and the War Party get their way. Whether they realize it or not, the street protesters are helping that establishment delegitimatize Trump and sabotage the one positive element in his program: peace with Russia.

Adjustments in the Enemy List

By its fatally flawed choices in the Middle East and in Ukraine, the United States foreign policy establishment has driven itself into a collision course with Russia. Unable to admit that the United States backed the wrong horse in Syria, the War Party sees no choice but to demonize and "punish" Russia, with the risk of dipping into the Pentagon's vast arsenal of argument-winning nuclear weapons. Anti-Russian propaganda has reached extremes exceeding those of the Cold War. What can put an end to this madness? What can serve to create normal attitudes and relations concerning that proud nation which aspires primarily simply to be respected and to promote old-fashioned international law based on national sovereignty? How can the United States make peace with Russia?

It is clear that in capitalist, chauvinist America there is no prospect of shifting to a peace policy by putting David Swanson in charge of U.S. foreign relations, however desirable that might be.

Realistically, the only way that capitalist America can make peace with Russia is through capitalist business. And that is what Trump proposes to do.

A bit of realism helps when dealing with reality. The choice of Exxon CEO Rex W. Tillerson as Secretary of State is the best step toward ending the current race toward war with Russia. "Make money not war" is the pragmatic American slogan for peace at this stage.

But the "resistance" to Trump is not likely to show support for this pragmatic peace policy. It is already encountering opposition in the war-loving Congress. Instead, by shouting "Trump is not my President!" the disoriented leftists are inadvertently strengthening that opposition, which is worse than Trump.

Avoiding war with Russia will not transform Washington into a haven of sweetness and light. Trump is an aggressive personality, and the opportunistic aggressive personalities of the establishment, notably his pro-Israel friends, will help him turn U.S. aggression in other directions. Trump's attachment to Israel is nothing new, but appears to be particularly uncompromising. In that context, Trump's extremely harsh words for Iran are ominous, and one must hope that his stated rejection of "regime change" war applies in that case as well as others. Trump's anti-China rhetoric also sounds bad, but in the long run there is little he or the United States can do to prevent China from becoming once again the "indispensable nation" it used to be during most of its long history. Tougher trade deals will not lead to the Apocalypse.

The Failure of the Intellectual Establishment

The sad image today of Americans as bad losers, unable to face reality, must be attributed in part to the ethical failure of the so-called 1968 generation of intellectuals. In a democratic society, the first duty of men and women with the time, inclination and capacity to study reality seriously is to share their knowledge and understanding with people who lack those privileges. The generation of academics whose political consciousness was temporarily raised by the tragedy of the Vietnam war should have realized that their duty was to use their position to educate the American people, notably about the world that Washington proposed to redesign and its history. However, the new phase of hedonistic capitalism offered the greatest opportunities for intellectuals in manipulating the masses rather than educating them. The consumer society marketing even invented a new phase of identity politics, with the youth market, the gay market, and so on. In the universities, a critical mass of "progressive" academics retreated into the abstract world of post-modernism and have ended up focusing the attention of youth on how to react to other people's sex lives or "gender identification." Such esoteric stuff feeds the publish or perish syndrome and prevents academics in the humanities from having to teach anything that might be deemed critical of U.S. military spending or its failing efforts to assert its eternal domination of the globalized world. The fiercest controversy coming out of academia concerns who should use which toilet.

If the intellectual snobs on the coasts can sneer with such self-satisfaction at the poor "deplorables" in flyover land, it is because they themselves have ignored their primary social duty of seeking truth and sharing it. Scolding people for their "wrong" attitudes while setting the social example of unrestrained personal promotion can only produce the anti-elite reaction called "populism." Trump is the revenge of people who feel manipulated, forgotten and despised. However flawed, he is the only choice they had to express their revolt in a rotten election. The United States is deeply divided ideologically, as well as economically. The United States is threatened, not by Russia, but by its own internal divisions and the inability of Americans not only to understand the world, but even to understand each other.

Trump Was Elected by Russia?

Mass Dementia in the
Western Establishment*

JULY 2018

Where to begin to analyze the madness of mainstream media in reaction to the Trump-Putin meeting in Helsinki? By focusing on the individual, psychology has neglected the problem of mass insanity, which has now overwhelmed the United States establishment, its mass media and most of its copycat European subsidiaries. The individuals may be sane, but as a herd they are ready to leap off the cliff.

For the past two years, a particular power group has sought to explain away its loss of power—or rather, its loss of the Presidency, as it still holds a predominance of institutional power—by creation of a myth. Mainstream media is known for its herd behavior, and in this case the editors, commentators, journalists have talked themselves into a story that initially they themselves could hardly take seriously.

Donald Trump was elected *by Russia?*

On the face of it, this is preposterous. Okay, the United States can manage to rig elections in Honduras, or Serbia, or even Ukraine, but the United States is a bit too big and complex to leave the choice of the Presidency to a barrage of electronic messages totally unread by most voters. If this were so, Russia wouldn't need to try to "undermine our democracy." It would mean that our democracy was already undermined, in tatters, dead. A standing corpse ready to be knocked over by a tweet.

Even if, as is alleged without evidence, an army of Russian bots (even bigger than the notorious Israeli army of bots) was besieging social media with its nefarious slanders against poor innocent Hillary Clinton, this could determine an election only in a vacuum, with no other

---

* First published in *Global Research,* July 20, 2018.

influences in the field. But there was a lot of other stuff going on in the 2016 election, some for Trump and some for Hillary, and Hillary herself scored a crucial own goal by denigrating millions of Americans as "deplorables" because they didn't fit into her identity politics constituencies.

The Russians could do nothing to build support for Trump, and there is not a hint of evidence that they tried. They might have done something to harm Hillary, because there was so much there: the private server emails, the Clinton foundation, the murder of Moammer Gaddafi, the call for a no-fly zone in Syria … they didn't have to invent it. It was there. So was the hanky panky at the Democratic National Committee, on which the Clintonite accusations focus, perhaps to cause everyone to forget much worse things.

When you come to think of it, the DNC scandal focused on Debbie Wasserman Schultz, not on Hillary herself. Screaming about "Russian hacking the DNC" has been a distraction from much more serious accusations against Hillary Clinton. Bernie Sanders supporters didn't need those "revelations" to make them stop loving Hillary or even to discover that the DNC was working against Bernie. It was always perfectly obvious.

So at worst, "the Russians" are accused of revealing some relatively minor facts concerning the Hillary Clinton campaign. Big deal.

But that is enough, after two years of fakery, to send the establishment into a frenzy of accusations of "treason" when Trump does what he said he would do while campaigning, try to normalize relations with Russia.

This screaming comes not only from the U.S. mainstream, but also from that European elite which has been housebroken for seventy years as obedient poodles, dachshunds or corgis in the American menagerie, via intense vetting by U.S. trans-Atlantic "cooperation" associations. They have based their careers on the illusion of sharing the world empire by following U.S. whims in the Middle East and transforming the mission of their armed forces from defense into foreign intervention units of NATO under U.S. command. Having not thought seriously about the implications of this for over half a century, they panic at the suggestion of being left to themselves.

The Western elite is now suffering from self-inflicted dementia.

Donald Trump is not particularly articulate, navigating through the language with a small repetitive vocabulary, but what he said at his Helsinki press conference was honest and even brave. As the hounds bay for his blood, he quite correctly refused to endorse the "findings" of U.S.

intelligence agencies, fourteen years after the same agencies "found" that Iraq was bursting with weapons of mass destruction. How in the world could anyone expect anything else?

But for the mainstream media, "the story" at the Helsinki summit, even the *only* story, was Trump's reaction to the, er, trumped-up charges of Russian interference in our democracy. Were you or were you not elected thanks to Russian hackers? All they wanted was a yes or no answer. Which could not possibly be yes. So they could write their reports in advance.

Anyone who has frequented mainstream journalists, especially those who cover the "big stories" on international affairs, is aware of their obligatory conformism, with few exceptions. To get the job, one must have important "sources," meaning government spokesmen who are willing to tell you what "the story" is, often without being identified. Once they know what "the story" is, competition sets in: competition as to how to tell it. That leads to an escalation of rhetoric, variations on the theme: "The President has betrayed our great country to the Russian enemy. Treason!"

This demented chorus on "Russian hacking" prevented mainstream media from even doing their job. Not even mentioning, much less analyzing, any of the real issues at the summit. To find analysis, one must go on line, away from the official fake news to independent reporting. For example, "the Moon of Alabama" site offers an intelligent interpretation of the Trump strategy, which sounds infinitely more plausible than "the story."[1] In short, Trump is trying to woo Russia away from China, in a reverse version of Kissinger's strategy forty years ago to woo China away from Russia, thus avoiding a continental alliance against the United States. This may not work because the United States has proven so untrustworthy that the cautious Russians are highly unlikely to abandon their alliance with China for shadows. But it makes perfect sense as an explanation of Trump's policy, unlike the caterwauling we've been hearing from Senators and talking heads on CNN.

Those people seem to have no idea of what diplomacy is about. They cannot conceive of agreements that would be beneficial to both sides. No, it's got to be a zero sum game, winner take all. If they win, we lose, and vice versa.

---

1 "Helsinki Talks: How Trump Tries to Rebalance the Global Triangle," July 17, 2018. https://www.moonofalabama.org/2018/07/helsinki-talks-how-trump-tries-to-rebalance-the-global-triangle/

They also have no idea of the harm to both sides if they do not agree. They have no project, no strategy. Just hate Trump.

He seems totally isolated, and every morning I look at the news to see if he has been assassinated yet.

It is unimaginable for our Manichean moralists that Putin might also be under fire at home for failing to chide the American president for U.S. violations of human rights in Guantanamo, murderous drone strikes against defenseless citizens throughout the Middle East, the destruction of Libya in violation of the U.N. mandate, interference in the elections of countless countries by government-financed "non-governmental organizations" (the National Endowment for Democracy), worldwide electronic spying, invasions of Iraq and Afghanistan, not to mention the world's greatest prison population and regular massacres of school children. But the diplomatic Russians know how to be polite.

Still, if Trump actually makes a "deal," there may be losers—neither the U.S. nor Russia but third parties. When two great powers reach agreement, it is often at somebody else's expense. The West Europeans are afraid it will be them, but such fears are groundless. All Putin wants is normal relations with the West, which is not much to ask.

Rather, candidate number one for paying the price are the Palestinians, or even Iran, in marginal ways. At the press conference, asked about possible areas of cooperation between the two nuclear powers, Trump suggested that the two could agree on helping Israel:

"We both spoke with Bibi Netanyahu. They would like to do certain things with respect to Syria, having to do with the safety of Israel. In that respect, we absolutely would like to work in order to help Israel. Israel will be working with us. So both countries would work jointly."

In political terms, Trump knows where political power lies, and is counting on the influence of the pro-Israel lobby, which recognizes the defeat in Syria and the rising influence of Russia, to save him from the liberal imperialists—a daring bet, but he does not have much choice.

On another subject, Trump said that "our militaries" get along with the Russians "better than our politicians." This is another daring bet, on military realism that could somehow neutralize military industrial congressional complex lobbying for more and more weapons.

In short, the only chance to end the nuclear war threat may depend on support for Trump from Israel and the Pentagon!

The hysterical neoliberal globalists seem to have ruled out any other possibility—and perhaps this one too.

"Constructive dialogue between the United States and Russia forwards the opportunity to open new pathways toward peace and stability in our world" Trump declared "I would rather take a political risk in pursuit of peace than to risk peace in pursuit of politics."

That is more than his political enemies can claim.

The 2020 Election

Bourgeois Democracy Meets
Global Governance*

AUGUST 2020

A small number of very rich men are quite sure they know what is best for the future of the world and have enough wealth and influence to believe they can make it happen. They can be called oligarchs, but the term is inadequate. They are a special category, the shapers of the Global Governance destined to replace bourgeois democracy. I can name two: one who is famous, notorious even, but very old, and another who is a generation younger, not yet so well known or so rich but probably even more influential.

The Global Governors

The old one is of course George Soros, who needs no introduction. He has no doubt that the world should be one big Open Society—in a word, globalization—in which borders and nation States dissolve into a kaleidoscopic mix of cultural identities in which major decisions are taken by brilliant financial oligarchs like himself.

The younger one is Nicolas Berggruen, the dashing 59-year-old Paris-born son of a leading German-Jewish art collector. Nicolas enjoys double U.S.-German citizenship and membership in the Council on Foreign Relations, the NYU Commission on Global Citizenship, the Brookings International Advisory Council, the Leadership Council at Harvard Kennedy School's Center for Public Leadership, the World Economic Forum—and on and on. He helped get Emmanuel Macron elected President of France and has friendly relations with Ursula von der Leyen, head of the European Union Commission.

---

* Published in *Consortium News,* August 28, 2020.

170

The billionaire has his own "think and action tank," the Berggruen Institute, to promote his interests which center on "global governance." He is particularly interested in technological ways to shape and guide the world of the future. The future for Berggruen belongs to digitalization and above all transhumanism. In a short video, he muses over whether or not the digital age makes us "less human."[1]

We are all connected and "less free" but we are all "part of something bigger—communities, families, friends"… The digital world "looks less human but it's still be created by us." (And who is "us" exactly?) Nicolas Berggruen's model of the future family may be seen in his own choice: two motherless children manufactured with donated ovules and born by two surrogate wombs.

Like European-born Soros and Berggruen, the United States is above all the current command and control center of the Western world still aspiring to be the nucleus of a global empire. U.S. elections are important to these world visionaries in staying the course of world transformation. For both of them, Donald Trump can only be an intolerable glitch in the screen. This must be corrected in 2020. The entire liberal elite is in overwhelming agreement.

The Transition Integrity Project

So it has been easy to arouse near panic in the Washington establishment and beyond over the notion that Trump might not be dislodged by the November 2020 election. Fear is being spread less that Trump might win the election (too unthinkable to think) than that he will lose the election but refuse to budge. This possibility received a big boost from a unique social event organized by Professor Rosa Brooks of Georgetown University, a leading champion of women's participation in the National Security State, and historian Nils Gilman, a head researcher at the Berggruen Institute. This well-connected pair easily enlisted dozens of power pointers to take part in what the Boston Globe called "a Washington version of Dungeons and Dragons," on the model of Pentagon planners who form teams to imagine what the U.S. and Russia might do in a nuclear war confrontation. They named their fun and games the Transition Integrity Project (TIP), clearly suggesting that the "integrity" of the anticipated transition from Trump to Biden was their main concern. Only a few of the 67 participants have been identified:

1 Berggruen Institute, *The Digital Human* video, August 1, 2020. https://berggruen.org/news/the-digital-human-video

anti-Trump Republican Michael Steele, Bill Clinton's White House chief of staff John Podesta, David Frum (ghost writer of President George W. Bush's "Axis of Evil" speech), and neoconservative political analyst William Kristol.

On August 3, the TIP issued its report, entitled "Preventing a Disrupted Presidential Election and Transition." This report resumed the results of the make-believe gaming scenarios, which provided imaginary support to the growing liberal Democratic hypothesis that Donald Trump is determined to steal the November election. "Like many authoritarian leaders, President Trump has begun to lay the groundwork for potentially ignoring or disrupting the voting process, by claiming, for instance, that any mail-in ballots will be fraudulent and that his opponents will seek to have non-citizens vote through fraud." It was taken for granted throughout that Trump's fears and accusations are fake whereas his opponents fears and accusations are soundly based.

The TIP report made a feeble attempt to appear neutral: "TIP takes no position on how Americans should cast their votes, or on the likely winner of the upcoming election; either party could prevail at the polls in November without resorting to 'dirty tricks'"—a neutrality consistently violated by the entire exercise.

The exercise comprised four scenarios: (1) an ambiguous voting result, (2) clear Biden victory, (3) clear Trump win, (4) narrow Biden win. The game was played by teams, primarily "Team Biden" and "Team Trump," but it is pretty clear that none of the players were pro-Trump, including the players on "Team Trump." But the games claimed to show how Trump supporters would react in these circumstances.

- Team Trump was consistently more ruthless than Team Biden—more willing to ignore existing democratic norms, to make use of disinformation, to deploy federal agencies to promote Trump's personal and electoral interests, and to engage in intimidation campaigns.

But "Team Biden" was much nicer:

- Team Biden generally felt constrained by a commitment to norms and a desire to tamp down violence and reduce instability.
- Team Biden often had the majority of the public on its side, and the ability to mobilize resentment about the

structural disenfranchisement in the way we conduct presidential elections.

Russiagate intruded into the gaming in an odd and even ludicrous way: "There was quite a bit of speculation that Trump might [...] attempt to rally nationalist feelings to himself, or placate foreign leaders to whom he may feel beholden, such as Vladimir Putin." Huh?

Nobody Dares Lose

A particularly alarming and disturbingly credible assumption of the TIP game is that in this election, neither side is prepared to accept defeat. The scenario exercises "revealed that for many Democrats and key Democratic constituencies, this election represents an existential crisis, the last chance to stop a rapid and potentially irreversible U.S. decline into authoritarianism and unbridled nativism." So, as much as Trump, many Democrats are ready to stop at nothing to win this election—for the best of reasons, of course.

Trump is depicted as equally desperate to win in order to avoid being treated as a criminal. An underlying assumption of this story-telling is that once out of office, Trump will be arrested and tried for unspecified crimes. This would indeed be an incentive for him not to lose.

At this point, it is necessary to recall that democratic election of national leaders depends on a degree of mutual trust that is being lost in America. The United States regularly insists that all foreign countries should elect their leaders by "fair and free elections." But there are many countries where, at some time of their historical development, this method is not advisable because one party, or tribe, fears for its very life if a rival party, or tribe, should take power. In such States, peace depends on the rule of a king, a mediator, a dictator. The United States can currently be seen to be regressing to just such a degree of mutual hatred and distrust.

No Compromise

It seems to me that if the Democratic establishment gave priority to a peaceful election and transition, against the possibility that Trump might reject the results, the smart and reasonable thing to do would be to reassure him on the two counts which they suggest might incite him to balk: postal vote fraud accusations and the threat of criminal charges against him.

As to the latter: "Participants in the scenario exercises universally believed that self-preservation for President Trump and his family will be Trump's first and possibly only priority if he is forced to concede electoral defeat." So it is a bit odd that the TIP goes on to report that: "During several of the TIP exercises, Team Biden attempted to enter into negotiations with Team Trump about a pardon and graceful transition, but those overtures were consistently rejected." Since there were no Trump supporters on either team, these game results merely reflect the intention of the Democratic establishment to assume that Donald Trump will be charged with "state crimes," as yet unspecified. No compromise deal is desired.

As for postal balloting, it should be conceivable that Trump's misgivings are justified. Trump is not against absentee ballots, which require identification of the voter, comparable to going to the polls, but is suspicious of mass mailings of ballots back and forth. In an age when anyone can photocopy any document, when mails are slow and when there are many ways in which ballots might be destroyed, such misgivings are not far-fetched. Indeed, in the course of Game #1, "a rogue individual destroyed a large number of ballots believed to have supported Biden." Why could the gamers imagine Biden ballots being destroyed, but rule out destruction of ballots supporting Trump?

For the sake of domestic peace, why not try to find a compromise? Kamala Harris has introduced legislation to generalize postal balloting. Why not, instead, extend polling time, opening polls not only on the second Tuesday in November but on the preceding Saturday and Sunday? This would provide time to allow voters afraid of covid-19 to keep distances from each other, as they do when they go to the supermarket. It would reduce the number of absentee ballots, the time needed for counting and above all the suspicions attached to postal voting. But the more wary Trump is of postal voting, the more Democrats insist on making it universal.

It becomes clearer and clearer that hatred of Trump has reached such a pitch, that for the Democratic establishment and its hangers-on, defeating Trump at the polls is not enough. They are practically inciting him to contest the election. Then they can have something more exciting and decisive: a genuine regime change.

Preparing for Regime Change

The classic regime change scenario involves a contested elections, mass street demonstrations including civil disobedience and finally, military intervention.

So, to start with, the gamers posit an authoritarian leader who won't step down. That's Trump.

Next, "a show of numbers in the streets—and actions in the streets—may be decisive factors in determining what the public perceives as a just and legitimate outcome." In an interview stressing "the flaws in our electoral system,"[2] TIP organizer Nils Gilman said that what we need "is for people to be prepared to take to the streets in nonviolent protest" if appeals to officials do not suffice. "We've learned over the last couple of months, since the Movement for Black Lives protest really took off again in the wake of George Floyd's murder, that taking to the streets and showing commitment to a democratic process beyond just the ballot box is a really important part of driving change." The demonstrations must be nonviolent, Gilman stressed.

As the TIP report put it, "the scale of recent demonstrations has increased the stakes for the Democratic Party to build strong ties with grassroots organizations and be responsive to the movement's demands." Certain of these grassroots organizations—MoveOn and Black Lives Matter—have enjoyed financial support from George Soros.

According to the scenarios, such protests could arise not only in case Trump refused to recognize a Biden win, but also, in Game #3, in case of a "comfortable Electoral College victory for President Trump—286–252—but also a significant popular vote win—52%–47%—for former Vice President Biden. The game play ended in a constitutional crisis, with threats of secession, and the potential for either a decline into authoritarianism or a radically revamped set of democratic rules that ensure the popular will prevails (abolishment of the Electoral College…)." The Biden Campaign retracted its initial concession, capitalizing "on the public's outrage that for the third time in 20 years a candidate lost the popular vote but won the Electoral College." The Biden Campaign encouraged California, Oregon and Washington to secede "unless Congressional Republicans agreed to a set of structural reforms to fix our democratic system to ensure majority rule." Congress

---

2 Zack Beauchamp, "How to avert a post-election nightmare," *Vox,* August 18, 2020. https://www.vox.com/policy-and-politics/2020/8/18/21371964/2020-transition-integrity-project-simulation-trump

supported Biden. "It was unclear what the military would do in this situation."

In reality, Democrats know that they have managed to keep the permanent State, including the military and intelligence agencies, on their side throughout Trump's presidency. Where are the forces that could carry out a pro-Trump coup d'état?

Whose Coup?

"During the exercises," the report notes, "winning 'the narrative' emerged as a potentially decisive factor. Either side can expand or contract the 'margin of contestation' if they succeed in substantially changing how key decision makers and the public view the 'facts,' the risks of action or inaction, or external events such as civil unrest." Winning the narrative appears to be a main purpose of the TIP, and it was quickly seconded in its efforts by top Democrats.

"Joe Biden should not concede under any circumstances because I think this is going to drag out, and eventually I do believe he will win if we don't give an inch and if we are as focused and relentless as the other side is," Hillary Clinton said in an interview on August 25.

A couple of days later, former Vice President and unsuccessful 2000 Democratic presidential candidate Al Gore chimed in. Trump, he said in a particularly loaded image, is "attempting to put his knee on the neck of democracy" by criticizing mail-in ballots.

"He seems to have no compunctions at all about trying to rip apart the social fabric and the political equilibrium of the American people, and he's strategically planting doubts in advance."

People ask whether Trump will leave office next January 20. "Well," said Gore, "it doesn't matter because it's not up to him. Because at noon on January 20th, if a new president is elected... the police force, the Secret Service, the military, all of the executive branch officers, will respond to the command and the direction of the new president."

The Bottom Line

Meanwhile, Americans can listen to the extravagant rhetoric of the two enemy camps, calling on them to choose between alleged "authoritarian white supremacy" (grossly exaggerated) and "radical Marxist socialism" (totally false) while offering absolutely nothing in terms of coherent public policy of benefit to the American people and the world.

The politicians claw to cling to ineffective office, while the future is being planned elsewhere.

Policy will be designed by the global governors, for instance at the next meeting in Davos of the World Economic Forum which, according to its founder and chairman Klaus Schwab, will lay out the "Great Reset" agenda for the Fourth Industrial Revolution that is destined to reshape all our lives. Nicolas Berggruen will be there with his ideas. So will other billionaires. They will not be "conspiring," but rather laying plans for what they consider best for the world. There is no political system enabling us to influence or even fully understand the projects they will sponsor. Surely these projects deserve to be sharply debated. But the politicians supposedly representing us are somewhere else, fighting furiously with each other over contrived issues.

The Electoral College is not the most fatal flaw in American democracy. Rather, it's the monopoly of political discourse by a Two-Party System fueled essentially by personal ambition, taking its cues from lobbies, the military industrial complex, Wall Street and the Global Governors.

Biden Exploits His Capitol Gains*

JANUARY 2021

What happened in the Capitol on January 6 was not surprising. It could have been avoided. It could have been prevented if the Democratic Establishment which held onto keys of power throughout Trump's mandate had truly wanted a smooth presidential transition. For months prior to the election, the elite Transition Integrity Project was spreading the alarm, loudly echoed by liberal media, that Trump would lose and refuse to acknowledge his loss.

There was a simple, obvious way to avoid such a drama. In an article for Consortium News last August, I suggested how this could be done by reassuring Trump on two crucial counts: postal vote fraud accusations and the threat of criminal charges against him. Instead of insisting on generalizing postal balloting, why not facilitate direct balloting, in particular scheduling voting on weekends, as other countries do? Isn't domestic peace worth seeking a compromise? But on the contrary, the Democratic Party establishment was doing everything to incite Trump to contest the election. That would enable them to have something more exciting and decisive: a genuine regime change.

So indeed what we got was something more exciting. Not exactly regime change, because we are seeing instead a powerful reaffirmation of the regime that was really still largely in control during Trump's largely deformed four-year term. The haste with which his aides and allies desert him in his last hour makes this clear. He was always a President without a team, operating on hunches, rhetoric and advice from his son-in-law and a few insiders who were really outsiders.

But what we are getting is indeed exciting: an alleged "insurrection" supposedly incited by Trump to "steal the election" (which there was

---

* Published in *Consortium News,* January 11, 2021.

absolutely no way of doing). The scenes of disorder have been instantly exploited to plunge him and his followers into an abyss of ignominy, if not criminal proceedings and imprisonment.

What happened on January 6 was not an insurrection. Anyone wanting to know what an insurrection is should look up the U.S.-sponsored armed uprising that overthrew duly elected Chilean President Salvador Allende on September 11, 1973. The Capitol disturbance was more like what happened when U.S.-trained "Otpor" militants broke into the Serbian parliament in the midst of that country's 2000 presidential election and set fire to ballot boxes. Or check out a particularly pertinent insurrection when truly violent demonstrators took over the Ukrainian Parliament in 2014 and overthrew the government, an event hailed by then U.S. Vice President Joe Biden as a great victory for democracy. Then there was the Hillary-endorsed coup in Honduras, the almost successful attempt to overthrow democracy in Bolivia, the U.S.-backed Guaido farce in Venezuela, etc., etc., etc.

No, an insurrection is not when a large crowd of people who feel their candidate has been cheated vent their indignation by managing to break into "their" parliament with no purpose in mind. Most of the intruders milled about taking selfies with no clear idea what to do next. By world standards, the "violence" on January 6 was very mild indeed, the only gun violence being the fatal shooting of an unarmed Trump enthusiast, Ashli Babbitt, who could easily have been pushed back from her adventurous attempt to climb over a barricade.

The intrusion was so far from carrying out a pro-Trump plan that it had the opposite effect. The immediate political result of the eruption of the undisciplined crowd was to prevent Republican Senators who were so inclined from presenting their arguments against the legitimacy of the November vote. If anything, the action worked in the favor of President-elect Biden.

One might think that in his moment of victory, a true statesman would demonstrate the qualities it takes to lead a nation by offering to bring all people together as fellow Americans. He did quite the opposite.

The very next day after the Capitol happening, in his small fiscal haven home state of Delaware, Joe Biden raged against his opponents as a terrorist mob, no less.

"They weren't protestors," he proclaimed. "Don't dare call them protesters. They were a riotous mob. Insurrectionists. Domestic terrorists. It's that basic. It's that simple."

Donald Trump, said Biden, "has unleashed an all-out assault on our institutions of democracy from the outset, and yesterday was but the culmination of that unrelenting attack." Trump had poisoned the political environment by using "language that autocrats and dictators use all over the world to hold on to power."

Biden's own language certainly sounded less like a magnanimous winner uniting his people than like that used by autocrats and dictators to hold onto power. Trump was trying to "deny the will of the American people," he said, much as Trump said of him. The whole problem was that "the will of the American people" was far from unanimous.

So even before his inauguration, President-elect Biden has given us a bitter taste of days ahead. There is to be no sacred unity, but deepened division between The Good (woke liberals), the Bad (Russians and other enemies of Our Democracy) and the Ugly Americans, to be labeled Domestic Terrorists, White Supremacists and fascists. The authoritarian center, ranging from opportunistic Republicans to The Squad, can rally around the necessary purge of Domestic Terrorists, silencing their communications and getting them properly fired from their jobs.

The Establishment has long been determined to crush Trump. But there is talk of "purging" all his followers as well. Biden is already speaking like a War President, calling for measures to combat the internal enemy such as during major wars.

The oligarchic nature of the American War Party is revealed by the haste with which privately owned social media enterprises silence dissent—even the still acting President of the United States. Indeed, who really rules the United States? Is the President only an agent of economic powers whose role is to serve their interests? And the trouble with Trump is that he had not been picked for the job.

Trump managed to appeal to millions of discontented Americans without offering any coherent practical program to replace the War Party with policies capable of transforming the nation into a haven of peace and prosperity. His confusion mirrored the ideological confusion of a population scandalously undereducated in history and political ideas. The illusion that Trump was the leader whom dissident Americans needed cost Ashli Babbitt her life and led thousands of Trump voters into what amounts to a trap. Trump himself was led into the trap.

A completely different approach to politics is needed to restore democracy to America. All appeals to identities and ideologies can only deepen the confusion and divisions, because they prevent people from understanding each other. The Biden administration appears intent on strengthening such confusion and divisions precisely by recourse to identities and ideologies. I firmly believe that only a scrupulously rational, open-minded, factual and pragmatic approach to clearly defined practical problems could bring peace to the United States, a peace that could favor peace in the world.

From outside the melee, it is easy to define the serious issues that should dominate political debate in the United States. But instead of that, we hear a torrential exchange of insults. The establishment elite cannot stoop to exchange viewpoints with populists denounced as deplorable, racist, misogynist, white supremacist, fascist and now even "terrorist." The populists' unfocused denunciation of the elite veers off into accusations of genocidal vaccination campaigns, occult pedophile rites and Satanism. Instead of anything resembling a clear political division, America is increasingly split by blind, burning mutual hatred.

What American political life needs is not more censorship, but the self-censorship of reason. That is very far away.

— PART V —
EUROPEAN POLITICS

Greece: Down and Out on the European Animal Farm[*]

FEBRUARY 2010

For Europe's poorest countries, European Union membership has long held out the promise of tranquil prosperity. The current Greek financial crisis ought to dispel some of their illusions.

There are two strikingly significant levels to the current crisis. While primarily economic, the European Economic Community also claims to be a community, based on solidarity—the sisterhood of nations and brotherhood of peoples. However, the economic deficit is nothing compared to the human deficit it exposes.

To put it simply, the Greek crisis shows what happens when a weak member of this Union is in trouble. It is the same as what happens on the world scale, where there is no such morally pretentious union perpetually congratulating itself on its devotion to human rights. The economically strong protect their own interests at the expense of the economically weak.

The crisis broke last autumn after George Papandreou's PASOK party won elections, took office and discovered that the cupboard was bare. The Greek government had cheated to get into the EU's euro zone in 2001 by cooking the books to cover deficits that would have disqualified it from membership in the common currency. The European Treaties capped the acceptable budget deficit at 3% and public debt at 60% of GDP respectively. In fact, this limit is being widely transgressed, quite openly by France. But major scandal arrived with revelations that Greece's budget deficit reached 12.7% in 2009, with a gross debt forecast for 2010 amounting to 125% of GDP.

---

[*] Original version: *CounterPunch,* March 1, 2010. https://www. counterpunch.org/2010/03/01/the-fall-of-greece/

Of course, European leaders got together to declare solidarity. But their speeches were designed not so much to reassure the increasingly angry and desperate Greek people as to soothe "the markets"—the real hidden almighty gods of the European Union. The markets, like the ancient gods, have a great old time tormenting mere mortals in trouble, so their response to the Greek problem was naturally to rush to profit from it. For instance, when Greece is obliged to issue new bonds this year, the markets can blithely demand that Greece double its interest rates, on grounds of increased "risk" that Greece won't pay, thus making it that much harder for Greece to pay. Such is the logic of the free market.

What the EU leaders meant by "solidarity" in their appeal to the gods was not that they were going to pour public money into Greece, as they poured it into their troubled banks, but that they intended to squeeze the money owed the banks out of the Greek people.

The squeezing is to take the forms made familiar over the past disastrous decades by the International Monetary Fund: the Greek State is enjoined to cut public expenses, which means firing public employees, cutting their overall earnings, delaying retirement, economizing on health care, raising taxes, and incidentally probably raising the jobless rate from 9.6% to around 16%, all with the glorious aim of bringing the deficit down to 8.7% this year and thus appeasing the almighty invisible gods of the market.

This just might propitiate both the gods and German leaders, who above all want to maintain the value of the euro. The financial markets will no doubt grab their pound of flesh in the form of increased interest rates, while the Greeks are bled by IMF-style "shock treatment."

And what about that great theater of human rights and universal brotherhood, the European Parliament? Well, in that august forum everyone gets to speak for a carefully clocked 1, 2, or 3 minutes, but when it comes to the most serious matter, the budget, the authoritative voices are all German.

Thus the chairman of the EP's special committee on the economic and financial crisis, Wolf Klinz, has called for sending a "high representative" of the EU to Greece, an "economies commissar" to make sure the Greeks carry out the austerity measures properly. The Greek crisis can allow the EU to put into practice for the first time its "Treaty instruments" concerning "supervision of budgetary and economic policy." Interest rates may go up because of "risk," but there is to be no risk. The pound of flesh will be delivered.

There was no such supervision of the financial fiddling which caused this mess. The EU statistics agency Eurostat recently discovered and revealed that in 2001, Goldman Sachs secretly ("but legally," protest its executive officers) helped the Greek government meet EU membership criteria by using a complicated "currency swap" that masked the extent of public deficit and national debt.

Who understands how that worked? I think it is fair to guess that not even Angela Merkel, who is trained as a scientist, understands clearly what went on, much less the incompetent Greek politicians who accepted the Goldman Sachs trickery. It allowed them to create an illusion of success—for a while. Success meant being a "member of the club" of the rich, and it can be argued that this notion of success has actually favored bad government at the national level. Belonging to the EU gave a false sense of security that contributed to the irresponsibility of incompetent political leaders.

Having euros to buy imported goods (notably from Germany) pleased rich consumers, while the euro priced Greek goods out of their previous markets. Now the debt trap is closing. The traditional way out for Greece would be to leave the euro and return to a devaluated drachma, in order to cut imports and favor exports. This way, the burden of necessary sacrifices would not be borne solely by the working class. But the embrace of EU "solidarity" is there to prevent this from happening. German authorities are preparing to lay down the law to the Greeks, after reducing the income of their own working class in order to benefit Germany's export-oriented economy.

Austerity measures are the opposite of what is needed in a time of looming depression. Rather, what is needed are Keynesian measures to stimulate employment and strengthen the domestic market. But Germany is firmly attached to the export model, for itself and everyone else ("globalization"). For a country like Greece, which cannot compete successfully within the EU, exports outside the EU are crippled by its use of a strong currency, the euro. Bound to the euro, Greece can neither stimulate its domestic market nor export successfully. But it is not going to be allowed to extricate itself from the debt trap and return to its traditional currency, the drachma. Poverty appears to be the only solution.

There is discontent within the German working class at their country's policies aimed at shrinking wages and social benefits for the sake of selling abroad. In an ideal "social Europe," workers in Germany would come to the aid of workers in Greece by demanding a radical revision of economic policy, away from catering to the international financial markets toward building a solid social democracy. The reality is quite different.

The Greek financial crisis exposes the absence of any real community spirit in the EU. The "solidarity" declared by the country's EU partners is a solidarity with their own investments. There is no popular solidarity between peoples. The EU has established a surrogate ideology of internationalism: rejection of the nation-state as source of all evil, a pompous pride in "Europe" as the center of human rights, giver of moral lessons to the world, which happens to fit in perfectly with its subservience to United States imperial foreign policy in the Middle East and beyond. The paradox is that European unification has coincided with decreasing curiosity in the larger EU states about what happens to their neighbors. Despite a certain amount of specialized training needed to create a Eurocrat class, the general population of each EU member is only superficially acquainted with the others. They see them as teams in soccer matches. They go on holiday around the Mediterranean, but this mostly involves meeting fellow tourists, and study of foreign languages has declined, except for English (omnipresent, if mangled). Mass media news reports are turned inward, featuring crime and scandal stories rather than significant political events in other EU member states.

Northern European media portray Greece practically as a Third World country, peripheral and picturesque, where people speak an impossible language, dance in circles on islands, and live beyond their means in their carefree way. The crickets in the Aesop fable, scorned by the assiduous ants. Media in Germany and the Netherlands imply that IMF-style shock treatment is almost too good for them. The widening polarization between rich and poor, between and within EU member states, is taken for granted.

The smaller indebted countries within the EU are amiably designated by the English-speaking financial priesthood as the PIGS—Portugal, Italy (perhaps Ireland), Greece, Spain—an appropriate designation for an animal farm where some are so much more equal than others.

All Power to the Banks!

The Winners-Take-All Regime of Emmanuel Macron*

MAY 2017

A ghost of the past was the real winner of the French presidential election. Emmanuel Macron won only because a majority felt they had to vote against the ghost of "fascism" allegedly embodied by his opponent, Marine Le Pen. Whether out of panic or out of the need to feel respectable, the French voted two to one in favor of a man whose program most of them either ignored or disliked. Now they are stuck with him for five years.

If people had voted on the issues, the majority would never have elected a man representing the trans-Atlantic elite totally committed to "globalization," using whatever is left of the power of national governments to weaken them still further, turning over decision-making to "the markets"—that is, to international capital, managed by the major banks and financial institutions, notably those located in the United States, such as Goldman-Sachs.

The significance of this election calls for a fairly thorough explanation, not only of the Macron project, but also of what the election of Marine Le Pen might have meant.

From a Two Party to a Single Party System

Despite the multiparty nature of French elections, for the past generation France has been essentially ruled by a two-party system, with government power alternating between the Socialist Party, roughly the

---

* Original version: *CounterPunch,* May 22, 2017. https://www. counterpunch.org/2017/05/22/all-power-to-the-banks-the-winners-take-all-regime-of-emmanuel-macron/

equivalent of the U.S. Democratic Party, and a party inherited from the Gaullist tradition which has gone through various name changes before recently settling on calling itself *Les Républicains* (LR), in obvious imitation of the United States. For decades, there has been nothing "socialist" about the Socialist Party and nothing Gaullist about The Republicans. In reality, both have adopted neoliberal economic policies, or more precisely, they have followed European Union directives requiring member states to adopt neoliberal economic policies. Especially since the adoption of the common currency, the euro, a little over fifteen years ago, those economic policies have become tangibly harmful to France, hastening its deindustrialization, the ruin of its farmers and the growing indebtedness of the State to private banks.

This has had inevitable political repercussions. The simplest reaction has been widespread reaction against both parties for continuing to pursue the same unpopular policies. The most thoughtful reaction has been to start realizing that it is the European Union itself that imposes this unpopular economic conformism.

To quell growing criticism of the European Union, the well-oiled Macron machine, labeled *"En Marche!"* has exploited the popular reaction against both governing parties. It has broken and absorbed large parts of both, in an obvious move to turn *En Marche!* into a single catch-all party loyal to Macron.

The destruction of the Socialist Party was easy. Since the "Socialist" government of President François Hollande was so unpopular that it could not hope to win, it was easy to lure prominent members of that party to jump the sinking ship and rally to Macron, who had been economics minister in that unpopular government, but who was advertised by all the media as "new" and "anti-system."

Weakening the Republicans was trickier. Thanks to the deep unpopularity of the outgoing Socialist government, the Republican candidate, François Fillon, looked like a shoo-in. But despite his pro-business economic policies, Fillon still cared about preserving France, and favored an independent foreign policy including good relations with Russia. It is unknown who dug into old records to come up with information about the apparently fake jobs Fillon gave to his wife and children in past years, and how they were passed on the weekly *Canard Enchaîné* to be revealed at a critical moment in the campaign. The uproar drowned out the issues. To an electorate already wary of "establishment politicians," these revelations were fatal. The impression that "politicians are all corrupt" played into the hands of Emmanuel Macron, too young to have done anything worse than make a few quick millions during his passage through the Rothschild Bank, and there's nothing illegal about that.

In France, the presidential election is followed by parliamentary elections, which normally give a majority to the party of the newly elected president. But Macron had no party, so he is creating one for the occasion, made up of defectors from the major defeated parties as well as his own innovation, candidates from "civil society," with no political experience, but loyal to him personally. These "civil society" newcomers tend to be successful individuals, winners in the game of globalized competition, who will have no trouble voting for anti-labor measures. Macron is thus confirming Marine Le Pen's longstanding assertion that the two main parties were really one big single party, whose rhetorical differences masked their political convergence.

The Macron victory demoralized Republicans. Weakening them further, Macron named a Republican, Edouard Philippe, as his Prime Minister, in a government with four Socialists and two Republicans, alongside his own selections from "civil society."

Transforming France

Macron won over older voters who were alarmed by his opponents' hints at leaving the European Union, which they have been indoctrinated to consider necessary to prevent renewal of Europe's old wars. But only the hysterical anti-fascist scare can explain why self-styled leftist "revolutionaries" such as François Ruffin, known for his successful anti-capitalist movie "Merci Patron," could join the stampede to vote for Macron—promising to "oppose him later." But how?

Later, after five years of Macron, opposition may be harder than ever. In recent decades, as manufacturing moves to low wage countries, including EU members such as Poland and Rumania, France has lost 40% of its industry. Loss of industry means loss of jobs and fewer workers. When industry is no longer essential, workers have lost their key power: stopping work to shut it down. Striking against public services annoys the public but does not cut into anyone's profits.

Emmanuel Macron has said that he wants to spend only a short time in political life, before getting back to business. He has a mission, and he is in a hurry. If he gains an absolute majority in the June parliamentary elections, he has a free hand to govern for five years. He says he will use this period not to "reform" the country, as his predecessors put their submission to EU dictates, but to "transform" France into a different sort of country. If he has his way, in five years France will no longer be a sovereign nation, but a reliable region in a federalized European Union, following a rigorous economic policy made in Germany by bankers and a bellicose foreign policy made in Washington by neocons.

As usual, the newly elected French president's first move was to rush to Berlin to assert loyalty to the increasingly lopsided "Franco-German partnership." He was most warmly welcomed by Chancellor Angela Merkel, thanks to his clear determination to force through the austerity measures demanded by the Frankfurt budget masters. Macron hopes that his fiscal obedience will be rewarded by German consent to a European investment fund for stimulating economic growth, but this implies a type of federalism that the pfennig-pinching Germans show little sign of accepting.

First of all, he has promised to complete the dismantling of the French labor code, which offers various protections to workers. This should save money for employers and the government. For Macron, the ruin of French industry and French farming seem to be welcome steps toward an economy of individual initiative, symbolized by startups.

The Macron program amounts to a profound ideological transformation of the French ideal of *égalité,* equality, from a horizontal concept, meaning equal benefits for all, to the vertical ideal of "equality of opportunity," meaning the theoretical chance of every individual to rise above the others. This is an ideal easily accepted in the United States with its longstanding myth of the self-made man. The French have traditionally been logical enough to understand that everyone can't rise above the others.

Horizontal equality in France has primarily meant institutional redistribution of wealth via universal access to benefits such as health care, pensions, communications and transportation facilities, allocations for families raising children, unemployment insurance, free education at all levels. These are the benefits that are under threat from the European Union in various ways. One way is the imposition of "competition" rules that ban governments from favoring their own industries. This favors privatization and foreign takeovers that transform public services into profit-seekers. Another is the imposition of public budget restrictions, along with the obligation of the State to seek private loans, increasing its debt, and the loss of tax revenue that all end up up making the State too poor to continue providing such services.

Very few French people would want to give up horizontal equality for the privilege of hoping to become a billionaire.

Macron is sufficiently Americanized, or, to be more precise, global-ized, to have declared that "there is no such thing as French culture." From this viewpoint, France is just a place open to diverse cultures, as well as to immigrants and of course foreign capital. He has clearly signaled his rejection of French independence in the foreign policy field. Unlike his leading rivals, who all called for improved relations with Russia, Macron echoes the Russophobic line of the neocons. He broke tradition on his inauguration by riding down the Champs-Elysées in a military vehicle. A change of tone is indicated by his cabinet nominations. The title of the new foreign minister, Jean-Yves Le Drian, who served as defense minister in the Hollande government, is "Minister of Europe and of Foreign Affairs," clearly giving Europe preference in the matter. Sylvie Goulard, an ardent Europe devotee who has remarked that "she does not feel French," has been named Minister of Armies and Minister of Defense. Clearly national defense is an afterthought, when the main idea is to deploy the armed forces in various joint Western interventions.

The Divided Opposition

Unless the June parliamentary elections produce stunning surprises, the opposition to Macron's catch-all governance party appears weak and fatally divided. The Socialist Party is almost wiped out. The Republicans are profoundly destabilized. Genuine opposition to the Macron regime can only be based on defense of French interests against EU economic dictates, starting with the euro, which prevents the country from pursu-ing an independent economic and foreign policy. In short, the genuine opposition would have to be *"souverainiste,"* concerned with preserving French sovereignty.

Two strong personalities emerged from the presidential election as potential leaders of that opposition: Jean-Luc Mélenchon and Marine Le Pen. But they are drastically opposed to each other.

Mélenchon ran a spectacularly popular campaign, leaving the Socialist Party far behind (the party he personally left behind years ago). Initially, as he seemed to be taking votes away from Le Pen as well as from the Socialists, he got friendly media coverage, but as he came clos-er to making it to the decisive second round, the tone started to change. Just as Le Pen was finally knocked out as a potential "fascist," there is little doubt that had Mélenchon been Macron's challenger, he would have been increasingly denounced as "communist."

Mélenchon is intelligent enough to have realized that the social pol-icies he advocates cannot be achieved unless France recovers control of its currency. He therefore took a stand against both NATO and the euro. So did Marine Le Pen. Mélenchon was embarrassed by the resemblance between their two programs, and contrary to other eliminated candidates, refrained from endorsing Macron, instead calling on his movement, *La France Insoumise,* to choose between Macron and abstention. Finally, 25% of Mélenchon voters abstained in the second round, but 62% voted for Macron—almost exclusively motivated by the alleged need to "stop fascism." That accounts for the final total results of 66% for Macron and 34 % for Le Pen.

That vote confirmed the impossibility of forming a unified *souverainiste* opposition and allows Marine Le Pen to strengthen her claim to be the leader of a genuine opposition to Macron. She has admitted her own mistakes in the campaign, particularly in her debate with Macron, who beat her hands down with his arrogant performance as the economic expert. But despite her mere 34%, she retains the most loyal base of supporters in a changing scene. The problem for Mélenchon is that his electorate is more versatile.

Despite his loud appeal to "youth," Macron was elected by France's huge population of old people. Among voters over 65, he won 80% against 20% for Le Pen. Marine Le Pen did better with the youngest age group, 18 to 24, winning 44% against Macron's 56%[1].

The differences were also significant between socio-professional categories. Macron won a whopping 83% of the votes coming from the "superior socio-professional categories"—categories where the "winners" in competitive society are largely ensconced. But in what are described as *"categories populaires,"* a French term for ordinary folk, with less education, the vote was 53% in favor of Le Pen. And she confirmed her position as favorite candidate of the working class, winning 63% of workers' votes.

Note that the "superior socio-professional categories" are where the significance of these results will be defined. Individuals from that category—journalists, commentators and show business personalities— are all in a position to spread the word that this vote indicates that the workers must be "racist," and therefore that we have narrowly escaped being taken over by "fascism."

One of the many odd things about the latest French presidential election is the rejoicing among foreign "leftists" over the fact that the

---

1 According to poll of 7,752 representative voters by Le Figaro/LCI, http://opinionlab.opinion-way.com/dokumenty/OpinionWay-SondageJourduVote-Tour2Presidentielle20177Mai2017.pdf

candidate of the rich roundly defeated the candidate of the poor. It used to be the other way around, but that was long ago. These days, the winners in the competitive game comfort themselves that they morally deserve their success, because they are in favor of diversity and against racism, whereas the less fortunate, the rural people and the working class, don't deserve much of anything, because they must be "racist" to be wary of mass immigration and globalization.

The fact that Paris voted 90% for Macron is natural, considering that real estate prices have increasingly pushed the working class out of the capital, much of whose population is now identified as "bobo"—the bohemian bourgeoisie, many employed in various branches of the dominant human rights ideology fabrication business: journalists, professors, teachers, consultants, the entertainment industry. In these milieux, hardly anyone would even dare speak a positive word about Marine Le Pen.

What if Marine Le Pen had won?

Since politics is largely fantasy, we may as well try to imagine the unimaginable: what if Marine Le Pen had won the election? This was never a realistic possibility, but it is worth imagining.

It could have had one, perhaps only one, extremely positive result: it could have freed France from its paralyzing obsession with the nonexistent "fascist threat." The ghost would be exorcised. If the word has any meaning, "fascism" implies single party rule, whereas Marine Le Pen made clear her desire to govern by coalition, and selected the leader of a small Gaullist party, Nicolas Dupont-Aignan, as her prospective prime minister. Poof! No fascism. That would have been an immeasurable benefit for political debate in France. At last genuine issues might matter. Real threats could be confronted.

Another advantage would have been the demise of the National Front. Since Marine Le Pen took over the notorious party founded by her reactionary father, it has kept a precarious balance between two opposing wings. There is the right wing in the southeast, along the Riviera, the bastion of the party's founder, Jean-Marie Le Pen, a region represented in the outgoing parliament by his conservative granddaughter Marion Maréchal Le Pen. In the old industrial northeast region, between Arras and Lille, Marine Le Pen has built her own bastion, as champion of ordinary working people, where she won a majority of votes in the presidential election.

This is not the only time in history when an heiress has gone away with the heritage to join someone of whom her father disapproves. All those who want to cling to their comforting hatred of the left's official Satan have trouble believing that Marine Le Pen broke with her reactionary father to go her own way (just as U.S. hawks couldn't believe in Gorbachev). This change owes everything to her encounter with Florian Philippot, an intellectual who gave up on the ability of the Socialists to face the real issues. Marine has the personal charisma of a leader, and Philippot provided the intellectual substance she needed. Marine has decisively chosen Philippot as her advisor and co-leader, despite grumblings by Jean-Marie that she has been led astray by a gay Marxist. Had Marine won, her left wing would have been strengthened enough to enable her and Philippot to scrap the National Front and found a new "Patriot Party."[2] However, by scoring below 40%, she has weakened her authority and must try to hold the troublesome party together in order to win seats in the new parliament—which will not be easy.

Marine Le Pen might have tried to enact measures to save French industry and the jobs it provides, provide various benefits for low-income people, withdraw from NATO, and even promote a peaceful world, starting with friendly relations with Russia. She would even have begun to prepare her compatriots for escape from the euro.

But not to worry, none of this "fascist" program would ever have come to pass. If she had won, bands of protesting "antifascists" would have invaded the streets, smashing windows and attacking police. The outgoing Socialist government was preparing to use the resulting chaos as a pretext to stay in power long enough to manage the parliamentary elections,[3] ensuring that President Marine Le Pen would be held in check. A "color revolution" was ready to be stirred up. The deep state is vigilant in NATOland.

---

2 Since she lost, Philippot was pushed out and formed a "Patriot Party" of his own, which has led antiwar demonstrations and remains marginal.

3 "Si Le Pen avait été élue... le plan secret pour 'protéger la République'," *Le Nouvel Observateur,* May 17, 2017 http://tempsreel.nouvelobs.com/presidentielle-2017/20170516.OBS9474/si-le-pen-avait-ete-elue-le-plan-secret-pour-proteger-la-republique.html

Regime Change in Budapest?

Disobedient Hungary: From the Soviet to the European Union*

SEPTEMBER 2018

CNN recently discovered a paradox. How was it possible, they asked, that in 1989, Viktor Orban, at the time a Western-acclaimed liberal opposition leader, was calling for Soviet troops to leave Hungary, and now that he is Prime Minister, he is cozying up to Vladimir Putin?

For the same reason, dummy.

Orban wanted his country to be independent then, and he wants it to be independent now.

In 1989, Hungary was a satellite of the Soviet Union. Whatever Hungarians wanted, they had to follow directives from Moscow and adhere to Soviet communist ideology.

Today, Hungary is ordered to follow directives from Brussels and adhere to the EU ideology, a k a "our common values."

But what exactly are those "common values"?

Not so very, very long ago, "the West," that is, both America and Europe, claimed devotion to "Christian values." Those values were evoked in Western condemnation of the Soviet Union.

That is out. These days, indeed, one of the reasons why Viktor Orban is considered a threat to our European values is his reference to a Hungarian conception of "the Christian character of Europe, the role of nations and cultures." The revival of Christianity in Hungary, as in Russia, is regarded in the West as deeply suspect.

So it's understood, Christianity is no longer a "Western value." What has taken its place? That should be obvious: today "our common values" essentially mean democracy and free elections.

---

* Published in *The Unz Review,* September 17, 2018.

Guess again. Orban was recently re-elected by a landslide. Leading EU liberal Guy Verhofstadt called this "an electoral mandate to roll back democracy in Hungary."

Since elections can "roll back democracy," they cannot be the essence of "our common values." People can vote wrong; that is called "populism" and is a bad thing.

The real, functional common values of the European Union are spelled out in its treaties: the four freedoms. No, not freedom of speech, since many Member States have laws against "hate speech," which can cover a lot of ground since its meaning is open to wide interpretation. No, the obligatory four freedoms of the EU are free movement of goods, services, persons and capital throughout the Union. Open borders. That is the essence of the European Union, the dogma of the Free Market.

The problem with the Open Border doctrine is that it doesn't know where to stop. Or it doesn't stop anywhere. When Angela Merkel announced that hundreds of thousands of refugees were welcome in Germany, the announcement was interpreted as an open invitation by immigrants of all sorts, who began to stream into Europe. This unilateral German decision automatically applied to the whole of the EU, with its lack of internal borders. Given German clout, Open Borders became the essential "European common value," and welcoming immigrants the essence of human rights.

Very contrasting ideological and practical considerations contribute to the idealization of Open Borders. To name a few:

• Economic liberals maintain that because Europe is aging, it needs young immigrant workers to pay for the pensions of retired workers.

• Many Jewish activists feel threatened by national majorities and feel safer in a society made up of ethnic minorities.

• More discreetly, certain entrepreneurs favor mass immigration because growing competition in the labor market brings down wages.

• Many artistically inclined people consider ethnic diversity to be more creative and more fun.

• Certain anarchist or Trotskyist sects believe that uprooted immigrants are the "agent" of the revolution that the Western proletariat failed to produce.

• Many Europeans accept the idea that nation states are the cause of war, concluding that every way of destroying them is welcome.

• International financial investors naturally want to remove all obstacles to their investments and thus promote Open Borders as The Future.

- There are even a few powerful schemers who see "diversity" as the basis of divide and rule, by breaking solidarity into ethnic pieces.
- There are good people who want to help all humanity in distress.

This combination of contrasting, even opposing motivations does not add up to a majority in every country. Notably not in Hungary.

It should be noted that Hungary is a small Central European country of less than ten million inhabitants, which never had a colonial empire and thus has no historic relationship with peoples in Africa and Asia as do Britain, France, the Netherlands, and Belgium. As one of the losers in World War I, Hungary lost a large amount of territory to its neighbors, notably to Romania. The rare and difficult Hungarian language would be seriously challenged by mass immigration. It is probably safe to say that the majority of people in Hungary tend to be attached to their national identity and feel it would be threatened by massive immigration from radically different cultures. It may not be nice of them, and like everyone they can change. But for now, that is how they vote.

In particular, they recently voted massively to re-elect Victor Orban, obviously endorsing his refusal of uncontrolled immigration. This is what has spurred scrutiny of Orban's leadership for signs of incumbent dictatorship. The EU is taking steps to strip Hungary of its political rights as a result. On September 14, Victor Orban made his position clear in a speech to the (largely rubber stamp) European Parliament in Strasbourg:

> Let's be frank. They want to condemn Hungary and the Hungarians who have decided that our country will not be an immigration country. With all due respect, but as firmly as possible, I reject the threats of the pro-immigration forces, their blackmail of Hungary and the Hungarians, all based on lies. I inform you respectfully that however you decide, Hungary will stop illegal immigration, and defend its borders, against you if necessary.

This was greeted with outrage.

Former Belgian prime minister Guy Verhofstadt, currently president of the Alliance of Liberals and Democrats for Europe Group in the European Parliament and an ardent European federalist, responded furiously that "we cannot let far right populist governments drag democratic European states into the orbit of Vladimir Putin!"

In a tweet to his EP colleagues, Verhofstadt warned: "We are in an existential battle for the survival of the European project. … For Europe's sake, we need to stop him!"

CNN approvingly ran an opinion piece from Verhofstadt describing Hungary as a "threat to international order."

"In the coming weeks and months, the international community— and the United States in particular—must heed our warning and act: Hungary's government is a threat to the rules-based international order," he wrote. "European governments and the U.S. have a moral obligation to intervene," he continued. "We cannot stand aside and let populist, far-right governments drag democratic European states into Vladimir Putin's orbit and undermine the postwar international norms."Next come sanctions: "Political and financial costs must be attached to governments pursuing an authoritarian path and support provided to civil society organizations…" Verhofstadt concluded: "This is not in the interests of the people of America or Europe. We need to stop him—now."

Verhofstadt's appeal to America to "stop" the Hungarian prime minister sounds like nothing so much as appeals to Brezhnev by hard-line communists to send the tanks into reformist Czechoslovakia in 1968.

However, this appeal for intervention was not addressed to President Trump, who is in the same doghouse as Orban among the Atlanticists, but rather to the deep state forces which the Belgian liberal fanatic assumes are still in power in Washington.

At the start of his CNN article, Verhofstadt paid tribute to "the late, great, John McCain, who once described Orban as 'a fascist in bed with Putin'…" That is the McCain who went around the world as head of the Republican branch of the National Endowment for Democracy (NED) encouraging and financing dissident groups to rebel against their respective governments, in preparation for U.S. intervention. Oh Senator McCain, where are you now that we need you for a little regime change in Budapest?

Orban's reputation in the West as dictator is unquestionably linked to his intense conflict with Hungarian-born financier George Soros, whose Open Society foundation finances all manner of initiatives to promote his dream of a borderless society, notably in Eastern Europe. Soros operations could be considered privatized U.S. foreign policy, along the same lines as McCain, and innocently "non-governmental." One Soros initiative is the private Budapest-based Central European University whose rector is open society advocate Michael Ignatieff. Hungary recently imposed a 25% tax on money spent by nongovernmental organizations on programs that "directly or indirectly aim to promote immigration," which affects the CEU. This is part of a recently adopted package of anti-immigration measures known as the "Stop Soros" bill.

Hungarian measures against Soros' interference are of course denounced in the West as a grave violation of human rights, while in the United States, prosecutors search frantically for the slightest indication of Russian interference or Russian agents.

In another blow against the international rules-based order, the Hungarian prime minister's office recently announced that the government will cease to fund university courses in gender studies, on the grounds that they "cannot be justified scientifically" and attract too few students to be worthwhile. Although privately funded and thus able to continue its own gender studies program, the CEU was "astonished" and called the measure "without any justification or antecedent."

Like the Soviet Union, the European Union is not merely an undemocratic institutional framework promoting a specific economic system; it is also the vehicle of an ideology and a planetary project. Both are based on a dogma as to what is good for the world: communism for the first, "openness" for the second. Both in varying ways demand of people virtues they may not share: a forced equality, a forced generosity. All this can sound good, but such ideals become methods of manipulation. Forcing ideals on people eventually runs up against stubborn resistance, all the more in that the practice rarely conforms to the ideals.

There are differing reasons to be against immigration just as to be for it. The idea of democracy was to sort out and choose between ideals and practical interests by free discussion and in the end a show of hands: an informed vote. The liberal Authoritarian Center represented by Verhofstadt seeks to impose its values, aspirations, even its version of the facts on citizens who are denounced as "populists" if they disagree. Under communism, dissidents were called "enemies of the people." For the liberal globalists, they are "populists"—that is, the people. If people are told constantly that the choice is between a left that advocates mass immigration and a right that rejects it, the swing to the right is unstoppable.

England Came and Went
*Leaving Europe in a Mess**

JANUARY 2020

Whew. Finally, at last, the United Kingdom is formally leaving the European Union on January 31. Here in Paris, the champions of French withdrawal from the EU are celebrating. They see Brexit as the harbinger of a future "Frexit," a French departure from undemocratic governance, and the beginning of the end of a failed project to unify Europe around the demands of neoliberal capitalism.

But the paradox is that the champions of European unification might be celebrating even more—if it weren't too late. Because years of British membership have already helped shatter the original dreams of a united European, whether the aspirations of the federalists for political unity or the project of a European confederation of independent States advocated by Charles De Gaulle some sixty years ago.

Way back then, when De Gaulle was meeting with the aged West German chancellor Konrad Adenauer to promote Franco-German reconciliation, the two old statesmen were thinking in terms of working gradually toward a partnership of core European states that would preserve their sovereignty within a confederation ensuring peace and cooperation.

From the start, the question of British membership appeared as a thorn in the side of European unity. Initially, London was opposed to the Common Market. In 1958, prime minister Harold MacMillan assailed it as "the Continental Blockade" (alluding to Napoleon's 1806 European policy) and said England would not stand for it. But as the project seemed to take shape, London sought accommodation.

De Gaulle warned from the start that Great Britain didn't belong in a unified Europe, geographically, economically or above all psychologically.

---

* First published in *Consortium News,* January 29, 2020.

The remark has become famous: in 1944, on the eve of the Normandy invasion, in a quarrelsome exchange, Churchill reportedly told De Gaulle that if Britain had to choose, it would always go for "the open sea" rather than the European continent.

Of course, Britain long ago lost both Churchill and its Empire. Nevertheless, the English remain psychologically wedded to their island status, the origin of their overwhelming maritime power that built the empire and has left traces of English-speaking nations and preferred trade relations all around the world. Brits do not normally feel part of "the continent" and the traditional policy of their governments was always to keep the continent divided and weak. This policy was passed on to London's pupils in Washington, echoed in the description of NATO's purpose: "to keep the Russians out, the Americans in and the Germans down"—the joke that tells the truth.

Sixty years ago, De Gaulle, who envisaged a European confederation as a way to achieve independence from the American liberators (who came to stay), saw very clearly that the UK would be America's Trojan horse in the European community. That is called vision, the quality of a statesman—a breed that seems to have died out in the West. He opposed British membership as long as he could, but the American influence was too great. And curiously enough, the ardent European federalists joined in promoting British membership, seemingly unaware that such membership was totally incompatible with the political unity they desired.

British leaders, firmly attached to their parliament, their royalty, their class system, and their unique role in the world—now largely passed on to their heirs in Washington—never would consider genuine political unity with the continent. But as a trading nation, they wanted to be part of a Europe that would favor free trade, period.

The United Kingdom first applied for membership in 1961, at a time when it comprised the central core made up of France, Germany, the Benelux countries and Italy. But as long as De Gaulle was President of France, this was not possible, despite U.S. support (the United States has always supported enlargement, notably Turkish membership, now considered out of the question). The United Kingdom joined the European Economic Community only on January first, 1973, bringing with it both Ireland and Denmark, another advocate of free trade.

Bringing in Britain was the decisive step toward making unified Europe into a vast free market, a step toward globalization. This was indeed the program of Jean Monnet, a totally Americanized French businessman who plotted the path to European unity through purely economic measures, indifferent to political issues. But it took British weight to pull Europe firmly in that direction, away from the original Common Market idea (removing trade barriers only between Member States) toward an open market, with minimum trade barriers, extending the benefits of its "free competition" doctrine to such giants as the United States and China.

In 1989, Margaret Thatcher appointed Leon Brittan to the post of European Commissioner for competition, where he stayed until 1999 in charge of trade and external affairs. In Brussels his was the most powerful influence in confirming the EU's role as chief enforcer of neo-liberal policies. At the same time, Thatcher demanded "her money back" and strengthened the UK's own freedom from European institutional constraints.

The UK never agreed to the Schengen agreement on EU borders and declined to scrap the pound sterling for the euro—a wise move, no doubt. But also symptomatic of the essential incapacity of England to fully merge with the continent.

At the same time, the presence of London has certainly contributed to the total inability of the EU to develop a foreign policy which deviates from that of Washington. Britain supported the enlargement to the East which has made the EU more politically disunited than ever and has been the strongest supporter of the paranoid Russophobia of Poland and the Baltic States which pushes other European countries into a dangerous conflict with Russia that is contrary to their own interests.

Not that Britain is responsible for everything that is wrong with the European Union today. A major mistake was made by French President François Mitterrand in the 1980s when he insisted on a "common European currency" under the illusion that this would help France contain Germany—when it turned out not only to do the contrary but to ruin Greece and cause ravages in Portugal, Spain and Italy.

And there are plenty of other mistakes that have been made, such as Angela Merkel's invitation to come to Europe, ostensibly addressed to Syrian war refugees but understood by millions of unfortunates in the Middle East and Africa as meant for themselves.

And certainly, there were and are a minority of Englishmen and women who sincerely identify with Europe and want to feel part of it. But they are a minority. England has for too many centuries cherished and celebrated its uniqueness for that to be erased by complex impersonal institutions.

As England returns to the uncertainties of the open sea, it leaves behind a European Union that is bureaucratically governed to serve the interests of financial capital. Member States, such as Macron's France, are governed according to EU decrees against the wishes of their people. British membership contributed to this denial of democracy, but paradoxically, the British people themselves are the first to reject it and demand a return to full national sovereignty.

Even the ardent fans of European unity increasingly insist that they want "a different Europe," recognizing that the project has failed to produce the wonders that were promised. But changing this particular Europe would require unanimity between the 27 remaining, and increasingly quarrelsome, Member States.

That is why the idea is growing that it may be time to give up this failed European union and start all over, seeking political understanding issue by issue between sovereign democracies rather than a nonfunctional economic unity as decreed by transnational capitalist bureaucracy.

France Stuck in the Extreme Center*

APRIL 2022

On Sunday, April 24, Emmanuel Macron was re-elected for a second five-year term as President of the French Republic with 58.54% of the vote. Just as in 2017, the candidate he defeated was Marine Le Pen, who got 41.46%. Sounds like *déjà vu* all over again.

From the outside, this can be seen either as showing that Macron is a popular President, and/or that France has once against been saved from the fascist threat. Neither of these impressions is correct. Mostly, it signifies that France is stuck in There Is No Alternative (TINA)—the neoliberal replacement of political experimentation by expertise governance.

Macron is not overwhelmingly popular. In the first eliminatory round of elections held on April 10, over 72% of voters chose one of the eleven other candidates.

Macron Personifies the Center

About four decades ago, when neoliberalism was just beginning to dictate its economic necessities, French political choices were defined by a traditional "left-right" alternance in government, between the nominally (but not really) "Gaullist" conservatives, later renamed The Republicans, and the Socialist Party. But this alternance lost its edge by the fact that whichever party was in office, regardless of its campaign promises, it carried out the same neoliberal policies favoring profits over wages and public services.

Five years ago, with the left-right distinction blurred by such conformity, the time was right to create a movement which was neither left nor right, or perhaps both, but was in perfect conformity with the

* Published in *Consortium News,* April 26, 2022.

neoliberal policies of the European Union. The handsome young banker Emmanuel Macron was initiated into government policy-making by highly influential individuals such as Jacques Attali and won support from international finance for this winning project. The 39-year-old's personal aura of vigorous youth in a hurry to get things done attracted political amateurs to support his movement *"En Marche"* (Let's go). That personification won him the 2017 election.

What Macron was accelerating were in fact the neoliberal reforms promoted by the EU. His policies facilitated privatization and deindustrialization, as well as cutbacks in public services such as hospitals and transport. This has caused most hardships in rural France, leading to the Yellow Vests protests, severely repressed by police.

Politics Marginalized as "Extremes"

Last April 10, in the first round of this year's Presidential election, the two erstwhile "government" parties, Republicans and Socialists, were nearly wiped out. The Republican candidate, Valérie Pécresse, who had started out high in the polls, came in short of the crucial 5% of the vote, which gives parties public funding. The fate of the Socialist Party was just as humiliating: Anne Hidalgo, famous as mayor of Paris for her chaotic efforts to eliminate cars in favor of bicycles and scooters, scored a pathetic 1.75%, even less than Communist Party candidate Fabien Roussel who got 2.28%.

The April 10 election produced three big voting blocs, around three candidates with weak parties, uncertain programs but strong personalities each representing an attitude: Emmanuel Macron 27.83%, Marine Le Pen 23.15%, Jean-Luc Mélenchon 21.95%. If JLM had come in second, facing Macron, there would surely have been a fear campaign stigmatizing him as dangerously "extreme," even "communist" and "an anti-European friend of Putin." Instead MLP came in second, and the fear campaign stigmatized her as "extreme right," even "fascist" and "an anti-European friend of Putin."

Politics outside the conformist center is dangerously "extreme."

Mélenchon Embodies the Left

Mélenchon's high score was the triumph of a strong personality over parties. Mélenchon's fiery rhetoric gained wide public recognition when he broke with the Socialist Party during the 2005 referendum on the EU draft Constitution. The Constitution was rejected by voters, but in defiance of the popular vote, parliamentarians went on to adopt the same measures in the Lisbon Treaty, confirming the neoliberal globalizing policies of the EU and its attachment to NATO.

In 2016 Mélenchon founded his own party *La France Insoumise* (Insubordinate France) whose main asset is his own vigorous oratory and cantankerous relationship with the media and adversaries. In the 2017 presidential race, he came in fourth with promises of bold policies defying EU constraints.

This time around Mélenchon adopted a program that lacked coherence but clearly aimed at gaining votes from all sections of France's divided and weakened left. He stressed lavishly generous measures to improve "purchasing power": higher minimum wage, lowering retirement age to 60, price controls on basic necessities—measures that seemed unrealistic even to many on the left. His measures to woo the green vote went all the way from all-bio free school lunches to phasing out nuclear power by 2045—against the growing trend in France to look to France's nuclear power industry as essential to survival. This succeeded in leaving the Green candidate Yannick Jadot, who had dreamed of emulating the success of the bellicose German Greens, with only 4.63% of the vote. For LGBTQI voters, Mélenchon spoke favorably of amending the Constitution to guarantee the right to change gender (a right that exists already). This might be seen as a bit contradictory to his efforts to gain support of the Muslim community.

Nevertheless, Muslim leaders issued a statement: "We, imams and preachers, call on French citizens of the Muslim faith to vote in the first round for the least worst of the candidates in that presidential election: Jean-Luc Mélenchon." According to exit polls, Mélenchon got nearly 70% of Muslim votes.

This may have overlapped somewhat with his high score among youth in cities and ethnically mixed suburbs: 38% of voters under 25. He called for lowering voting age to 16.

All in all Mélenchon's vote corresponded most clearly to the identity politics vote focused on societal rather than socio-economic issues, although he did well with the working class (27% of workers and 22% of employees) but Marine Le Pen did better (33% and 36%).

Asked why they voted for Mélenchon, about 40% said it was a "useful" vote—not to support his program, but rather because he was the candidate on the left who might have eliminated Marine Le Pen. He now dreams of sweeping the legislative elections in June to become the leader of the opposition—or even prime minister.

JLM's last word to his followers on the evening of April 10 was imperative: "Not one vote for Marine Le Pen!"

Marine Le Pen, the Outsider

An enemy is always a unifying factor, and for the fractured French left, Marine Le Pen is the unifier. She inherited this role from her father, Jean-Marie Le Pen.

In the early 1980s, when President Mitterrand abruptly abandoned the socializing Common Program that got him elected with strong Communist Party support, the Socialist Party switched its ideological focus to "anti-racism." Anti-racism gradually mutated into support for immigration and even open borders, on the grounds that any restrictions on immigration must be motivated by "racist hate." This was not the traditional attitude of the left. In the early 1930s, and for decades afterwards, opposition to mass immigration was a key policy of the Marxist left and the labor movement, which saw mass immigration as a technique of capital to split worker solidarity and lower wages.

Immigration evolved into a key issue only since the institutionalized left abandoned its economic program in order to go along with neoliberalism imposed by the European Union. As it happens, open borders is a position that is totally compatible with neoliberal economics, and the two can flourish together, tending toward identity politics.

In the 1980s, the closest the Socialists could find as racist villain was Jean-Marie Le Pen, who was opposed to large scale immigration primarily for reasons of national identity. His diverse party, the National Front, included remnants of moribund ultraright groups, although JMLP was more facetious than fascist. His enemies blew up his remark that "Gas chambers were a detail of World War II" into proof of complicity in the Holocaust. More proactive enemies blew up his apartment, making an impression on his then 8-year-old daughter Marine.

Marine went on to career as a lawyer, two marriages and three children before turning to politics and virtually inheriting her father's political party as he retired. Jean-Marie had enjoyed being provocative. Marine wanted to win hearts and minds. She purged the most extremist elements of the party, successfully ran for parliament in the depressed Northern town of Henin-Beaumont, changed the party's name from *Front National* to the looser *Rassemblement National* and increasingly took her distance from the party itself. She tried to warm up to Jewish organizations. Her program called for a popular referendum on controlling immigration, which among other things would allow France to expel foreigners convicted of serious crimes. Her most controversial (and probably impossible) proposals concerned "eradicating Islamic extremist ideology" (distinguished from conventional Islam).

Jean-Marie Le Pen was fiercely anti-de Gaulle, not least because President de Gaulle conceded independence to Algeria. That is ancient history to his daughter's generation. Marine Le Pen has increasingly identified with Gaullism: patriotism, national independence, and a social conservatism that respects the interests of the working class. She has called for France to leave the joint command of NATO, as did de Gaulle in 1966. (President Sarkozy rejoined in 2009.). She has also advocated an independent foreign policy, normalizing relations with Russia—a point she reiterated even after the Russian invasion of Ukraine.

Meanwhile, various wars, especially the 2011 destruction of Libya, have accelerated illegal immigration. While the brain drain—notably of medical personnel from poor countries—is always welcome, the economy is currently not able to absorb unqualified labor, which inevitably leads to social problems. The refusal of the left to acknowledge the existence of such problems makes it extremely difficult to raise the issue without being labeled "racist." But the questions raised are there.

Zemmour, the Surprise Candidate

In reality, opposition to mass immigration suddenly dominated this presidential campaign as the political writer and tv commentator Eric Zemmour set out to steal the issue away from Marine Le Pen and run with it all the way to the presidency. Zemmour is a sort of anti-BHL, the very opposite of the rich "philosopher" Bernard Henri Lévy—both of Algerian Jewish origin. In the Mitterrand 1980s, BHL won fame as leading anti-communist liberal leftist, castigating France for its latent fascism and anti-Semitism. If the U.S. and NATO can wage a war in Afghanistan, Bosnia, Libya or Ukraine, he is all for it. BHL is tall and means to be glamorous. Zemmour is small and mousy but speaks more reasonably than the flamboyant BHL. In contrast to BHL's moral lectures to the French, Zemmour has embraced his French homeland with ardent love and wishes to defend it from the perils of mass immigration and Islamic extremism.

His initial rallies drew enthusiastic crowds, notably drawing many well-educated young men. While Marine Le Pen appeals to the working class in small towns and rural areas, Zemmour won his followers among the upper class educated, calling for a "Reconquest" of France from the "great replacement" of the French by immigration. Zemmour came in fourth with a little over 7% in the first round compared to Le Pen's 23.15%. His ambition is to lead formation of a new right-wing party. He scored relatively well in the rich Western sections of Paris and came in first among overseas French living in Israel and other countries of the region.

Zemmour's political emergence corresponds to a broad shift of Zionist Jews from the left to the right.

It seems that Zemmour bit slightly into the upper income vote which finally went fairly solidly to Macron. The class division was clear in the final election—Macron got the votes of the prosperous, Marine was the favorite of the forgotten.

In the final election, Marine Le Pen swept France's overseas territories in the West Indies, scoring 70% in Guadeloupe and 60% in Martinique and French Guyana. Since 93% of Guadeloupe's population is of African origin, this vote seems to confirm that, whatever others may say or think, Marine Le Pen's supporters do not consider her to be "racist."

Personality matters in politics. Just as Mélenchon's popularity owes a lot to his irascible nature, Marine Le Pen's popularity owes a lot to her public personality: a woman who appears warm, good humored, and resilient. The Marine vote is for the cat-lover rather than for an ideology.

Stop Fascism!

After first issuing the order, "Not one vote for Le Pen!" Mélenchon went on to exhort his first round voters not to abstain, in effect endorsing Macron. The implication was that electing Le Pen would put an end to our freedoms once and for all.

Over 350 NGOs signed a statement by the Movement Against Racism and for Friendship among Peoples (MRAP) warning that her election would "abolish the state of law."

Small groups of anarchist students temporarily occupied the Sorbonne and a couple of other elite universities in Paris and tore things up to show their discontent, a warning of what might come later.

The General Confederation of Labor (CGT) declared that: "History shows there is a difference of nature between republican parties that gain power and give it up and the extreme right which, once in power, confiscates it."

And how would she do that? Her party is not very strong and entirely based on electoral politics. There is no militia organized to use force for political purposes (as in the case of real historic fascists). There are

212 WORLD WATCHER: ON MANUFACTURING WAR

plenty of counter-powers in France, including political parties, hostile media, a largely left-leaning magistrature, the armed forces (linked to NATO), big business and finance which have never supported Le Pen, the entertainment industry, etc., etc.

In reality, the real danger of Marine Le Pen being elected was quite the opposite: the difficulty she would have had in governing. In her campaign, she made it clear she would want to share power, but with whom? Certain groups were promising to raise hell in the streets. Much of her proposed legislation would be impossible to enact or would face opposition in the courts.

The Hypothesis of Compromise

Let us just imagine a different context, where "left" is no longer defined by "absolute refusal to have anything to do with anyone on the right."

Macron's program for the next five years further speeds up the EU-sponsored neoliberal reforms, notably lengthening the age of retirement from 62, as it is now, to 65. Mélenchon actually called for lowering retirement age to 60. Meanwhile, Marine Le Pen emphasized her support for retaining a lower retirement age, with special concern for all those who have worked in physically demanding jobs since an early age. This position helped her come in first with working class voters.

In an imaginary different context, a Mélenchon could have proposed a compromise with Le Pen, in order to defeat Macron and carry out a somewhat more social program. Since the two largely agreed on the crucial issue of foreign policy—in particular, avoiding war with Russia—it might be possible to work out some sort of "Gaullist" policy in common that would break the hold of the extreme center, with its unshakable loyalty to the Atlantic Alliance. This would not have led to "confiscation of power" but would shake things up. It would be reintroducing alternance into political life.

But in reality as it is, Mélenchon gave the election to Macron. And now he aspires to lead the opposition to Macron. But so do Marine Le Pen... and Eric Zemmour.

The Election and the War in Ukraine

When Russian forces moved into Ukraine last February 24, the prediction was that this would solidify Macron's position as head of state in a military crisis. As media and politicians rushed to express solidarity with

Ukraine against Russia, both Marine Le Pen and Jean-Luc Mélenchon were denounced for their well-known attitude toward improving relations with Russia. A photo of Marine Le Pen with Vladimir Putin was widely circulated by Green adversaries in the expectation that this would destroy her chances.

It didn't happen that way. In fact, both those "Putin-understanders" saw their approval ratings rise as the war continued.

Moreover, Fabien Roussel, the rather fresh and young Communist Party candidate was edging toward a mild comeback for his party when the war began, but started to sink after he took the conventional Western anti-Russian pro-Ukrainian position.

The Green candidate Yannick Jadot, who had hoped to emulate the success of the German Greens, and Valérie Pécresse, candidate of the once powerful Republicans, both followed the official Western line on the war. Neither of them reached 5%.

In the first round, then, the war was not an issue—at least not at open issue, but it may have been a hidden issue, indicating that French voters are not as Russophobic as they are supposed to be.

However, in their three-hour televised debate on April 20, Macron took a low road to attack Le Pen. Unlike Macron, whose campaigns can always count on generous donors, Marine Le Pen is chronically hard up for funding. In 2014, when no French bank would lend her money for the upcoming regional elections, she took out a loan of 9.4 million euros with the First Czech Russian Bank (FCRB). The bank has since failed, and she continues to pay to its creditors. During their debate, Macron abruptly referred to that loan, which is public knowledge, telling Le Pen that "when you speak to Putin you are talking to your banker." She reacted indignantly, stressing that she was a free woman.

Alexei Navalny followed up with a statement from his Russian prison in support of Macron.

Three European prime ministers, Olaf Scholz of Germany, Pedro Sanchez of Spain and Antonio Costa of Portugal wrote an open letter opposing Marine Le Pen as "an extreme-right candidate who openly sides with those who attack our freedom and democracy, values based on the French ideas of Enlightenment." European leaders naturally rushed to congratulate Macron for his victory as a commitment to European construction.

Marine Le Pen had insisted that the significant political division was no longer between left and right but between preservation of the nation and globalization. The drastic division of the world resulting from the

Ukraine crisis is seen by some as ending the myth of globalization, and concern for the welfare of the nation is inevitably growing. Nevertheless, in this election globalization won over conservation of the nation.

The war was not a major issue in France largely because Macron himself is perhaps the least Russophobic among leaders of major European countries. His efforts to encourage Ukraine to negotiate the settlement of the Donbass problem according to the Minsk accords failed, but at least he made those efforts, or seemed to make those efforts. He appears to wish to salvage what he can of his position as potential negotiator, even as all prospects for negotiations are blocked by U.S. insistence on using the Ukraine crisis to defeat (and even destroy) Russia.

Government by Consultancy Firms

On March 17, the French Senate issued a report that revealed the profoundly technocratic nature of the Macron regime. In the last four years, the Macron government has paid at least 2.43 billion euros to international (largely American) consultancy firms to design policies or procedures in all fields, especially public health. For example, McKinsey consultancy charges the Ministry of Health 2,700 euros per day, a sum equal to the monthly salary for a public hospital employee.

This amounts to a form of very expensive privatization of the government. Even more serious, it means turning over the intellectual capacity of the French government to agencies adept in fashioning the uniform Western narrative in all matters. This is how technocratic "governance" destroys political government.

After his victory, Macron celebrated under the European flag. Marine Le Pen had called for a French foreign policy independent of the "Franco-German couple." Macron promises to preserve the close partnership with Germany—even as tendencies in the two countries diverge more and more visibly. The prospects of an independent "Gaullist" French foreign policy remain remote.

— PART VI —
PERPETUATING WAR IN EUROPE

Tightening the U.S. Grip on Western Europe

Washington's Iron Curtain in Ukraine[*]

JUNE 2014

NATO leaders are currently acting out a deliberate charade in Europe, designed to reconstruct an Iron Curtain between Russia and the West.

With astonishing unanimity, NATO leaders feign surprise at events they planned months in advance. Events that they deliberately triggered are being misrepresented as sudden, astonishing, unjustified "Russian aggression." The United States and the European Union undertook an aggressive provocation in Ukraine that they knew would force Russia to react defensively, one way or another.

They could not be sure exactly how Russian president Vladimir Putin would react when he saw that the United States was manipulating political conflict in Ukraine to install a pro-Western government intent on joining NATO. This was not a mere matter of a "sphere of influence" in Russia's "near abroad," but a matter of life and death to the Russian Navy, as well as a grave national security threat on Russia's border.

A trap was thereby set for Putin. He was damned if he did, and damned if he didn't. He could underreact, and betray Russia's basic national interests, allowing NATO to advance its hostile forces to an ideal attack position.

Or he could overreact, by sending Russian forces to invade Ukraine. The West was ready for this, prepared to scream that Putin was "the new Hitler," poised to overrun poor, helpless Europe, which could only be saved (again) by the generous Americans.

---

[*] Original version: *CounterPunch* Weekend Edition, June 6–8, 2014. https://www.counterpunch.org/2014/06/06/washingtons-iron-curtain-in-ukraine-2/

217

In reality, the Russian defensive move was a very reasonable middle course. Thanks to the fact that the overwhelming majority of Crimeans felt Russian, having been Russian citizens until Khrushchev frivolously bestowed the territory on Ukraine in 1954, a peaceful democratic solution was found. Crimeans voted for their return to Russia in a referendum which was perfectly legal according to international law, although in violation of the Ukrainian constitution, which was by then in tatters having just been violated by the overthrow of the country's duly elected president, Victor Yanukovych, facilitated by violent militias. The change of status of Crimea was achieved without bloodshed, by the ballot box.

Nevertheless, the cries of indignation from the West were every bit as hysterically hostile as if Putin had overreacted and subjected Ukraine to a U.S.-style bombing campaign, or invaded the country outright—which they may have expected him to do.

U.S. Secretary of State John Kerry led the chorus of self-righteous indignation, accusing Russia of the sort of thing his own government is in the habit of doing. "You just don't invade another country on phony pretext in order to assert your interests. This is an act of aggression that is completely trumped up in terms of its pretext," Kerry pontificated. "It's really 19th century behavior in the 21st century." Instead of laughing at this hypocrisy, U.S. media, politicians and punditry zealously took up the theme of Putin's unacceptable expansionist aggression. The Europeans followed with a weak, obedient echo.

It Was All Planned at Yalta

In September 2013, one of Ukraine's richest oligarchs, Viktor Pinchuk, paid for an elite strategic conference on Ukraine's future that was held in the same Palace in Yalta, Crimea, where Roosevelt, Stalin and Churchill met to decide the future of Europe in 1945. The Economist, one of the elite media reporting on what it called a "display of fierce diplomacy," stated that: "The future of Ukraine, a country of 48m people, and of Europe was being decided in real time." The participants included Bill and Hillary Clinton, former CIA head General David Petraeus, former U.S. Treasury secretary Lawrence Summers, former World Bank head Robert Zoellick, Swedish foreign minister Carl Bildt, Shimon Peres, Tony Blair, Gerhard Schröder, Dominique Strauss-Kahn, Mario Monti, Lithuanian president Dalia Grybauskaite, and Poland's influential foreign minister Radek Sikorski. Both President Viktor Yanukovych, deposed five months later, and his subsequently elected successor Petro Poroshenko were present. Former U.S. energy secretary

Bill Richardson was there to talk about the shale-gas revolution which the United States hopes to use to weaken Russia by substituting fracking for Russia's natural gas reserves. The center of discussion was the "Deep and Comprehensive Free Trade Agreement" (DCFTA) between Ukraine and the European Union, and the prospect of Ukraine's integration with the West. The general tone was euphoria over the prospect of breaking Ukraine's ties with Russia in favor of the West.

Conspiracy against Russia? Not at all. Unlike Bilderberg, the proceedings were not secret. Facing a dozen or so American VIPs and a large sampling of the European political elite was a Putin adviser named Sergei Glazyev, who made Russia's position perfectly clear.

Glazyev injected a note of political and economic realism into the conference. *Forbes* reported at the time on the "stark difference" between the Russian and Western views "not over the advisability of Ukraine's integration with the EU but over its likely *impact.*" In contrast to Western euphoria, the Russian view was based on "very specific and pointed economic criticisms" about the Trade Agreement's impact on Ukraine's economy, noting that Ukraine was running an enormous foreign accounts deficit, funded with foreign borrowing, and that the resulting substantial increase in Western imports could only swell the deficit. Ukraine "will either default on its debts or require a sizable bailout."

The Forbes reporter concluded that "the Russian position is far closer to the truth than the happy talk coming from Brussels and Kiev."

As for the political impact, Glazyev pointed out that the Russian-speaking minority in Eastern Ukraine might move to split the country in protest against cutting ties with Russia, and that Russia would be legally entitled to support them, according to *The Times* of London.

In short, while planning to incorporate Ukraine into the Western sphere, Western leaders were perfectly aware that this move would entail serious problems with Russian-speaking Ukrainians, and with Russia itself. Rather than seeking to work out a compromise, Western leaders decided to forge ahead and to blame Russia for whatever would go wrong. What went wrong first was that Yanukovych got cold feet faced with the economic collapse implied by the Trade Agreement with the European Union. He postponed signing, hoping for a better deal. Since none of this was explained clearly to the Ukrainian public, outraged protests ensued, which were rapidly exploited by the United States... against Russia.

Ukraine as Bridge...Or Achilles Heel

Ukraine, a term meaning borderland, is a country without clearly fixed historical borders that has been stretched too far to the East and too far to the West. The Soviet Union was responsible for this, but the Soviet Union no longer exists, and the result is a country without a unified identity and which emerges as a problem for itself and for its neighbors.

It was extended too far East, incorporating territory that might as well have been Russian, as part of a general Soviet policy to distinguish the USSR from the Tsarist empire, enlarging Ukraine at the expense of its Russian component and demonstrating that the Soviet Union was really a union among equal socialist republics. So long as the whole Soviet Union was run by the Communist leadership, these borders didn't matter too much.

It was extended too far West at the end of World War II. The victorious Soviet Union extended Ukraine's border to include Western regions, dominated by the city variously named Lviv, Lwow, Lemberg or Lvov, depending on whether it belonged to Lithuania, Poland, the Habsburg Empire or the USSR, a region which was a hotbed of anti-Russian sentiments. This was no doubt conceived as a defensive move, to neutralize hostile elements, but it created the fundamentally divided nation that today constitutes the perfect troubled waters for hostile fishing.

The Forbes report cited above pointed out that: "For most of the past five years, Ukraine was basically playing a double game, telling the EU that it was interested in signing the DCFTA while telling the Russians that it was interested in joining the customs union." Either Yanukovych could not make up his mind, or was trying to squeeze the best deal out of both sides, or was seeking the highest bidder. In any case, he was never "Moscow's man," and his downfall owes a lot no doubt to his own role in playing both ends against the middle. His was a dangerous game of pitting greater powers against each other.

It is safe to say that what was needed was something that so far seems totally lacking in Ukraine: a leadership that recognizes the divided nature of the country and works diplomatically to find a solution that satisfies both the local populations and their historic ties with the Catholic West and with Russia. In short, Ukraine could be a bridge between East and West—and this, incidentally, has been precisely the Russian position. The Russian position has not been to split Ukraine, much less to conquer it, but to facilitate the country's role as bridge. This would involve a degree of federalism, of local government, which so far is entirely lacking in the country, with local governors selected not by election but by the central government in Kiev. A federal Ukraine could both develop relations with the EU and maintain its vital (and profitable) economic relations with Russia.

But this arrangement calls for Western readiness to cooperate with Russia. The United States has plainly vetoed this possibility, preferring to exploit the crisis to brand Russia "the enemy."

Plan A and Plan B

U.S. policy, already evident at the September 2013 Yalta meeting, was carried out on the ground by Victoria Nuland, former advisor to Dick Cheney, deputy ambassador to NATO, spokeswoman for Hillary Clinton, wife of neocon theorist Robert Kagan. Her leading role in the Ukraine events proves that the neo-con influence in the State Department, established under Bush II, was retained by Obama, whose only visible contribution to foreign policy change has been the presence of a man of African descent in the presidency, calculated to impress the world with U.S. multicultural virtue. Like most other recent presidents, Obama is there as a temporary salesman for policies made and executed by others.

As Victoria Nuland boasted in Washington, since the dissolution of the Soviet Union in 1991, the United States has spent five billion dollars to gain political influence in Ukraine (this is called "promoting democracy"). This investment is not "for oil," or for any immediate economic advantage. The primary motives are geopolitical, because Ukraine is Russia's Achilles' heel, the territory with the greatest potential for causing trouble to Russia.

What called public attention to Victoria Nuland's role in the Ukrainian crisis was her use of a naughty word, when she told the U.S. ambassador, "Fuck the EU." But the fuss over her bad language veiled her bad intentions. The issue was who should take power away from the elected president Viktor Yanukovych. German Chancellor Angela Merkel's party been promoting former boxer Vitaly Klitschko as its candidate. Nuland's rude rebuff signified that the United States, not Germany or the EU, was to choose the next leader, and that was not Klitschko but "Yats." And indeed it was Yats, Arseniy Yatsenyuk, a second-string U.S.-sponsored technocrat known for his enthusiasm for IMF austerity policies and NATO membership, who got the job. This put a U.S. sponsored government, enforced in the streets by fascist militia with little electoral clout but plenty of armed meanness, in a position to manage the May 25 elections, from which the Russophone East was largely excluded.

Plan A for the Victoria Nuland putsch was probably to install, rapidly, a government in Kiev that would join NATO, thus formally setting the stage for the United States to take possession of Russia's indispensable Black Sea naval base at Sebastopol in Crimea. Reincorporating Crimea into Russia was Putin's necessary defensive move to prevent this.

But the Nuland gambit was in fact a win-win ploy. If Russia failed to defend itself, it risked losing its entire southern fleet—a total national disaster. On the other hand, if Russia reacted, as was most likely, the U.S. thereby won a political victory that was perhaps its main objective. Putin's totally defensive move is portrayed by the Western mainstream media, echoing political leaders, as unprovoked "Russian expansionism," which the propaganda machine compares to Hitler grabbing Czechoslovakia and Poland.

Thus a blatant Western provocation, using Ukrainian political confusion against a fundamentally defensive Russia, has astonishingly succeeded in producing a total change in the artificial Zeitgeist produced by Western mass media. Suddenly, we are told that the "freedom-loving West" is faced with the threat of "aggressive Russian expansionism." Some 25 years ago, Soviet leaders gave away the store under the illusion that peaceful renunciation on their part could lead to a friendly partnership with the West, and especially with the United States. But those in the United States who never wanted to end the Cold War are having their revenge. Never mind "communism"; if, instead of advocating the dictatorship of the proletariat, Russia's current leader is simply old-fashioned in certain ways, Western media can fabricate a monster out of that. The United States needs an enemy to save the world from.

The Protection Racket Returns

But first of all, the United States needs Russia as an enemy in order to "save Europe," which is another way of saying, in order to continue to dominate Europe. Washington policy-makers seemed to be worried that Obama's swing to Asia and neglect of Europe might weaken U.S. control of its NATO allies. The May 25 European Parliament elections revealed a large measure of disaffection with the European Union. This disaffection, notably in France, is linked to a growing realization that the EU, far from being a potential alternative to the United States, is in reality a mechanism that locks European countries into U.S.-defined globalization, economic decline and U.S. foreign policy, wars and all.

Ukraine is not the only entity that has been overextended. So has the EU. With 28 members of diverse language, culture, history and mentality, the EU is unable to agree on any foreign policy other than the one Washington imposes. The extension of the EU to former Eastern European satellites has totally broken whatever deep consensus might have been possible among the countries of the original Economic Community: France, Germany, Italy and the Benelux states. Poland and the Baltic States see EU membership as useful, but their hearts are in America—where many of their most influential leaders have been educated and trained. Washington is able to exploit the anti-communist, anti-Russian and even pro-Nazi nostalgia of northeastern Europe to raise the false cry of "the Russians are coming!" in order to obstruct the growing economic partnership between the old EU, notably Germany, and Russia.

Russia is no threat. But to vociferous Russophobes in the Baltic States, Western Ukraine and Poland, the very existence of Russia is a threat. Encouraged by the United States and NATO, this endemic hostility is the political basis for the new "iron curtain" meant to achieve the aim spelled out in 1997 by Zbigniew Brzezinski in *The Grand Chessboard:* keeping the Eurasian continent divided in order to perpetuate U.S. world hegemony. The old Cold War served that purpose, cementing U.S. military presence and political influence in Western Europe. A new Cold War can prevent U.S. influence from being diluted by good relations between Western Europe and Russia.

Obama has come to Europe ostentatiously promising to "protect" Europe by basing more troops in regions as close as possible to Russia, while at the same time ordering Russia to withdraw its own troops, on its own territory, still farther away from troubled Ukraine. This appears designed to humiliate Putin and deprive him of political support at home, at a time when protests are rising in Eastern Ukraine against the Russian leader for abandoning them to killers sent from Kiev.

To tighten the U.S. grip on Europe, the United States is using the artificial crisis to demand that its indebted allies spend more on "defense," notably by purchasing U.S. weapons systems. Although the U.S. is still far from being able to meet Europe's energy needs from the new U.S. fracking boom, this prospect is being hailed as a substitute for Russia's natural gas sales —stigmatized as a "way of exercising political pressure," something of which hypothetic U.S. energy sales are presumed to be innocent. Pressure is being brought against Bulgaria and even Serbia to block construction of the South Stream pipeline that would bring Russian gas into the Balkans and southern Europe.

From D-Day to Dooms Day

Today, June 6, the seventieth anniversary of the D-Day landing is being played in Normandy as a gigantic celebration of American domination, with Obama heading an all-star cast of European leaders. The last of the aged surviving soldiers and aviators present are like the ghosts of a more innocent age when the United States was only at the start of its new career as world master. They were real, but the rest is a charade. French television is awash with the tears of young villagers in Normandy who have been taught that the United States is some sort of Guardian Angel, which sent its boys to die on the shores of Normandy out of pure love for France. This idealized image of the past is implicitly projected on the future. In seventy years, the Cold War, a dominant propaganda narrative and above all Hollywood have convinced the French, and most of the West, that D-Day was the turning point that won World War II and saved Europe from Nazi Germany.

Vladimir Putin came to the celebration, and has been elaborately shunned by Obama, self-appointed arbiter of Virtue. The Russians are paying tribute to the D-Day operation which liberated France from Nazi occupation, but they—and historians—know what most of the West has forgotten: that the Wehrmacht was decisively defeated not by the Normandy landing, but by the Red Army. If the vast bulk of German forces had not been pinned down fighting a losing war on the Eastern front, nobody would celebrate D-Day as it is being celebrated today.

Putin is widely credited as being "the best chess player," who won the first round of the Ukrainian crisis. He has no doubt done the best he could, faced with the crisis foisted on him. But the U.S. has whole ranks of pawns which Putin does not have. And this is not only a chess game, but chess combined with poker combined with Russian roulette. The United States is ready to take risks that the more prudent Russian leaders prefer to avoid… as long as possible.

Perhaps the most extraordinary aspect of the current charade is the servility of the "old" Europeans. Apparently abandoning all Europe's accumulated wisdom, drawn from its wars and tragedies, and even oblivious to their own best interests, today's European leaders seem ready to follow their American protectors to another D-Day … D for Doom.

Can the presence of a peace-seeking Russian leader in Normandy make a difference? All it would take would be for mass media to tell the truth, and for Europe to produce reasonably wise and courageous leaders, for the whole fake war machine to lose its luster, and for truth to begin to dawn. A peaceful Europe is still possible, but for how long?

To Understand or Not to Understand Putin*

MAY 2014

In Germany these days, very many citizens object to the endless Russia-bashing of the NATO-oriented mainstream media. They may point out that the U.S.-backed regime change in Kiev, putting in power an ultra-right transitional government eager to join NATO, posed an urgent threat to preservation of Russia's only warm water naval base in Crimea. Under the circumstances, and inasmuch as the Crimean population overwhelmingly approved, reinstating Crimea in the Russian federation was a necessary defensive move.

In Germany, anyone who says thing like that can be denigrated as a *"Putinversteher"* (a Putin understander).

That says it all. We are not supposed to understand. We are supposed to hate. The media are there to see to that.

While the West doggedly refuses to understand Putin and Russia, Vladimir Putin, on the other hand, seems to understand things pretty well.

He seems to understand that he and his nation are being systematically lured into a death trap by an enemy which excels in the contemporary art of "communication." In a war situation, NATO communication means that it doesn't matter who does what. The only thing that matters is who tells the story. The Western media are telling the story in a way which depends on not understanding Russia, and not understanding Putin. Putin and Russia become fictional villains in the Western version, just the latest reincarnation of Hitler and Nazi Germany.

The horrific massacre in Odessa on May 2 proved this. The photographic evidence, the testimony of numerous eye witnesses, the

---

* Original version: *CounterPunch,* May 8, 2014. https://www.counterpunch.org/2014/05/08/to-understand-or-not-to-understand-putin/

smoldering bodies and the shouts of the killers are all there to prove what happened. Tents erected to collect signatures in favor of a referendum to introduce a federal system into Ukraine (now a politically divided but totally centralized state) were set on fire by a militia of fascist thugs who attacked the local federalists as "separatists" (accusing them of wanting to "separate" from Ukraine to join Russia, when that is not what they are seeking). The local activists fled into the big trade union building on the square where they were pursued, assaulted, murdered and set on fire by "Ukrainian nationalists," acting on behalf of the illegitimate Kiev regime supported by the West.

No matter how vicious the assaults, Western media saw no evil, heard no evil, spoke no evil. They deplored a "tragedy" which just sort of happened.

Odessa is proof that whatever happens, the NATO political class, political leaders and media united, have decided on their story and are sticking to it. The nationalists that seized power in Kiev are the good guys, the people being assaulted in Odessa and in Eastern Ukraine are "pro-Russian" and therefore the "bad guys."

Understanding Putin

So despite everything, let's try to understand President Putin, which is really not very hard. Behind every conscious action there should be a motive. Let's look at motives. Today, UK Foreign Secretary William Hague, who certainly gives every sign of never understanding—or wanting to understand—anything, parroted the NATO line that Russia was "trying to orchestrate conflict and provocation" in Ukraine's east and south.

That makes no sense. Putin has absolutely no motive to want civil war to rage in neighboring Ukraine, and very strong reasons to do all he can to avoid it. It confronts him with a serious dilemma. Ongoing vicious attacks by fanatic nationalists from Western Ukraine on citizens in the east and south of the country can only incite the victimized Russian-speaking Ukrainians to call on Russia for help. But at the same time, Putin must know that those Russophone Ukrainians do not really want to be invaded by Russia. Perhaps they want something impossible. And it is perfectly obvious that any use of Russia's military force to protect people in Ukraine would let loose an even wilder demonization of Putin as "the new Hitler" who is invading countries "for no reason." And NATO would use this, as it has already used the reunification of Crimea with Russia, as "proof" that Europe must tighten its alliance, establish military bases throughout Eastern Europe and (above all) spend more money on "defense" (buying U.S. military equipment).

The Western takeover of the Kiev government is clearly a provocation to draw Putin into a trap that certain Western strategists (Zbigniew Brzezinski being the chief theorist) hope will cause Putin's downfall and plunge Russia into a crisis that can lead to its eventual dismemberment.

Putin can only wish to find a peaceful solution to the Ukrainian mess.

While Washington reverts to Cold War "containment" policy to "isolate" Russia, Putin today held talks in Moscow with Didier Burkhalter, the Swiss president and current chairman of the Organization for Security and Co-operation in Europe (OSCE), in hope of initiating some sort of peaceful mediation.

Putin Pulls Back From False Flag Plan?

On this occasion, Putin announced that he had pulled back Russian forces from the border with Ukraine. He indicated that this was to ease concerns over their positioning, meaning claims that Russia was preparing an invasion. He also advised against holding referendums for greater autonomy in the Russophone areas until "conditions for dialogue" can be created.

However, news reports indicated that this reported military pullback caused new concerns among some Ukrainians, who felt Russia was abandoning them in their hour of need, and among some Russians, who feared the President was backing down under Western pressure.

It is not impossible that the pullback order was linked to a Novosti RIA report dated May 6, which indicated that the Ukrainian secret service was planning an imminent false flag operation in order to accuse Russia of violating the border with Ukraine.

Novosti said it had learned from security circles in Kiev that the Ukrainian secret service SBU had secretly shipped about 200 Russian army uniforms and some 70 forged Russian officer ID into the Eastern Ukrainian protest stronghold of Donetz, to be used to stage a false attack on Ukrainian border patrols.

Novosti said the reports were unconfirmed, but they could nevertheless be taken seriously by the Russians. "The plan would be to simulate an attack on Ukrainian border troops and to film it for the media," the report said. In connection with the plan, a dozen or so combatants from the ultranationalist Right Sector were to cross the border and kidnap a

Russian soldier in order to present him as "proof" of Russian military incursion. The operation was scheduled for May 8 or 9.

By pulling Russian troops farther away from the border, Putin could hope to make the false flag operation less plausible and perhaps to forestall it.

The whole Ukrainian operation, at least partly directed by Victoria Nuland of the U.S. State Department, has been rife with false flag operations, most notoriously by the snipers who suddenly spread murder and terror in Maidan square in Kiev, effectively wrecking the internationally sponsored transition agreement. "Pro-West" insurgents accused President Yanukovych of sending the killers and forced a rump parliament to give government power to Ms Nuland's protégé, Arseniy "Yats" Yatsenyuk. However, there has been plenty of evidence to show that the mysterious snipers were pro-West mercenaries: photographic evidence, followed by the telephone statement by the Estonian foreign minister to that effect, and finally by the German television channel ARD whose Monitor documentary concluded that the snipers came from the extreme right anti-Russian groups involved in the Maidan uprising. Indeed, all known evidence points to a fascist false flag operation, and yet Western media and politicians continue to blame everything on Russia.

So whatever he does, Putin now has to realize that he will be deliberately "misunderstood" and misrepresented by Western leaders and media. Over the heads of the American people, over the heads of the Germans, French and other Europeans, a private consensus has obviously been reached among persons we may describe as our own Western "oligarchs" to revive the Cold War in order to provide the West with an "enemy" serious enough to save the military-industrial complex and unite the transatlantic community against the rest of the world.

This is what Russian leaders are obliged to understand. What they need most to save the world from endless and useless conflict is the understanding of all those Americans and Europeans who have never been consulted or informed about this perilous shift in strategy, and who, if they understood, would surely say no.

At the Annual Munich Security Conference

The West Displays Its Insecurity Complex*

FEBRUARY 2020

"The West is winning!" U.S. leaders proclaimed at the high-level Annual Security Conference held in Munich last weekend.

Not everybody was quite so sure.

There was a lot of insecurity displayed at a conference billed as "the West's family meeting"—enlarged to 70 participating nations, including U.S.-designated "losers."

Trump's crude Secretary of State Mike Pompeo made nobody feel particularly secure by treating the world as a huge video game which "we are winning." Thanks to our "values," he proclaimed, the West is winning against the other players that Washington has forced into its zero-sum game: Russia and China, whose alleged desires for "empire" are being thwarted.

The Munich Security Conference (MSC) is a private gathering founded in 1963 by Ewald-Heinrich von Kleist-Schmenzin, a member of the aristocratic Wehrmacht officer class who plotted to get rid of Hitler when their estates in Eastern Germany were already being lost to the Red Army (to become part of Poland). The conference was evidently conceived as a means to enable Germans to get a word into strategic discussions from which they had been excluded by defeat in World War II.

The Munich conference knew its greatest hour of glory in February 2007, when Russian president Vladimir Putin shocked the assemblage by declaring his opposition to a "unipolar world" as "not only unacceptable but also impossible in today's world." Putin declared that NATO expansion up to Russian borders had nothing to do with ensuring security in

---

* Published in *Consortium News,* February 18, 2020.

Europe. Russia, he said then, "would like to interact with responsible and independent partners with whom we could work together in constructing a fair and democratic world order that would ensure security and prosperity not only for a select few, but for all."

This speech was taken as a major challenge, redefining capitalist Russia as the new enemy of the West and its "values."

What Is "the West"?

The term "the West" could mean a number of things. The conference organizers define it by "values" that are supposed to be essentially Western: democracy, human rights, a market-based economy and "international cooperation in international institutions." In fact, what is meant is a particular interpretation of all those "values," an interpretation based on Anglo-American history. And indeed, in historic terms, this particular "West" is essentially the heir and continuation of the British empire, centered in Washington after London was obliged to abdicate after World War II, while retaining its role as imperial tutor and closest partner. It implies the worldwide hegemony of the English language and English ideas of "liberalism" and is "multicultural" as empires always are. While the United States is the power center, many of the most ardent subjects of this empire are not American but European, starting with the Norwegian secretary general of NATO. Its imperial power is expressed by military bases all around the world offering "protection" to its subjects.

As for protection, the United States is currently shipping 20,000 military personnel to reinvade Germany on their way to unprecedented military maneuvers next month in ten countries right up to Russia's borders. Some 40,000 troops will take part in this exercise, on the totally imaginary pretext of a "Russian threat" to invade neighboring countries. This delights Washington's enthusiastic vassals in Poland and the Baltic States but is making many people nervous in Germany itself and other core European Union countries, wondering where this provocation of Russia may lead. But they hardly dare say so in violation of "western solidarity." The only complaint allowed is that the United States might not defend us enough, when the greater danger comes from being defended too much.

Opening this year's conference, the President of the German Federal Republic Frank-Walter Steinmeier, expressed Germany's strategic frustration more openly than usual. Steinmeier accused Washington, Beijing and Moscow of "great power competition" leading to more mistrust, more armament, more insecurity, leading "all the way to a new nuclear arms race." He didn't specify who started all that.

Overwhelming establishment distaste for Trump has provided a novel opportunity for leaders of U.S.-occupied countries to criticize Washington, or at least the White House. Steinmeier dared say that "our closest ally, the United States of America, under the present administration, rejects the idea of an international community." But he made up for this by accusing Russia of "making military violence and the violent change of borders on the European continent a political tool once again" by annexing Crimea—forgetting the NATO violent detachment of Kosovo from Serbia and ignoring the referendum in which an overwhelming majority of Crimeans voted to return to Russia, without a shot fired.

French President Emmanuel Macron also expressed frustration at Europe's dependence on Washington. He would like the European Union to develop its own military defense and security policy. "We cannot be the United States' junior partner," he said, although that is certainly what Europe is. While repeating the usual NATO line about the Russian threat, he noted that the policy of threats and sanctions against Russia had accomplished nothing and called for a "closer dialogue" to resolve problems. In that, he was surely echoing the consensus of the French elite which sees absolutely no French interest in the ongoing U.S.-inspired feud with Moscow.

Macron openly aspires to building a more independent EU military defense. The first obstacle lies in EU Treaties, which tie the Union to NATO. With the UK out of the EU, France is its strongest military power and its sole possessor of nuclear arms. There are indications that some German leaders might like to absorb France's nuclear arsenal into a joint European force—which would surely arouse a "nationalist" uproar in France.

Playing the Game

Aside from providing protection, the Empire calls on everybody to play the game of international trade—so long as they consent to lose.

On Saturday in Munich, both Nancy Pelosi and Defense Secretary Mark Esper lit into China for daring to emerge as a trade giant and technological center. "China is seeking to export its digital autocracy through its telecommunication giant Huawei," Pelosi warned.

Huawei has overtaken Russian natural gas as the export Washington condemns most vigorously as nefarious interference in the internal affairs of importers.

Esper gave a long speech damning Beijing's "bad behavior," "malign activity," authoritarianism and, of course, Huawei. The Pentagon chief concluded his diatribe against America's number one economic rival by a moralizing sermon on "our values, sense of fairness, and culture of opportunity," which "unleash the very best of human intellect, spirit, and innovation."

"Maybe, just maybe, we can get them on the right path," Esper suggested benevolently. "Again, make no mistake, we do not seek conflict with China."

In general, said Esper, "we simply ask of Beijing what we ask of every nation: to play by the rules, abide by international norms, and respect the rights and sovereignty of others."

(He could say, what we ask of every nation except our own.)

The Department of Defense, he said, is doing its share: "focused on deterring bad behavior, reassuring our friends and allies, and defending the global commons." We want China to "behave like a normal country" but, said Esper, if it "will not change its ways," then we must make "greater investments in our common defense; by making the hard economic and commercial choices needed to prioritize our shared security … prepared to deter any threat, defend any Ally, and defeat any foe."

In short, China's economic progress provides another excuse to increase the Pentagon budget and pressure European allies into more military spending. This could only please such major sponsors of this conference as Raytheon and Lockheed Martin (and probably did not displease Goldman Sachs and all the other major Western industries backing this get-together).

Chinese foreign minister Wang Yi replied to Esper's harangue with some lessons of his own for the West, concerning "multilateralism."

"It is not multilateralism if only the Western countries prosper while the non-Western countries lag behind forever. It would not achieve the common progress of mankind," said Wang. "China's modernization is the necessity of history." China's history and culture meant that it could not copy the Western pattern nor seek hegemony as major powers in the past.

Wang said the West should discard its subconscious mentality of civilization supremacy, give up its bias and anxiety over China, and accept and welcome the development and revitalization of a country from the East with a system different from that of the West.

The West at Munich did not appear particularly ready to follow this advice. Nor that of Russian foreign minister Sergei Lavrov who was also allowed his few minutes to address deaf ears. Lavrov lamented that "the structure of the Cold War rivalry is being recreated" as NATO continues to advance eastward, carrying on military exercises of unprecedented scope near the Russian borders, and inflating arms budgets. Lavrov invited the West to stop promoting the phantom of the Russian or any other "threat" and remember "what unites us all" before it's too late.

But the self-appointed representatives of "the West" hadn't come to hear that. They were much more ready to listen respectfully to representatives of such friendly arms purchasers as Qatar and Saudi Arabia whose acceptance of "Western values" was not called into question.

"Westlessness"

It had evidently been decided who belongs to "the West" and who is threatening it: China and Russia. "China's rapid ascent has stirred much debate over the primacy of the United States and the West in the 21st century," Esper remarked. Indeed, the "Munich Security Report" published for the conference was devoted to the odd theme of "Westlessness," lamenting a new "decline of the West" (in echo of Oswald Spengler's famous *Der Untergang des Abendlandes* of a century ago). The world was becoming less Western—and even worse, so was the West itself.

This complaint had two sides, material and ideological. In material terms, the West feels challenged by foreign economic and technological development, especially in China. It is notable that, while Western powers vigorously promoted international trade-based economies, they seem unable to react to the results except in terms of power rivalry and ideological conflict. As long as Western dominance was ensured, international trade was celebrated as the necessary basis for a peaceful world. But the moment a non-Western trader is doing too well, its exports are ominously denounced as means to exert malign influence over its customers. The prime example was Russian natural gas. Chinese technology is the next. Both are decried, especially by U.S. spokespeople, as treacherous means to make other countries "dependent."

Of course, trade does imply mutual dependence, and with it, a certain degree of political influence. Certainly, the overwhelming U.S. dominance of the entertainment industry (movies, TV series, popular music) exercises an enormous ideological influence on much of the world. The U.S. influence via Internet is also considerable.

But the avoidance of such nefarious foreign influence would call for precisely an "inward-looking" nationalism that the MSC denounced as destructive of our Western values.

The Western strategists see themselves threatened by too much globalization abroad, in the terms of China rising, and not enough enthusiasm for globalization at home. Enthusiasm is waning for foreign military expeditions to impose "values"—an essential aspect of Western identity.

The Report deplored the rise of "inward-looking" nationalism in Europe, which could be called patriotism, since it has none of the aggressive tendencies associated with nationalism. In fact, some of these European "nationalists" actually favor less intervention in the Middle East and would like to promote peaceful relations with Russia.

When the alleged threat to the West was "godless communism," Western values were relatively conservative. Today, the liberal West is threatened by conservatism, by people who more or less want to preserve their traditional lifestyle.

Finally, the MSC acknowledged that "the defenders of an open, liberal West, ... so far seem unable to find an adequate answer to the illiberal-nationalist challenge..." Part of the reason "may be found in the long almost unshakable conviction that all obstacles to liberalization were only minor setbacks, as liberalism's eventual triumph was seen as inevitable." Politicians have presented their policies as without alternative. As a result, there is growing "resistance against a system allegedly run by liberal experts and international institutions, which in the eyes of some amounts to a 'new authoritarianism'..."

Isn't "liberal authoritarianism" an oxymoron? But what do you call it when Macron's police enjoy impunity when they shoot out the eyes of Yellow Vest citizens peacefully protesting against massively unpopular social policies, when the UK holds Julian Assange in a dungeon despite denunciation of his cruel treatment by the U.N. Special Rapporteur on Torture? When the United States holds a record number of people in prison, including Chelsea Manning, simply to force her to testify against her will, and with no end in sight?

The day may come when it is accepted that the world is round, and "West" is only a relative geographic term, depending on where you are.

Replaying the End of World War II as World War III*

SEPTEMBER 2022

The European Union is girding for a long war against Russia that appears clearly contrary to European economic interests and social stability. A war that is apparently irrational—as many are—has deep emotional roots and claims ideological justification. Such wars are hard to end because outside the range of rationality.

The Late Arrival of German Revanchism

For decades after the Soviet Union entered Berlin and decisively defeated the Third Reich, Soviet leaders worried about the threat of "German revanchism." Since World War II could be seen as German revenge for being deprived of victory in World War I, couldn't aggressive German *Drang nach Osten* be revived, especially if it enjoyed Anglo-American support? There had always been a minority in U.S. and UK power circles that would have liked to provide their own victorious end to Hitler's war against the Soviet Union.

It was not the desire to spread communism but the need for a buffer zone to stand in the way of such dangers that was the primary motivation for the ongoing Soviet political and military clampdown on the tier of countries from Poland to Bulgaria that the Red Army had wrested from Nazi occupation.

This concern waned considerably in the early 1980s as a young German generation took to the streets in peace demonstrations against the stationing of nuclear "Euromissiles" which could increase the risk of nuclear war on German soil. The movement created the image of a new

---

* First published in *Consortium News,* September 12, 2022.

peaceful Germany. I believe that Mikhail Gorbachev took this transformation seriously. On June 15, 1989, Gorbachev came to Bonn which was then the modest capital of a deceptively modest West Germany. Apparently delighted with the warm and friendly welcome, Gorbachev stopped to shake hands with people along the way in that peaceful university town that had been the scene of large peace demonstrations. I was there and experienced his unusually warm, firm handshake and eager smile. I have no doubt that Gorbachev sincerely believed in a "common European home" where East and West Europe could live happily side by side united by some sort of democratic socialism.

Gorbachev died at age 91 on August 30. His dream of Russia and Germany living happily in their "common European home" had soon been fatally undermined by the Clinton administration's go-ahead to eastward expansion of NATO. But the day before Gorbachev's death, leading German politicians in Prague wiped out any hope of such a happy end by proclaiming their leadership of a Europe dedicated to combating the Russian enemy. These were politicians from the very parties—the SPD (social democratic party) and the Greens—that took the lead in the 1980s peace movement.

German Europe Must Expand Eastward

German Chancellor Olaf Scholz is a colorless SPD politician but his August 29 speech in Prague was inflammatory in its implications. Scholz called for an expanded, militarized European Union under German leadership. He claimed that the Russian operation in Ukraine raised the question "where the dividing line will be in the future between this free Europe and a neo-imperial autocracy." We cannot simply watch, he said, "as free countries are wiped off the map and disappear behind walls or iron curtains."

In reality, the conflict in Ukraine is clearly the unfinished business of the collapse of the Soviet Union, aggravated by malicious outside provocation. As in the Cold War, Moscow's defensive reactions are interpreted as harbingers of Russian invasion of Europe, and thus a pretext for arms buildups.

To meet the imaginary Russian threat, Germany will lead an expanded, militarized EU. First, Scholz told his European audience in the Czech capital, "I am committed to the enlargement of the European Union to include the states of the Western Balkans, Ukraine, Moldova and, in the long term, Georgia." Worrying about Russia moving the dividing line West is a bit odd while planning to incorporate three former

Soviet States, one of which (Georgia) is geographically and culturally very remote from Europe but on Russia's doorstep.

Adding these member states will achieve "a stronger, more sovereign, geopolitical European Union," said Scholz. A "more geopolitical Germany" is more like it. As the EU grows eastward, Germany is "in the center" and can expect to dominate the newcomers. So, in addition to enlargement, Scholz calls for "a gradual shift to majority decisions in common foreign policy" to replace the unanimity required today.

What this means should be obvious to the French. Historically, the French have defended the consensus rule so as not to be dragged into a foreign policy they don't want. French leaders have exalted the mythical "Franco-German couple" as guarantor of European harmony, mainly to keep German ambitions under control. But Scholz says he doesn't want "an EU of exclusive states or directorates," which implies the final divorce of that "couple." With an EU of 30 or 36 states, he notes, "fast and pragmatic action is needed." And he can be sure that German influence on most of these poor, indebted and often corrupt new Member States will produce the needed majority.

France has always hoped for an EU security force separate from NATO in which the French military would play a leading role. But Germany has other ideas. "NATO remains the guarantor of our security," said Scholz, rejoicing that President Biden is "a convinced transatlanticist."

"Every improvement, every unification of European defense structures within the EU framework strengthens NATO," Scholz said. "Together with other EU partners, Germany will therefore ensure that the EU's planned rapid reaction force is operational in 2025 and will then also provide its core. This requires a clear command structure. Germany will face up to this responsibility when we lead the rapid reaction force in 2025." It has already been decided that Germany will support Lithuania with a rapidly deployable brigade and NATO with further forces in a high state of readiness.

Serving to Lead ... Where?

In short, Germany's military buildup will give substance to Robert Habeck's notorious statement in Washington last March that: "The stronger Germany serves, the greater its role." Habeck is the Green economics minister and the second most powerful figure in Germany's current government. The strange remark meant that by subservience to the U.S. empire, Germany is strengthening its role as European leader. Just as the

U.S. arms, trains and occupies Germany, Germany will provide the same services for smaller EU states, notably to its east.

Since the start of the Russian operation in Ukraine, German politician Ursula von der Leyen has used her position as head of the EU Commission to impose ever more drastic sanctions on Russia, leading to the threat of a serious energy crisis this winter. Her hostility to Russia seems boundless. In Kiev last April she called for rapid EU membership for Ukraine, notoriously the most corrupt country in Europe and far from meeting EU entrance standards. She proclaimed that "Russia will descend into economic, financial and technological decay, while Ukraine is marching towards a European future." For von der Leyen, Ukraine is "fighting our war." This presumption to speak for the EU's 27 Members goes far beyond her legal authority, but nobody stops her.

Germany's Green Party foreign minister Annalena Baerbock is every bit as intent on "ruining Russia." Proponent of a "feminist foreign policy," Baerbock expresses policy in personal terms. "If I give the promise to people in Ukraine, we stand with you as long as you need us," she told the NED-sponsored Forum 2000 in Prague on August 31, speaking in English. "Then I want to deliver no matter what my German voters think, but I want to deliver to the people of Ukraine."

"People will go on the street and say, we cannot pay our energy prices, and I will say, Yes I know so we will help you with social measures. […] We will stand with Ukraine and this means the sanctions will stay also til winter time even if it gets really tough for politicians."

Certainly, support for Ukraine is strong in Germany, but perhaps because of the looming energy shortage, a recent Forsa poll indicates that some 77% of Germans would favor diplomatic efforts to end the war—which should be the business of the foreign minister. But Baerbock shows no interest in diplomacy, only in "strategic failure" for Russia—however long it takes.

In the 1980s peace movement, a generation of Germans was distancing itself from that of their parents and vowed to overcome "enemy images" inherited from past wars. Curiously, Annalena Baerbock, born in 1980, has referred to her grandfather who fought in the Wehrmacht as somehow having contributed to European unity. Is this the generational pendulum?

The Little Revanchists

There is reason to surmise that current German Russophobia draws much of its legitimization from the revanchism that flourished among former Nazi allies in smaller European countries and were incorporated into United States Cold War operations. Those little revanchisms were not subjected to the denazification gestures or Holocaust guilt imposed on Germany. Rather, they were welcomed by the CIA, Radio Free Europe and Congressional committees for their fervent anticommunism. They were strengthened politically in the United States by anticommunist diasporas from Eastern Europe.

Of these, the Ukrainian diaspora was surely the largest, the most intensely political and the most influential, in both Canada and the American Middle West. Ukrainian fascists who had previously collaborated with Nazi invaders were the most numerous and active, leading the Bloc of Anti-Bolshevik Nations with links to German, British and U.S. intelligence.

Eastern European Galicia, not to be confused with Spanish Galicia, has been back and forth between Russia and Poland for centuries and after World War II was divided between Poland and Ukraine. Ukrainian Galicia is the center of a virulent brand of Ukrainian nationalism, whose principal World War II hero was Stepan Bandera. This nationalism can properly be called "fascist" not simply because of superficial signs—its symbols, salutes or tatoos—but because it has always been fundamentally racist and violent. Incited by Western Catholic powers, notably the Habsburg Empire, the key to Ukrainian nationalism was its claim to be *Western,* and thus superior. Since Ukrainians and Russians stem from the same population, pro-Western Ukrainian ultra-nationalism was built on imaginary myths of racial differences: Ukrainians were the true Western whatever-it-was, whereas Russians were mixed with "Mongols" and thus an inferior race. Banderist Ukrainian nationalists have openly called for elimination of Russians *as such,* as inferior beings.

So long as the Soviet Union existed, Ukrainian racial hatred of Russians had anticommunism as its cover, and Western intelligence agencies could support them on the "pure" ideological grounds of the fight against Bolshevism/Communism. But now that Russia is no longer ruled by communists, the mask has fallen, and the racist nature of Ukrainian ultra-nationalism is visible—for all who want to see it.

However, Western leaders and media are determined not to notice.

Ukraine is not just like any Western country. It is deeply and dramatically divided between Donbass in the East, Russian territories attributed to the Ukrainian Socialist Republic within the Soviet Union, and the anti-Russian West. Russia's defense of Donbass, wise or unwise, by no means indicates a Russian intention to invade other countries. This false alarm is the pretext for the remilitarization of Germany in alliance with the Anglo-Saxon powers against Russia.

The Yugoslav Prelude

This process began in the 1990s, with the breakup of Yugoslavia.

Yugoslavia was not a member of the Soviet bloc. Precisely for that reason, the country got loans from the West which in the 1970s led to a debt crisis in which the leaders of each of the six federated republics wanted to shove the debt onto others. This favored separatist tendencies in the relatively rich Slovenian and Croatian republics, tendencies enforced by ethnic chauvinism and encouragement from outside powers, especially Germany.

During World War II, German occupation had split the country apart. Serbia, allied to France and Britain in World War I, was subject to a punishing occupation. Idyllic Slovenia was absorbed into the Third Reich, while Germany supported an independent Croatia, ruled by the fascist Ustasha party, which included most of Bosnia, scene of the bloodiest internal fighting. When the war ended, many Croatian Ustasha emigrated to Germany, the United States and Canada, never giving up the hope of reviving secessionist Croatian nationalism.

In Washington in the 1990s, members of Congress got their impressions of Yugoslavia from a single expert: 35-year-old Croatian-American Mira Baratta, assistant to Senator Bob Dole (Republican presidential candidate in 1996). Baratta's grandfather had been an important Ustasha officer in Bosnia and her father was active in the Croatian diaspora in California. Baratta won over not only Dole but virtually the whole Congress to the Croatian version of Yugoslav conflicts blaming everything on the Serbs.

In Europe, Germans and Austrians, most notably Otto von Habsburg, heir to the defunct Austro-Hungarian Empire and member of the European Parliament from Bavaria, succeeded in portraying Serbs as the villains, thus achieving an effective revenge against their historic World War I enemy, Serbia. In the West, it became usual to identify Serbia as "Russia's historic ally," forgetting that in recent history Serbia's closest allies were Britain and especially France.

In September 1991, a German constitutional lawyer and former Defense Minister, Rupert Scholz, explained why Germany should promote the breakup of Yugoslavia by recognizing the Slovenian and Croat secessionist Yugoslav republics.[1] By ending the division of Germany, he said, "we have, so to speak, overcome and mastered the most important consequences of the Second World War ... but in other areas we are still dealing with the consequences of the First World War"—which, he noted "started in Serbia."

"Yugoslavia, as a consequence of the First World War, is a very artificial construction, never compatible with the idea of self-determination." He concluded: "In my opinion, Slovenia and Croatia must be immediately recognized internationally. (...) When this recognition has taken place, the Yugoslavian conflict will no longer be a domestic Yugoslav problem, where no international intervention can be permitted."

And indeed, recognition was followed by massive Western intervention which continues to this day. By taking sides, Germany, the United States and NATO ultimately produced a disastrous result, a half dozen statelets, with many unsettled issues and heavily dependent on Western powers. Bosnia-Herzegovina is under military occupation as well as the dictates of a "High Representative" who happens to be German. It has lost about half its population to emigration. Only Serbia shows signs of independence, refusing to join in Western sanctions on Russia, despite heavy pressure. For Washington strategists the breakup of Yugoslavia was an exercise in using ethnic divisions to break up larger entities, with an eye to the USSR and then Russia.

Western politicians and media persuaded the public that the 1999 NATO bombing of Serbia was a "humanitarian" war, generously waged to "protect the Kosovars."

But the real point of the Kosovo war was that it transformed NATO from a defensive into an aggressive alliance, ready to wage war anywhere, without U.N. mandate, on whatever pretext it chose. As soon as Serbian President Milosevic, to save his country's infrastructure from NATO destruction, agreed to allow NATO troops to enter Kosovo, the U.S. unceremoniously grabbed a huge swath territory to build its first big U.S. military base in the Balkans.

This lesson was clear to the Russians. After the Kosovo war, NATO could no longer credibly claim that it was a purely "defensive" alliance.

Just as the United States rushed to build a huge military base in Kosovo, it was clear what to expect of the United States after it succeeded in 2014 in installing a government in Kiev eager to join NATO.

---

    1   Former CDU Minister of Defense, Rupert Scholz, at the 6th Fürstenfeldbrucker Symposium for the Leadership of the German Military and Business, held September 23–24, 1991.

This would be the opportunity for the United States to take over the Russian naval base in Crimea. Since it was known that the majority of the population in Crimea wanted to return to being part of Russia (as it had from 1783 to 1954), Putin was able to forestall this threat by holding a popular referendum confirming this return.

East European Revanchism Captures the EU

The European Union enlargements to twelve new members in 2004 and 2007 brought into EU institutions a new wave of Russophobia in the guise of fanatic anticommunism, even though Russia was no more communist than the other Soviet successor states.

The European Parliament, obsessed with virtue signaling in regard to human rights, was particularly receptive to the zealous anti-totalitarianism of its new Eastern European members.

As an aspect of anticommunist lustration, or purges, Eastern European States sponsored "Memory Institutes" devoted to denouncing the crimes of communism. Of course, such campaigns were used by far right politicians to cast suspicion on the left in general. As explained by European scholar Zoltan Dujisin,[2] "anticommunist memory entrepreneurs" at the head of these institutes succeeded in lifting their public information activities from the national to the European Union level, using Western bans on Holocaust denial to complain that while Nazi crimes had been condemned and punished at Nuremberg, communist crimes had not. The tactic of the anticommunist entrepreneurs was to demand that references to the Holocaust be accompanied by denunciations of the Gulag. This campaign had to deal with a delicate contradiction since it tended to challenge the uniqueness of the Holocaust, a dogma essential to gaining financial and political support from West European memory institutes.

In 2008, the EP adopted a resolution establishing August 23 as "European Day of Remembrance for the victims of Stalinism and Nazism"—for the first time adopting what had been a fairly isolated far right equation. A 2009 EP resolution on "European Conscience and Totalitarianism" called for support of national institutes specializing in totalitarian history.

---

2   Zoltan Dujisin, "A history of post-communist remembrance: from memory politics to the emergence of a field of anticommunism," *Theory and Society,* volume 50, pages 65–96 (2021) https://link.springer.com/article/10.1007/s11186-020-09401-5

Dujisin explains, "Europe is now haunted by the specter of a new memory. The Holocaust's singular standing as a negative founding formula of European integration, the culmination of long-standing efforts from prominent Western leaders ... is increasingly challenged by a memory of communism, which disputes its uniqueness." East European memory institutes together formed the "Platform of European Memory and Conscience" which between 2012 and 2016 organized a series of exhibits on "Totalitarianism in Europe: Fascism—Nazism—Communism," travelling to museums, memorials, foundations, city halls, parliaments, cultural centers, and universities in 15 European countries, supposedly to "improve public awareness and education about the gravest crimes committed by the totalitarian dictatorships."

Under this influence, the European Parliament on September 19, 2019, adopted a resolution "on the importance of European Remembrance for the Future of Europe" that went far beyond equating political crimes by proclaiming a distinctly Polish interpretation of history as European Union policy. It goes so far as to proclaim that the Molotov-Ribbentrop pact is responsible for World War II—and thus Soviet Russia is as guilty of the war as Nazi Germany.

The resolution:

> "Stresses that the Second World War, the most devastating war in Europe's history, was started as an immediate result of the notorious Nazi-Soviet Treaty on Non-Aggression of 23 August 1939, also known as the Molotov-Ribbentrop Pact, and its secret protocols, whereby two totalitarian regimes that shared the goal of world conquest divided Europe into two zones of influence;"

It further:

> "Recalls that the Nazi and communist regimes carried out mass murders, genocide and deportations and caused a loss of life and freedom in the 20th century on a scale unseen in human history, and recalls the horrific crime of the Holocaust perpetrated by the Nazi regime; condemns in the strongest terms the acts of aggression, crimes against humanity and mass human

*rights violations perpetrated by the Nazi, communist
and other totalitarian regimes;"*

This of course not only directly contradicts the Russian celebration of the "Great Patriotic War" to defeat the Nazi invasion, it also took issue with recent effort of Russian President Vladimir Putin to put the Molotov-Ribbentrop agreement in the context of prior refusals of Eastern European states, notably Poland, to ally with Moscow against Hitler.

But the EP resolution:

*"Is deeply concerned about the efforts of the current
Russian leadership to distort historical facts and
whitewash crimes committed by the Soviet totalitarian
regime and considers them a dangerous component of
the information war waged against democratic Europe
that aims to divide Europe, and therefore calls on the
Commission to decisively counteract these efforts;"*

Thus the importance of "Memory" for the future, turns out to be an ideological declaration of war against Russia based on interpretations of World War II, especially since the memory entrepreneurs implicitly suggest that the past crimes of communism deserve punishment—like the crimes of Nazism. It is not impossible that this line of thought arouses some tacit satisfaction among certain individuals in Germany.

When Western leaders speak of "economic war against Russia," or "ruining Russia" by arming and supporting Ukraine, one wonders whether they are consciously preparing World War III, or trying to provide a new ending to World War II. Or will the two merge?

As it shapes up, with NATO openly trying to "overextend" and thus defeat Russia in a war of attrition in Ukraine, it is a bit as if Britain and the United States, some 80 years later, switched sides and joined German-dominated Europe to wage war against Russia, alongside the heirs to Eastern European anticommunism, some of whom were allied to Nazi Germany.

Memory is Not the Key to Peace

History may help understand events, but the cult of memory easily becomes the cult of revenge. Revenge is a circle with no end. It uses the past to kill the future. Europe needs clear heads looking to the future able to understand the present.

Omerta in the NATO Gangster War*

SEPTEMBER 2022

Imperialist wars are waged to conquer lands, peoples, territories. Gangster wars are waged to remove competitors. In gangster wars you issue an obscure warning, then you smash the windows or burn the place down.

Gangster war is what you wage when you already are the boss and won't let any outsider muscle in on your territory. For the dons in Washington, our territory can be just about everywhere, but its core is occupied Europe.

By an uncanny coincidence, Joe Biden just happens to look like a mafia boss, to talk like a mafia boss, to wear a little lopsided half smile like a mafia boss. Just watch the now famous video.[1]

> Pres. Biden: "If Russia invades...then there will be no longer a Nord Stream 2. We will bring an end to it."
> Reporter: "But how will you do that, exactly, since... the project is in Germany's control?"
> Biden: "I promise you, we will be able to do that."

Able for sure.

It cost billions of dollars to lay the Nord Stream 2 pipeline across the Baltic Sea, from near Saint Petersburg to the port of Greifsfeld in Germany. The idea was to ensure safe natural gas supplies to Germany and other European partners by going around troublesome Ukraine, known for readiness to use its transit rights to siphon off gas for itself

---

* Published in *Consortium News,* September 28, 2022.

1 Posted by ABC News on *X,* February 7, 2022. https://twitter.com/i/status/1490792461979078662

or blackmail clients. Of course, Ukraine was always vehemently hostile to the project. So was the United States. And so were Poland, the three Baltic States, Finland and Sweden, all attentive to what went on in their sea.

The Baltic Sea is a nearly closed body of water, with narrow access to the Atlantic through Danish and Swedish straits. The waters near the Danish island of Bornholm where the Nord Stream pipelines were sabotaged by massive underwater explosions is under constant military surveillance by these neighbors.

"It seems completely impossible that a state actor could carry out a major naval operation in the middle of this densely monitored area without being noticed by the countless active and passive sensors of the littoral states; certainly not directly off the island of Bornholm, where Danes, Swedes and Germans have a rendezvous in monitoring the surface and undersea activities," writes Jens Berger in the excellent German website *NachDenkSeiten.*[2]

Last June, Berger reports, "the annual NATO maneuver Baltops took place in the Baltic Sea. Under the command of the U.S. 6th Fleet, 47 warships participated in the exercise this year, including the U.S. fleet force around the helicopter carrier USS *Kearsarge.* Of particular significance is one particular maneuver conducted by the 6th Fleet's Task Force 68—a special unit for explosive ordnance disposal and underwater operations of the U.S. Marines, the very unit that would be the first address for an act of sabotage on an undersea pipeline." In June this year this very unit was engaged in a maneuver off the island of Bornholm, operating with unmanned underwater vehicles.

Berger considers that a major sabotage operation "could not have been carried out directly under the noses of several littoral states without anyone noticing." But he adds this clever observation: "if you want to hide something, it is best to do so in public."

> In order to be able to attach explosive devices to a gas pipeline halfway unnoticed, one would need a plausible distraction—a reason for diving near Bornholm without immediately being suspected of committing an act of sabotage. It doesn't even have to be directly related in time to the attacks. Modern explosive devices can, of course, be detonated remotely. So who has

2 https://www.nachdenkseiten.de/?p=88603

been conducting such operations in the maritime area in recent weeks? As luck would have it, exactly the same task force around the USS Kearsarge was again in the sea area around Bornholm last week.

In short, during NATO maneuvers, some participant could have laid the explosives, to be blown up at a later chosen moment.

By an odd coincidence, only a few hours after the sabotage of Nord Stream 1 and 2, ceremonies began opening the new Baltic Pipe carrying gas from Norway to Denmark and Poland.

The Political Significance of the Sabotage

Due to Western sanctions against Russia, gas was not being delivered through the destroyed pipelines. However gas inside the pipelines is leaking dangerously. The pipelines remained ready for use whenever an agreement could be reached. And the first, dramatic significance of the sabotage is that henceforth, no agreement can be reached. Nord Stream 2 would have been the key to some sort of settlement between Russia and the Europeans. The sabotage has virtually announced that the war can only intensify with no end in sight.

In Germany, the Czech Republic and some other countries, movements were beginning to grow calling for an end to the sanctions, specifically to solve the energy crisis by putting Nord Stream 2 into operation for the first time. The sabotage has thus invalidated the leading demand of potential peace movements in Germany and Europe.

This act of sabotage is above all a deliberate sabotage of any prospect of a negotiated peace in Europe. The next move from the West has been for NATO governments to call on all their citizens to leave Russia immediately. In preparation of what?

The Russians Did It

In this catastrophic situation, Western mainstream media are all wondering who could be the guilty party, and suspicion automatically fixes on… Russia. Motive? "To raise the price of gas," or "to destabilize Europe"—things that were happening anyway. Any far-fetched notion will do.

European opinion-makers are showing the result of seventy years of Americanization. Especially in Germany, but also in France and elsewhere, for decades the United States has systematically spotted up and coming young people, invited them to become "young leaders," invited them to the United States, indoctrinated them in "our values" and made them feel like members of the great transatlantic family. They are networked into top positions in politics and media. In recent years, great alarm is raised about alleged Russian efforts to exert "influence" in European countries, while Europeans bathe in perpetual American influence: movies, Netflix, pop culture, influence in universities, media, everywhere.

When disaster strikes Europe, it can't be blamed on America (except for Trump, because the American establishment despised and rejected him, so Europeans must do the same). It has to be the bad guy in the movie, Putin.

The fanatically anti-Russian former Polish foreign minister Radek Sikorsky couldn't restrain himself and joyously greeted the massive natural gas leaks from the destroyed pipeline with a cheerful tweet, "Thank you, USA." But Poland was certainly also willing, and perhaps even able. So perhaps were some others in NATOland. But they all prefer to publicly "suspect" Russia.

Officially, so far, no NATO government knows who dunnit. Or maybe they all know. Maybe this is like the famous Agatha Christie mystery on the Orient Express train, where suspicion falls on all the passengers, and are all guilty. And all united in Omerta.

Germans Down and Russians Out[*]

MARCH 2023

On the purpose of NATO: "To keep the Americans in, the Russians out, and the Germans down."

— saying attributed to Lord Hastings Ismay,
the secretary general of NATO 1952–1957

Divide and rule is the eternal law of Empire.

Above all, don't let other big guys get together. Keep them at each other's throats. Half a century ago, stuck in the unwinnable Vietnam war, President Richard M. Nixon heeded Henry Kissinger's advice to open relations with Beijing in order to deepen the split between the Soviet Union and China.

But which big guys, and when? Priorities have evidently shifted. Eight years ago, America's most influential, private geostrategic analyst, George Friedman, defined the current dominant U.S. *divide et impera* priority, at work in Ukraine.

"The primordial interest of the United States is the relationship between Germany and Russia, because united, they're the only force that could threaten us," Friedman explained.

Russia's main interest has always been to have a neutral buffer zone in Eastern Europe. But the U.S. purpose is to build a hostile *cordon sanitaire* from the Baltic to the Black Sea, as a definitive barrier separating Russia from Germany.

"Russia knows it. Russia believes the United States intends to break the Russian Federation," said Friedman, jokingly adding that he thought the intention was not to kill Russia but only to make it suffer.

---

[*] Published in *Consortium News,* March 21, 2023. https://consortiumnews.com/2023/03/21/diana-johnstone-germans-down-russians-out/#

Speaking to an elite group in Chicago on April 13, 2015, Friedman noted that the U.S. Army commander in Europe, General Ben Hodges, had just visited Ukraine, decorating Ukrainian soldiers and promising them trainers. He was doing this outside NATO, said Friedman, because NATO membership required 100 percent approval and Ukraine risked being vetoed, so the U.S. was going ahead on its own.

What the U.S. has long dreaded, said Friedman, is the combination of German capital and technology with Russian resources and labor. The Nord Stream pipeline was leading in that direction, toward mutual trade and security arrangements that would no long require either the dollar or NATO.

"For Russia," said Friedman, "the status of Ukraine is an existential threat. And the Russians cannot afford to let it go." For the United States, however, it is a means to an end: separating Russia from Germany.

Friedman concluded that the big question was, how will the Germans react?

So far, German leaders have been reacting like the loyal managers of a country under U.S. occupation—which it is.

The German Peace Movement Threat

Any sign of sympathy with Russia has been so demonized, repressed, even criminalized since the Russian invasion began on Feb. 24, 2022, that most German protests initially avoided taking any position on the war itself and focused on the economic hardships caused by sanctions.

But on Jan. 25 of this year, Chancellor Olaf Scholz gave in to U.S. pressure to send German Leopard 2 tanks to Ukraine, about the same time that German Foreign Minister Annalena Baerbock, of the Green Party, casually told an international meeting that "we are fighting a war against Russia."

This jolted people into action.

Spontaneous demonstrations broke out in large and small cities all over Germany with slogans such as "Ami (Americans) Go Home!," "Greens to the Front!," "Make Peace Without German Weapons." Speakers condemned the tank deliveries for "crossing a red line," accused the United States of forcing Germany into war with Russia, and called for Baerbock's resignation.

The wave of demonstrations peaked one month later on Feb. 25 when up to 50,000 people rallied to the "Uprising for Peace" (*Aufstand für Frieden*) in Berlin, called on the initiative of two women, left politician Sahra Wagenknecht and veteran feminist writer and editor Alice Schwartzer.

Over half a million people signed their "Manifesto for Peace" calling on Chancellor Scholz to "stop the escalation of arms deliveries" and work for a ceasefire and negotiations. Organizers called for reconstruction of a massive German peace movement, on the model of the anti-nuclear missile movement of the 1980s that led up to Russian acceptance of German reunification.

However, building a peace movement in Germany today faces many obstacles. Under U.S. military occupation since the end of World War II, German institutions and media are permeated with American influence, as is the legal order. Paradoxically, the trans-Atlantic American grip seems only to have tightened since German reunification.

Monitoring "Extremes"

Germany monitors political "extremism" through a domestic intelligence agency, the Federal Office for the Protection of the Constitution, BfV (*Bundesamt für Verfassungsschutz*). Although strictly speaking Germany does not have a constitution, it has a strong Constitutional Court designed specifically to prevent any reversion to Nazi power practices.

Instead of a constitution, a transitional Basic Law approved by the Western occupying powers (the U.S., Britain and France) in 1949 enabled the Federal Republic to assume the government of West Germany. Upon reunification, the Basic Law was extended to all of Germany.

In the spirit of liberal "antitotalitarianism," the BfV monitors both "left-wing extremism" and "right-wing extremism" as potential threats. "Islamic extremism" has more recently come under supervision. The underlying political implication is that "right-wing extremism" designates Nazi tendencies, while "left-wing extremism" leans toward Soviet-style communism.

This 20th century political topography implicitly establishes "the center" as an innocent middle-ground where citizens can feel at ease. Even the most radical militarism is not "extreme" in this scheme of things.

Article 5 of the Basic Law grants individuals the right to express opinions, but there are numerous limitations in the Criminal Code, with punishment for "inciting hatred," racism, anti-Semitism and prison terms for Holocaust denial. Also prohibited are propaganda or symbols of "unconstitutional" organizations, disparagement of the State and its symbols, blasphemy against established religions and especially failure to respect "human dignity."

Of course, what matters in all these laws is how they are interpreted. The ban on "rewarding and approving crimes" (Section 140), that was originally intended to apply to convictions for violent civil crimes, has now been extended to the geopolitical sphere, namely, outlawing "approval or support" of what it terms "aggressive war."

Antiwar activist Heinrich Bücker's speech in Berlin last June 22 calling for good relations with Russia on the anniversary of the 1941 Nazi invasion of the Soviet Union was condemned by a Berlin court for "approving Russia's crime of invasion." In practice, any effort to clarify the Russian position by referring to NATO expansion and Kiev regime attacks on Donbass since 2014 can be interpreted as such "approval or support."

Needless to say, Germans were never threatened with criminal prosecution for approving the U.S. invasions of Vietnam, Iraq or Afghanistan, much less the totally aggressive and illegal 1999 bombing of Serbia, in which they enthusiastically took part. Widely celebrated as a laudable act of humanitarianism, that bombing campaign, killing civilians and destroying infrastructure, forced Serbia to allow NATO to occupy its province of Kosovo, where the Americans built themselves a huge military base. Ethnic Albanian rebels declared independence and thousands of non-Albanians were driven out.

German Police Enforce Centrist Conformity

As demonstrators gathered for the "Uprising for Peace" demonstration in Berlin, an organizer appeared on the speakers' platform to read out a long list of things banned by police. The list included numerous symbols or signs related to the Soviet Union, Russia, Belarus or Donbass; Russian military songs; "endorsement of the war of aggression currently being waged by Russia against Ukraine," etc.

The day before, Berlin police had delivered to the organizers a detailed explanation justifying these prohibitions, specifying that "public safety was in imminent danger." Police said that according to their information, "the participants of your meeting will mainly consist of people with an old-left, pro-Russian basic attitude, who are against the arms deliveries of the German government to Ukraine, the geopolitics of the 'West/the USA' and against NATO in general."

The police had reason to believe that the Feb. 25 meeting would attract "very heterogeneous" participants "with their own views (state delegitimizers, conspiracy believers, supporters of the Putin regime, etc.)" and therefore, precautions must be taken.

The Cross-Front Threat

Police referred to a comparable meeting a month earlier, on Jan. 27, whose organizers were accused by leftist and antifascist groups of having "tolerated cross-thinkers (*Querdenker*) and people of the right scene at their meeting." A cross-thinker is one who crosses the enemy front lines between left and right, an offense called "cross-front," also referred to as "red-brown."

What is remarkable is that in Germany, the establishment, the media, the BfV and notably the police have taken up the term "cross-front" (*Querfront*) with the same opprobrium as the Antifa movement where it is used ostensibly to enforce the ideological purity of the left. Initially it meant a rightwing appropriation of leftwing themes intended to seduce and mislead leftists into fascist combinations. The historical basis of the term lies in unsuccessful coalition attempts of rightwingers in the late Weimar Republic in a context of intense rivalry between strong Nazi and Communist movements vying for working class support, totally unlike the political atmosphere of today.

In the absence of either a strong Nazi or Communist movement, the term is currently used to denounce any cooperation, or even contact, between leftists and movements or individuals described as "extreme right." This label is frequently based on not much more than opposition to unlimited immigration, denounced as racism.

By this standard, the Alternative for Germany (AfD) opposition party (with 78 out of 736 seats in the current Bundestag) is "extreme right." Since most Bundestag members critical of arming Ukraine come either from Die Linke (Left) party or the AfD, the anti-crossfront vigilance condemns in advance a broad, open antiwar opposition.

Subjective Evaluations by Police

According to the Feb. 24 Berlin police warning, "The approval of the war of aggression against international law, which the Russian Federation is currently waging against Ukraine, is punishable under Section 140 ..." Such approval can be expressed not only by words but by a number of signs and symbols. In particular, the display of the letter "Z" (supposedly standing for the Russian expression *za pobyedu* – for victory) would constitute a criminal offense.

Even more far-fetched, the flag of the defunct U.S.S.R. is also crim-inalized, because, according to police: "the U.S.S.R. flag symbolizes a Russia within the borders of the former Soviet Union." This, according to Berlin police, "is seen by experts as the actual desired goal of Russian President Vladimir Putin" and explains his attack on Ukraine.

"The present restrictions are expressly not directed against the content of expressions of opinion, which may not be prevented within the framework of Article 5 of the Basic Law, but are intended, from a contextual point of view, to prevent your assembly, in the manner in which it is conducted, from being suitable or intended for conveying a readiness to use violence and thereby having an intimidating effect, or from violating the moral sensibilities of citizens and fundamental social or ethical views in a significant manner."

A Cautious Demonstration

The "Uprising for Peace" in the end provided no opportunities for police interventions or arrests. Like the "Manifesto for Peace," the German speeches largely avoided references to U.S. and NATO provo-cations leading to the war.

Only Jeffrey Sachs, whose opening speech in English was broadcast to the crowd on a screen, dared speak of the background to the Russian invasion: the 2014 Kiev coup, the U.S. arming of Ukraine, the U.S. op-position to peace negotiations, the likelihood that the U.S. was responsi-ble for blowing up the Nord Stream pipelines and other facts susceptible of offending certain sensibilities. But there was no chance that Berlin police would arrest Sachs, who was not in Germany.

The other speakers largely ignored the origins of the war, concen-trating instead on fears of where it might lead: constant escalation of arms deliveries, even nuclear war. The huge crowd was bundled up against the icy cold and light snow. Flags mostly portrayed peace doves and slogans called for diplomacy, for peace negotiations instead of arms deliveries, for avoidance of nuclear war. Neo-Nazis and extreme right-ists were declared unwelcome and must have come in disguise as they were scarcely visible. The whole event could hardly have been more well-behaved and respectable.

Attacking Wagenknecht

Despite all this niceness, the demonstration and its organizers were fiercely attacked by politicians and media. Sahra Wagenknecht is a popular figure, being pushed out of her dwindling Left Party (*Die Linke*) by leaders who tend to follow the increasingly bellicose Greens in the hope of being included in leftwing coalition governments.

Wagenknecht, married to Oskar Lafontaine, who as a leading Social Democrat was prominent in the antimissile movement of the 1980s, is rumored to be preparing to found a party of her own. This would fill a yawning gap in the current German political scene: an antiwar party firmly on the left. She must therefore be seen as the main political threat to the reigning coalition.

Thus Wagenknecht has been vehemently attacked for the fact that her antiwar speeches have been applauded in parliament by members of the AfD. And despite having repeatedly condemned the Russian invasion for breaking international law, other things she has said have been described as "close to the narrative" of Russian President Vladimir Putin.

Despite her caution, she is blamed for "understanding" the Russian viewpoint, which is unacceptable.

In a major hit piece, journalist Markus Decker called Wagenknecht the most influential enemy of democracy in Germany. Wagenknecht, he wrote, "is the personified embodiment of what intelligence officers have been warning about for years: the blurring of the boundaries between the political fringes and the extremes."

In other words, she should be monitored by the BfV as a sponsor of the dreaded cross-front. "Wagenknecht, who has been systematically blurring the lines between dictatorship and democracy since the beginning of the Russian attack on Ukraine, is not about peace. It's about destroying democracy. Wagenknecht is probably its most influential enemy in Germany," Decker wrote.

In the past few years, as hostility toward Russia has been building in the West, the Antifa exclusionary dogma has strengthened within the left. The result is that the left is less interested in winning over conservatives than in excluding them. This is a sort of essentialist identity politics: anyone "on the right" must be inherently an irreconcilable enemy.

There is no thought that perhaps some people may vote for the Alternative for Germany because they feel let down by other parties, for instance by the Left Party. This could be especially true in East Germany, where both parties have roots.

Freedom of Opinion Under Threat

On March 15, a group of leftist artists and intellectuals released a petition calling for the defense of free expression. It reads:

> Germany is in a deep crisis. ... Disinformation and manipulation of the population largely determine the current media culture. Anyone who does not share the prescribed official opinion on the Ukraine war, criticizes it and makes this known publicly, is defamed, threatened and sanctioned or ostracized. ... In such an atmosphere, open debates, the exchange and presentation of differing views in the media, science, art, culture and other areas are hardly possible anymore. A truly free formation of opinion by weighing different arguments is impossible. Bias and ignorance, but also intimidation, fear, self-censorship and hypocrisy are the consequences. This is incompatible with human dignity and personal freedom.

Last month, Federal Interior Minister Nancy Faeser (SPD) introduced a new law making it possible to dismiss "enemies of the constitution" from the civil service by a simple administrative act. "We will not allow our democratic constitutional state to be sabotaged from within by extremists," Faeser said. But in the view of the German Civil Servants' Association, the bill "sends a message of mistrust to both employees and citizens."

A war atmosphere is supposed to unite a nation. But imposed artificially, it exposes and creates deep divisions.

Bear Baiting: U.S. Foreign Policy is a Cruel Sport*

FEBRUARY 2022

In the time of the first Queen Elizabeth, British royal circles enjoyed watching fierce dogs torment a captive bear for the fun of it. The bear had done no harm to anyone, but the dogs were trained to provoke the imprisoned beast and goad it into fighting back. Blood flowing from the excited animals delighted the spectators.

This cruel practice has long since been banned as inhumane.

And yet today, a version of bear baiting is being practiced every day against whole nations on a gigantic international scale. It is called United States foreign policy. It has become the regular practice of the absurd international sports club called NATO.

United States leaders, secure in their arrogance as "the indispensable nation," have no more respect for other countries than the Elizabethans had for the animals they tormented. The list is long of targets of U.S. bear baiting, but Russia stands out as prime example of constant harassment. And this is no accident. The baiting is deliberately and elaborately planned.

As evidence, I call attention to a 2019 report by the RAND corporation to the U.S. Army chief of staff entitled "Extending Russia." Actually, the RAND study itself is fairly cautious in its recommendations and warns that many perfidious tricks might not work. However, I consider the very existence of this report scandalous, not so much for its content as for the fact that this is what the Pentagon pays its top intellectuals to do: figure out ways to lure other nations into troubles U.S. leaders hope to exploit.

The official U.S. line is that the Kremlin threatens Europe by its aggressive expansionism, but when the strategists talk among themselves

---

* First published in *Consortium News,* February 22, 2022.

the story is very different. Their goal is to use sanctions, propaganda and other measures to *provoke* Russia into taking the very sort of negative measures ("over-extension") that the U.S. can exploit to Russia's detriment.

The RAND study explains its goals:

> We examine a range of nonviolent measures that could exploit Russia's actual vulnerabilities and anxieties as a way of stressing Russia's military and economy and the regime's political standing at home and abroad. The steps we examine would not have either defense or deterrence as their prime purpose, although they might contribute to both. Rather, these steps are conceived of as elements in a campaign designed to unbalance the adversary, leading Russia to compete in domains or regions where the United States has a competitive advantage, and causing Russia to overextend itself militarily or economically or causing the regime to lose domestic and/or international prestige and influence.

Clearly, in U.S. ruling circles, this is considered "normal" behavior, just as teasing is normal behavior for the schoolyard bully, and sting operations are normal for corrupt FBI agents.

This description perfectly fits U.S. operations in Ukraine, intended to "exploit Russia's vulnerabilities and anxieties" by advancing a hostile military alliance onto its doorstep, while describing Russia's totally predictable reactions as gratuitous aggression. Diplomacy involves understanding the position of the other party. But verbal bear baiting requires total refusal to understand the other, and constant deliberate misinterpretation of whatever the other party says or does.

What is truly diabolical is that, while constantly accusing the Russian bear of plotting to expand, the whole policy is directed at goading it into expanding! Because then we can issue punishing sanctions, raise the Pentagon budge a few notches higher and tighten the NATO Protection Racket noose tighter around our precious European "allies."

For a generation, Russian leaders have made extraordinary efforts to build a peaceful partnership with "the West," institutionalized as the European Union and above all, NATO. They truly believed that the end of the artificial Cold War could produce a peace-loving European neighborhood. But arrogant United States leaders, despite contrary advice from their best experts, rejected treating Russia as the great nation it is, and preferred to treat it as the harassed bear in a circus.

The expansion of NATO was a form of bear-baiting, the clear way to transform a potential friend into an enemy. That was the way chosen by Clinton and following administrations. Moscow had accepted the independence of former members of the Soviet Union. Bear-baiting involved constantly accusing Moscow of plotting to take them back by force.

Russia's Borderland

Ukraine is a word meaning borderlands, essentially the borderlands between Russia and the territories to the West that were sometimes part of Poland, or Lithuania, or Habsburg lands. As a part of the USSR, Ukraine was expanded to include large swaths of both. History had created very contrasting identities on the two extremities, with the result that the independent nation of Ukraine, which came into existence only in 1991, was deeply divided from the start. And from the start, Washington strategies, in cahoots with a large, hyperactive anti-communist anti-Russian diaspora in the U.S. and Canada, contrived to use the bitterness of Ukraine's divisions to weaken first the USSR and then Russia. Billions of dollars were invested in order to "strengthen democracy"—meaning the pro-Western west of Ukraine against its semi-Russian east.

The 2014 U.S.-backed coup that overthrew President Viktor Yanukovych, who was solidly supported by the east of the country, brought to power pro-West forces determined to bring Ukraine into NATO, whose designation of Russia as prime enemy had become ever more blatant. This raised the prospect of an eventual NATO capture of Russia's major naval base at Sebastopol, on the Crimean peninsula. Since the Crimean population had never wanted to be part of Ukraine, the peril was averted by organizing a referendum in which an overwhelming majority of Crimeans voted to return to Russia, from which they had been severed by an autocratic Khrushchev ruling in 1954. Western propagandists relentlessly denounced this act of self-determination as a "Russian invasion" foreshadowing a program of Russian military conquest of its Western neighbors—a fantasy supported by neither facts nor motivation.

Appalled by the coup overthrowing the President they had voted for by nationalists threatening to outlaw the Russian language they spoke, the people of the eastern provinces of Donetsk and Lugansk declared their independence. Russia did not support this move, but instead supported the Minsk agreement, signed in February 2015 and endorsed by a

U.N. Security Council resolution. The gist of the accord was to preserve the territorial integrity of Ukraine by a federalization process that would return the breakaway republics in return for their local autonomy.

The Minsk agreement set out a few steps to end the internal Ukrainian crisis. First, Ukraine was supposed to immediately adopt a law granting self-government to eastern regions (in March 2015). Next, Kiev would negotiate with eastern territories over guidelines for local elections to be held that year under OSCE supervision. Then Kiev would implement a constitutional reform guaranteeing eastern right. After the elections, Kiev would take full control of Donetsk and Lugansk, including border with Russia. A general amnesty would cover soldiers on both sides.

However, although it signed the agreement, Kiev has never implemented any of these points and refuses to negotiate with the eastern rebels. Under the so-called Normandy agreement, France and Germany were expected to put pressure on Kiev to accept this peaceful settlement, but nothing happened. Instead, the West has accused Russia of failing to implement the agreement, which makes no sense inasmuch as the obligations to implement fall on Kiev, not on Moscow. Kiev officials regularly reiterate their refusal to negotiate with the rebels, while demanding more and more weaponry from NATO powers in order to deal with the problem in their own way.

Meanwhile, major parties in the Russian Duma and public opinion have long expressed concern for the Russian-speaking population of the eastern provinces, suffering from privations and military attack from the central government for eight years. This concern is naturally interpreted in the West as a remake of Hitler's drive to conquest neighboring countries. However, as usual the inevitable Hitler analogy is baseless. For one thing, Russia is much too large to need to conquer *Lebensraum.*

You Want an Enemy? Now You've Got One

Germany has found the perfect formula for Western relations with Russia: Are you or are you not a *"Putinversteher,"* a "Putin understander." By Putin they mean Russia, since the standard Western propaganda ploy is to personify the targeted country with the name of its President, necessarily a dictatorial autocrat. If you "understand" Putin, or Russia, then you are under deep suspicion of disloyalty to the West. So, all together now, let us make sure that we DO NOT UNDERSTAND Russia!

Russian leaders claim to feel threatened by members of a huge hostile alliance, holding regular military manoeuvers on their doorstep? They feel uneasy about nuclear missiles aimed at their territory from nearby NATO member states? Why, that's just paranoia, or a sign of sly, aggressive intentions. There is nothing to understand.

So the West has treated Russia like a baited bear. And what it's getting is a nuclear-armed, militarily powerful adversary nation led by people vastly more thoughtful and intelligent than the mediocre politicians in office in Washington, London and a few other places.

Biden and his deep state never wanted a peaceful solution in Ukraine, because troubled Ukraine acts as a permanent barrier between Russia and Western Europe, ensuring U.S. control over the latter. They have spent years treating Russia as an adversary, and Russia is now drawing the inevitable conclusion that the West will accept it only as an adversary. The patience is at an end. And this is a game changer.

First reaction: the West will punish the bear with sanctions! Germany is stopping certification of the Nordstream 2 natural gas pipeline. Germany thus refuses to buy the Russian gas it needs in order to make sure Russia won't be able to cut off the gas it needs sometime in the future. Now that's a clever trick, isn't it! And meanwhile, with a growing gas shortage and rising prices, Russia will have no trouble selling its gas somewhere else in Asia.

When "our values" include refusal to understand, there is no limit to how much we can fail to understand.

To be continued.

D-Day 2024:
A Reversal of Alliances?*

JUNE 2024

Ceremonies were held last week commemorating the 80th anniversary of Operation Overlord, the Anglo-American landing on the beaches of Normandy that took place on June 6, 1944, known as D-Day. For the very first time, the Russians were ostentatiously *not* invited to take part in the ceremonies.

The Russian absence symbolically altered the meaning of the festivities. Certainly, the significance of Operation Overlord as the first step in the domination of Western Europe by the English-speaking world was more pertinent than ever. But without Russia, the event was symbolically taken out of the original context of World War II.

Ukrainian president Vladimir Zelensky was invited to give a video address to the French Parliament in honor of the occasion. Zelensky pulled out all the rhetorical stops to demonize Putin, describing the Russian President as the "common enemy" of Ukraine and Europe. Russia, he claimed "is a territory where life no longer has any value… It's the opposite of Europe, it's the anti-Europe."

So after 80 years, D-Day symbolically celebrated a different alliance and a different war—or perhaps, the same old war, but with the attempt to change the ending.

Here was a shift in alliances which would have pleased a good part of the prewar British upper class. From the time he took power, Hitler had many admirers in Britain's aristocracy and even in its royal family. Many saw Hitler as the effective antidote to Russian "judeo-bolshevism." At the end of the war, there were those who would have favored "finishing the job" by turning against Russia. It has taken 80 years to make it happen. But the seeds of the reversal were always there.

---

* First published in *Consortium News*, June 14, 2024.

262

D-Day and the Russians

In June 1941, without so much as a pretext or false flag, Nazi Germany massively invaded the Soviet Union. In December, the United States was brought into the war by the Japanese attack on Pearl Harbor. As the war raged on the Eastern front, Moscow pleaded with its Western allies, the U.S. and Britain, to open a second front in order to divide German forces. By the time the Western Allies landed in Normandy, the Red Army had already decisively defeated the Nazi invaders in Russia and was on the verge of opening a gigantic front in Soviet Belarus that dwarfed the Normandy battle.

The Red Army launched Operation Bagration on June 22, 1944, and by August 19 had destroyed 28 of 34 divisions, completely shattering the German front line. It was the biggest defeat in German military history, with around 450,000 German casualties. After liberating Minsk, the Red Army advanced on to victories in Lithuania, Poland and Rumania.

The Red Army offensive in the East undoubtedly ensured the success of the Anglo-American-Canadian Allied forces against much weaker German forces in Normandy.

D-Day and the French

As decided by the Anglo-Americans, the only role for the French in Operation Overlord was that of civilian casualties. In preparation for the landings, British and American bombers pounded French railway towns and seaports, causing massive destruction and tens of thousands of French civilian casualties. In the course of operations in Normandy, numerous villages, the town of St Lô and the city of Caen were destroyed by Anglo-American aviation.

The Free French armed forces under the supreme command of General Charles de Gaulle were deliberately excluded from taking part in Operation Overlord. De Gaulle recalled to his biographer Alain Peyrefitte how he was informed.

"Churchill summoned me to London on June 4, like a squire summoning his butler. And he told me about the landings, without any French unit having been scheduled to take part. I criticized him for taking orders from Roosevelt, instead of imposing a European will on him. He then shouted at me with all the force of his lungs: 'De Gaulle, you must understand that when I have to choose between you and Roosevelt, I'll always prefer Roosevelt. When we have to choose between the French and the Americans, we'll always prefer the Americans.'"

As a result, De Gaulle adamantly refused to take part in D-Day memorial ceremonies. "The June 6th landings were an Anglo-Saxon affair, from which France was excluded. They were determined to set themselves up in France as if it were enemy territory! As they had just done in Italy and were about to do in Germany!" [...] "And you want me to go and commemorate their landing, when it was the prelude to a second occupation of the country? No, no, don't count on me!"

Excluded from the Normandy operation, in August the Free French First Army joined the Allied invasion of Southern France. The Americans had made plans to impose a military government on France, through AMGOT (Allied Military Government of Occupied Territories). This was avoided by the stubbornness of de Gaulle, who ordered the Resistance to restore independent political structures throughout France, and who succeeded in persuading supreme Allied commander General Eisenhower to allow Free French forces and a Resistance uprising to liberate Paris in late August 1944.

D-Day in Hollywood

France has always celebrated the Normandy landing as a liberation. Polls show, however, that views of its significance have evolved over the decades. Soon after the end of the war, public opinion was grateful to the Anglo-Americans but overwhelming attributed the final victory in World War II to the Red Army. Increasingly, opinion has shifted to the idea that D-Day was the decisive battle and that the war was won primarily by the Americans with help from the British. This evolution can be largely credited to Hollywood.

The Marshall Plan and French indebtedness provided the context for post-war commercial deals with both financial and political aspects. On 28 May 1946, U.S. Secretary of State James Byrnes and French representative Léon Blum signed a deal concerning motion pictures. The Blum-Byrnes agreement stipulated that French movie theatres were required to show French-made films for only four out of every thirteen weeks, while the remaining nine weeks were open to foreign competition, in practice mostly filled by American productions. Hollywood had a huge backlog, already amortized on the home market and thus cheap. As a result, in the first half of 1947, 340 American films were shown compared to 40 French ones. France reaped financial benefits from this deal in the form of credits, but the flood of Hollywood productions contributed heavily to a cultural Americanization, influencing both "the way of life" and historic realities.

The Normandy landing was indeed a dramatic battle suitable to be portrayed in many movies. However, the cinematic focus on D-Day has inevitably fostered the widespread impression that the United States rather than the Soviet Union defeated Nazi Germany. Polls show that in May 1945, 57% of French named the Soviet Union as having contributed most to the defeat of Germany, with 20% naming the United States and 12% naming Britain. By 2004, 58% gave the main credit to the United States, with the USSR down to 20% and the UK at 16%.

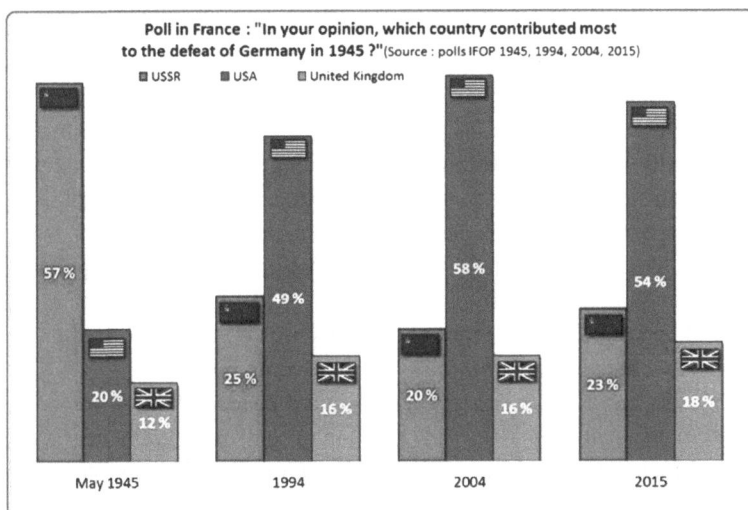

Poll in France : "In your opinion, which country contributed most to the defeat of Germany in 1945 ?"(Source : polls IFOP 1945, 1994, 2004, 2015)

Olivier Berruyer, www.les-crises.fr

Alliance Reversal 1—The British

By June 1944, with the Red Army well on the way to decisively defeating the Wehrmacht, Operation Overlord was hailed by Soviet leaders as a helpful second front. For Anglo-American strategists, it was also a way to block the Soviet Westward advance. British leaders, and Churchill in particular, actually contemplated moving Eastward against the Red Army once the Wehrmacht was defeated.

It must be recalled that in the 19th century, British imperialists saw Russia as a potential threat to its rule over India and further expansion in Central Asia, and developed strategic planning based on the concept of Russia as its principal enemy on the Eurasian continent. This attitude persisted.

At the very moment of Germany's defeat in May 1945, British Prime Minister Winston Churchill ordered the British Armed Forces'

Joint Planning Staff to develop plans for a surprise Anglo-American attack on the forces of their Soviet ally in Germany. Top secret until 1998, the plans even included arming defeated Wehrmacht and SS troops to take part. This fantasy was code-named Operation Unthinkable[1], which coincides with the judgment of the British Chefs of Staff, who rejected it as out of the question.

At the February Yalta meeting just three months earlier, Churchill had praised Stalin as "a friend whom we can trust." The reverse was certainly not true. One might assume that Franklin D. Roosevelt would have dismissed any such plans had he not died in April. Roosevelt seemed confident that the war-exhausted Soviet Union was no threat to the United States, which was indeed true.

In fact, Stalin always scrupulously respected the sphere of influence agreements with the Western allies, refusing to support the communist liberation movement in Greece (which angered Tito, contributing to Moscow's split with Yugoslavia) and consistently urged the strong Communist Parties in Italy and France to go easy in their political demands. While those parties were treated as dangerous threats by the right, they were fiercely opposed by ultra-leftists for staying within the system as urged by Moscow rather than pursuing revolution.

Soviet and Russian leaders truly wanted peace with their erstwhile Western allies and never had any ambition to control the entire continent. They understood the Yalta agreement as authorizing their insistence on imposing a defensive buffer zone on the string of Eastern European States liberated from Nazi control by the Red Army.

Russia had undergone more than one devastating invasion from the West. It responded with a repressive defensiveness which the Atlantic powers, intent on access everywhere, saw as potentially aggressive. The Soviet clampdown on their satellites only hardened in response to the Western challenge eloquently announced by Winston Churchill ten months after the end of the war. The spark was lit to a dynamic of endless and futile hostility.

Churchill was voted out of office by a Labour Party landslide in July 1945. But his influence as wartime leader remained overwhelming in the United States. On March 6, 1946, Churchill gave an historic speech at a small college in Missouri, the home state of Roosevelt's inexperienced and influenceable successor, Harry Truman. The speech was meant to

---

1   https://en.wikipedia.org/wiki/Operation_Unthinkable

renew the wartime Anglo-American alliance—this time against the third great wartime ally, Soviet Russia.

Churchill titled his speech, "Sinews of Peace." In reality, it announced the Cold War in the historic phrase: "From Stettin in the Baltic to Trieste in the Adriatic, an *iron curtain* has descended across the Continent."

The Iron Curtain designated the Soviet sphere, essentially defensive and static. The problem for Churchill was the loss of influence in that part of the world. A curtain, even if "iron," is essentially defensive, but his words were picked up as warning of a threat.

"Nobody knows what Soviet Russia and its Communist international organisation intends to do in the immediate future, or what are the limits, if any, to their expansive and proselytising tendencies." (This despite the fact that Stalin had dissolved the Communist International[2] on May 15, 1943.) In America, this uncertainty was soon transformed into a ubiquitous "communist threat" that needed to be hunted down and eradicated in the State Department, trade unions and Hollywood.

Alliance Reversal 2: The Americans

The alleged need to contain the Soviet threat provided an argument for U.S. government planners, notably Paul Nitze in NSC-68[3], to renew and expand the U.S. arms industry, which had the political advantage of putting a decisive end to the economic depression of the 1930s.

Throughout Eastern Europe, Nazi collaborators could be welcomed in the United States, where intellectuals became leading "Russia experts." In this way, Russophobia was institutionalized, as old-school WASP diplomats, editors and scholars who had nothing in particular against Russians made way to newcomers with old grudges.

Among the old grudges, none were more vehement and persistent than that of the Ukrainian nationalists from Galicia, the far west of Ukraine, whose hostility to Russia had been promoted during the time that their territory was ruled by the Habsburg Empire. Fanatically devoted to denying their divided country's deep historic connection to Russia, Ukrainian ultra-nationalists were nurtured for decades by the CIA in Ukraine itself and in the large North American diaspora.

---

2 The Soviet Union founded a sort of successor, the Cominform, in 1947 to counter the influence of the Marshall Plan in Eastern Europe. It never tried to spread revolution and was dissolved in 1956.

3 https://fr.wikipedia.org/wiki/NSC-68

We saw the culmination of this process when the talented comedian Vladimir Zelensky, in his greatest role as tragedian, claimed to be "the heir to the Normandy" invasion and described Russian President Vladimir Putin as the reincarnation of Adolf Hitler, out to conquer the world—already an exaggeration for Hitler, who mainly wanted to conquer Russia. Which is what the U.S. and Germany apparently want to do today.

Alliance Reversal 3: Germany

While the Russians and Anglo-Americans joined in condemning top Nazi leaders at the Nuremberg trials, denazification proceeded very differently in the respective zones occupied by the victorious powers. In the Federal Republic established in the Western zones, very few officials, officers or judges were actually purged for their Nazi past. Their official repentance centered on persecution of the Jews, expressed in monetary compensation to individual victims and especially to Israel. While immediately after the war, the war itself was considered the major Nazi crime, over the years the impression spread through the West that the worst crime and even the primary purpose of Nazi rule had been the persecution of the Jews. The Holocaust, the Shoah were names with religious connotations that set it apart from the rest of history. The Holocaust was the unpardonable crime, acknowledged by the Federal Republic so emphatically that it tended to erase all others. As for the war itself, Germans could easily consider it their own misfortune, considering the extent of their losses.

It was not Germans but the American occupiers who determined to create a new German army, the Bundeswehr, safely ensconced in an alliance under U.S. control. Germans themselves had had enough. But the Americans were intent on solidifying their control of Western Europe through the North Atlantic Treaty Organization. NATO's first secretary general, Lord Ismay—who had been Churchill's chief military assistant during World War II—succinctly defined its mission: "to keep the Americans in, the Russians out, and the Germans down."

The United States government wasted no time in selecting qualified Germans for their own alliance reversal. German experts who had gathered intelligence or planned military operations against the Soviet Union on behalf of the Third Reich were welcome to continue their professional activities, henceforth on behalf of Western liberal democracy as defined in Washington.

This transformation is personified by Wehrmacht Major General Reinhard Gehlen, who had been head of military intelligence on the Eastern Front. In June 1946, U.S. occupation authorities established a new intelligence agency in Pullach, near Munich, employing former members of the German Army General Staff and headed by Gehlen, to spy on the Soviet bloc.

The Gehlen Organization recruited agents among anti-communist East European émigré organizations, in close collaboration with the CIA. The Organization employed hundreds of former Nazis. It contributed to the domestic West German political scene by hunting down communists (the German Communist Party was banned). The Gehlen Organization's activities were put under the authority of the Federal Republic government in 1956 and absorbed into the Bundesnachrichtendienst (BND or Federal Intelligence Service).

In short, for decades, under U.S. occupation, the Federal Republic of Germany has fostered the structures of the Alliance Reversal, directed against Russia. The old pretext was the threat of communism. But Russia is no longer communist. The Soviet Union surprisingly dissolved itself and turned to the West in search of lasting peace.

In retrospect, it becomes stunningly clear that the "communist threat" was indeed only a pretext for the United States to rearm and dominate Western Europe. There was never a Russian threat, but there was Russia with all its land and resources. Great powers to its West have repeatedly looked at Russia in the way mountain-climbers proverbially look at mountains. Why must you climb that mountain? Because it's there. Because it's too big, it has all that space and all those resources. And oh yes, we must defend "our values."

It's nothing new. The dynamic is deeply institutionalized. It's just the same old war, based on illusions, lies and manufactured hatred, leading us to greater disaster.

Is it too late to stop?

For Washington,
War Never Ends[*]

MARCH 2022

It goes on and on. The "war to end war" of 1914–1918 led to the war of 1939–1945, known as World War II. And that one has never ended either, mainly because for Washington, it was the Good War, the war that made The American Century: why not the American Millenium?

The conflict in Ukraine may be the spark that sets off what we already call World War III.

But this is not a new war. It is the same old war, an extension of the one we call World War II, which was not the same war for all those who took part.

The Russian war and the American war were very, very different.

Russia's World War II

For Russians, the war was an experience of massive suffering, grief and destruction. The Nazi invasion of the Soviet Union was utterly ruthless, propelled by a racist ideology of contempt for the Slavs and hatred of "Jewish Bolsheviks." An estimated 27 million died, about two thirds of them civilians. Despite overwhelming losses and suffering, the Red Army succeeded in turning the Nazi tide of conquest that had subdued most of Europe. This gigantic struggle to drive the German invaders from their soil is known to Russians as the Great Patriotic War, nourishing a national pride that helped console the people for all they had been through. But whatever the pride in victory, the horrors of the war inspired a genuine desire for peace.

---

* Published in *Consortium News,* March 15, 2022.

America's World War II

America's World War II (like World War I) happened somewhere else. That is a very big difference. The war enabled the United States to emerge as the richest and most powerful nation on earth. Americans were taught never to compromise, neither to prevent war ("Munich") nor to end one ("unconditional surrender" was the American way). Righteous intransigence was the fitting attitude of Good in its battle against Evil. The war economy brought the U.S. out of the depression. Military Keynesianism emerged as the key to prosperity. The Military-Industrial-Complex was born. To continue providing Pentagon contracts to every congressional constituency and guaranteed profits to Wall Street investors, it needed a new enemy. The Communist scare—the very same scare that had contributed to creating fascism—did the trick.

The Cold War: World War II continued

In short, after 1945, for Russia, World War II was over. For the United States, it was not. What we call the Cold War was its voluntary continuation by leaders in Washington. It was perpetuated by the theory that Russia's defensive "Iron Curtain" constituted a military threat to the rest of Europe.

At the end of the war, the main security concern of Stalin was to prevent such an invasion from ever happening again. Contrary to Western interpretations, Moscow's ongoing control of Eastern European countries it had occupied on its way to victory in Berlin was not inspired so much by communist ideology as by determination to create a buffer zone as an obstacle to repeated invasion from the West. Stalin respected the Yalta lines between East and West and declined to support the life and death struggle of Greek communists. Moscow cautioned leaders of large Western European Communist Parties to eschew revolution and play by the rules of bourgeois democracy. The Soviet occupation could be brutal but was resolutely defensive. Soviet sponsorship of peace movements was perfectly genuine.

The formation of the North Atlantic Treaty Organization (NATO) and the rearmament of Germany confirmed that for the United States, the war in Europe was not entirely over. The lackadaisical U.S. "de-Nazification" of its sector of occupied Germany was accompanied by an organized brain drain of Germans who could be useful to the United States in its rearmament and espionage (from Wernher von Braun to Reinhard Gehlen).

America's Ideological Victory

Throughout the Cold War, the United States devoted its science and industry to building a gigantic arsenal of deadly weapons, which wreaked devastation without bringing U.S. victory in Korea or Vietnam. But military defeat did not cancel America's ideological victory. The greatest triumph of American imperialism has been in spreading its self-justifying images and ideology, primarily in Europe. The dominance of the American entertainment industry has spread its particular blend of self-indulgence and moral dualism around the world, especially among youth. Hollywood convinced the West that World War II was won essentially by the U.S. forces and their allies in the Normandy invasion. America sold itself as the final force for Good as well as the only fun place to live. Russians were drab and sinister.

In the Soviet Union itself, many people were not immune to the attractions of American self-glorification. Some apparently even thought that the Cold War was all a big misunderstanding, and that if we are very nice and friendly, the West will be nice and friendly too. Mikhail Gorbachev was susceptible to this optimism. Former U.S. ambassador to Moscow Jack Matlock recounts that the desire to liberate Russia from the perceived burden of the Soviet Union was widespread within the Russian elite in the 1980s. It was the leadership rather than the masses who accomplished the self-destruction of the Soviet Union, leaving Russia as the successor State, with the nuclear weapons and U.N. veto of the USSR, under the alcohol-soaked presidency of Boris Yeltsin—and overwhelming U.S. influence during the 1990s.

The New NATO

Russia's modernization over the past three centuries has been marked by controversy between "Westernizers"—those who see Russia's progress in emulation of the more advanced West—and "Slavophiles," who consider that the nation's material backwardness is compensated by some sort of spiritual superiority, perhaps based in the simple democracy of the traditional village. In Russia, Marxism was a Westernizing concept. But official Marxism did not erase admiration for the "capitalist" West and in particular for America. Gorbachev dreamed of "our common European home" living some sort of social democracy. In the 1990s, Russia asked only to be part of the West.

What happened next proved that the whole "communist scare" justifying the Cold War was false. A pretext. A fake designed to perpetuate military Keynesianism and America's special war to maintain its own economic and ideological hegemony.

There was no longer any Soviet Union. There was no more Soviet communism. There was no Soviet bloc, no Warsaw Pact. NATO had no more reason to exist.

But in 1999, NATO celebrated its 50th anniversary by bombing Yugoslavia and thereby transforming itself from a defensive to an aggressive military alliance. Yugoslavia had been non-aligned, belonging neither to NATO nor the Warsaw Pact. It threatened no other country. The NATO aggression violated international law. At the very same time, in violation of unwritten but fervent diplomatic promises to Russian leaders, NATO welcomed Poland, Hungary and the Czech Republic as new members.

Five years later, in 2004, NATO took in Romania, Bulgaria, Slovakia, Slovenia and the three Baltic Republics. Meanwhile, NATO members were being dragged into war in Afghanistan, the first and only "defense of a NATO member"—namely, of the United States.

Understanding Putin—Or Not

Meanwhile, Vladimir Putin had been chosen by Yeltsin as his successor, partly no doubt because as a former KGB officer in East Germany he had some knowledge and understanding of the West. Putin pulled Russia out of the shambles caused by Yeltsin's acceptance of American-designed economic shock treatment. Putin put a stop to the most egregious rip-offs, incurring the wrath of dispossessed oligarchs who used their troubles with the law to convince the West that they were victims of persecution (example: the ridiculous Magnitsky Act).

On February 11, 2007, the Russian Westernizer Putin went to a center of Western power, the Munich Security Conference, and asked to be understood by the West. It is easy to understand, if one wants to.[1] Putin challenged the "unipolar world" being imposed by the United States and emphasized Russia's desire to "interact with responsible and independent partners with whom we could work together in constructing a fair and democratic world order that would ensure security and prosperity not only for a select few, but for all."

The reaction of the leading Western partners was indignation, rejection, and a 15-year media campaign portraying Putin as some sort of demonic creature.

---

1 http://en.kremlin.ru/events/president/transcripts/24034

Indeed, since that speech there have been no limits to Western media's insults directed at Putin and Russia. And in this scornful treatment we see the two versions of World War II. In 2014, world leaders gathered in Normandy to commemorate the 70th anniversary of the D-Day landings by U.S. and British forces. In fact, that 1944 invasion ran into difficulties, even though German forces were mainly concentrated on the Eastern front, where they were losing the war to the Red Army. Moscow launched a special operation precisely to draw German forces away from the Normandy front. Even so, Allied progress could not beat the Red Army to Berlin.

However, thanks to Hollywood, many in the West consider D-Day to be the decisive operation of World War II. To honor the event, Vladimir Putin was there and so was German Chancellor Angela Merkel.

Then, in the following year, world leaders were invited to a lavish victory parade held in Moscow celebrating the 70th anniversary of the end of World War II. Leaders of the United States, Britain and Germany chose not to participate.

This was consistent with an endless series of Western gestures of disdain for Russia and its decisive contribution to the defeat of Nazi Germany (it destroyed 80 percent of the Wehrmacht).

On September 19, 2019, the European Parliament adopted a resolution on "the importance of European remembrance for the future of Europe" which jointly accused the Soviet Union and Nazi Germany of unleashing World War II. Vladimir Putin responded to this gratuitous affront in a long article on "The Lessons of World War II" published in English in *The National Interest*[2] on the occasion of the 75th anniversary of the end of the war.

Putin answered with a careful analysis of the causes of the war and its profound effect on the lives of the people trapped in the murderous 872-day Nazi siege of Leningrad (now Saint Petersburg), including his own parents whose two-year-old son was one of the 800,000 who perished. Clearly, Putin was deeply offended by continual Western refusal to grasp the meaning of the war in Russia. "Desecrating and insulting the memory is mean," Putin wrote. "Meanness can be deliberate, hypocritical and pretty much intentional as in the situation when declarations commemorating the 75th anniversary of the end of the Second World

---

2 "Vladimir Putin: The Real Lessons of the 75th Anniversary of World War II," *National Interest*, June 18, 2020. https://nationalinterest.org/feature/vladimir-putin-real-lessons-75th-anniversary-world-war-ii-162982

War mention all participants in the anti-Hitler coalition except for the Soviet Union."

And all this time, NATO continued to expand eastward, more and more openly targeting Russia in its massive war exercises on its land and sea borders.

The U.S. Seizure of Ukraine

The encirclement of Russia took a qualitative leap ahead with the 2014 seizure of Ukraine by the United States. Western media recounted this complex event as a popular uprising, but popular uprisings can be taken over by forces with their own aims, and this one was. The elected president Yanukovych was overthrown by violence a day after he had agreed to early elections in an accord with European leaders. Billions of U.S. dollars and murderous shootings by extreme right militants enforced a regime change openly directed by U.S. Assistant Secretary of State Victoria Nuland ("F___ the EU") producing a leadership in Kiev largely selected in Washington, and eager to join NATO.

By the end of the year, the government of "democratic Ukraine" was largely in the hands of U.S.-approved foreigners. The new minister of finance was a U.S. citizen of Ukrainian origin, Natalia Iaresko, who had worked for the State Department before going into private business. The minister of economy was a Lithuanian, Aïvaras Arbomavitchous, a former basketball champion. The ministry of health was taken by a former Georgian minister of health and labor, Sandro Kvitachvili. Later, disgraced former Georgian president Mikheil Saakashvili was called in to take charge of the troubled port of Odessa. And Vice President Joe Biden was directly involved in reshuffling the Kiev cabinet as his son, Hunter Biden, was granted a profitable position on the Ukrainian gas company Barisma.

The vehemently anti-Russian thrust of this regime change aroused resistance in the southeastern parts of the country, largely inhabited by ethnic Russians. Protesters were burned alive in Odessa, as the provinces of Lugansk and Donetsk moved to secede in resistance to the coup.

The U.S.-installed regime in Kiev then launched a war against the provinces that continued for eight years, killing thousands of civilians.

And a referendum returned Crimea to Russia.

The peaceful return of Crimea was obviously vital to preserve Russia's main naval base at Sebastopol from threatened NATO takeover. And since the population of Crimea had never approved the peninsula's transfer to Ukraine by Khrushchev in 1954, the return was accomplished by a democratic vote, without bloodshed. This was in stark contrast to the detachment of the province of Kosovo from Serbia, accomplished in 1999 by weeks of NATO bombing.

But to the United States and most of the West, what was a humanitarian action in Kosovo was an unforgivable aggression in Crimea.

The Oval Office Back Door to NATO

Russia kept warning that NATO enlargement must not encompass Ukraine. Western leaders vacillated between asserting Ukraine's "right" to join whatever alliance it chose and saying it would not happen right away. It was always possible that Ukraine's membership would be vetoed by a NATO member, perhaps France or even Germany.

But meanwhile, on September first, 2021, Ukraine was adopted by the White House as Washington's special geostrategic pet. NATO membership was reduced to a belated formality. A Joint Statement on the U.S.-Ukraine Strategic Partnership issued by the White House announced that "Ukraine's success is central to the global struggle between democracy and autocracy"—Washington's current self-justifying ideological dualism, replacing the Free World versus Communism. It went on to spell out a permanent *casus belli* against Russia:

> *In the 21st century, nations cannot be allowed to redraw borders by force. Russia violated this ground rule in Ukraine. Sovereign states have the right to make their own decisions and choose their own alliances. The United States stands with Ukraine and will continue to work to hold Russia accountable for its aggression. America's support for Ukraine's sovereignty and territorial integrity is unwavering.*

The Statement also clearly described the war in Donbass as a "Russian aggression." And it made this uncompromising assertion: "The United States does not and *will never* recognize Russia's purported annexation of Crimea…" (*my emphasis*). This is followed by promises to strengthen Ukraine's military capacities, clearly in view of recovery of Donbass and Crimea.

Since 2014, the United States and Britain have surreptitiously transformed Ukraine into a NATO auxiliary, psychologically and militarily turned against Russia. To Russian leaders this looked increasingly like nothing other than a buildup for an all-out military assault on Russia,

Operation Barbarossa all over again. Many of us who tried to "understand Putin" failed to foresee the Russian "special military operation" invasion for the simple reason that we did not believe it to be in the Russian interest. But the Russians saw the conflict as inevitable and chose the moment.

Ambiguous Echoes

Putin justified Russia's February 2022 "operation" in Ukraine as necessary to stop genocide in Lugansk and Donetsk. This echoed the U.S.-promoted R2P, Responsibility to Protect doctrine, notably the U.S./NATO bombing of Yugoslavia, allegedly to prevent "genocide" in Kosovo. In reality, the situation, both legal and especially human, is vastly more dire in Donbass than it ever was in Kosovo. However, in the West, any attempt at comparison of Donbass with Kosovo is denounced as "false equivalence" or what-about-ism.

But the Kosovo war is much more than an analogy with the Russian invasion of Donbass: it is part of the *cause*.

Above all, the Kosovo war made it clear that NATO was no longer a defensive alliance. Instead, it had become an offensive force, under U.S. command, that could authorize itself to bomb, invade or destroy any country it chose. The pretext could always be invented: a danger of genocide, a violation of human rights, a leader threatening to "kill his own people." Any dramatic lie would do. With NATO spreading its tentacles, nobody was safe. Libya provided a second example.

Putin's announced goal of "denazification" also might have been expected to ring a bell in the West. But if anything, it illustrates the fact that "Nazi" does not mean quite the same thing in East and West. In Western countries, Germany or the United States, "Nazi" has come to mean primarily anti-Semitic. Nazi racism applies to Jews, to Roma, perhaps to homosexuals.

But for the Ukrainian Nazis, racism applies to Russians. The racism of the Azov battalion, which has been incorporated into Ukrainian security forces, armed and trained by the Americans and the British, echoes that of the Nazis: the Russians are a mixed race, partly "Asiatic" due to the Medieval Mongol conquest, whereas the Ukrainians are pure white Europeans. Some of these fanatics proclaim that their mission is to destroy Russia. In Afghanistan and elsewhere, the United States supported Islamic fanatics, in Kosovo they supported gangsters. Who cares what they think if they fight on our side against the Slavs?

Conflicting War Aims

For Russian leaders, their military "operation" is intended to *prevent* the Western invasion they fear. They still want to negotiate Ukrainian neutrality. For the Americans, whose strategist Zbigniew Brzezinski boasted of having lured the Russians into the Afghanistan trap (giving them "their Vietnam"), this is a psychological victory in their endless war. The Western world is united as never before in hating Putin. Propaganda and censorship surpass even World War levels. The Russians surely want this "operation" to end soon, as it is costly to them in many ways. The Americans rejected any effort to prevent it, did everything to provoke it, and will extract whatever advantages they can from its continuation.

On March 16, Volodymyr Zelensky implored the U.S. Congress to give Ukraine more military aid. The aid will keep the war going. Anthony Blinken told NPR that the United States is responding by "denying Russia the technology it needs to modernize its country, to modernize key industries: defense and aerospace, its high-tech sector, energy exploration."

The NATO war aim is not to spare Ukraine, but to ruin Russia. That takes time.

The danger is that the Russians won't be able to end this war, and the NATO leaders will do all they can to keep it going.

Index

9/11 attacks, 14–20, 152
2004 U.S. elections, 88
2016 U.S. elections, 165–169
2020 U.S. elections, 40–41, 170–177

A
Abdic, Fikret, 74n
Abraham Lincoln Brigade, 26
Adelson, Sheldon, 140
Adenauer, Konrad, 202
Adriatic Sea, 52, 55n, 83, 267
Afghanistan, 23, 76, 99, 104, 106,
    107, 134, 151, 152, 168, 210,
    252, 273, 277, 278
Africa, 64, 84, 126, 134, 154, 199,
    204
African-Americans, 142
AMGOT (Allied Military
    Government of Occupied
    Territories), 264
Ahmadinejad, Mahmoud, 130
AIG (American International Group),
    107
Al Bashir, Omar, 23
Alexa, 42–43
Albania, 51–53, 57n, 68n, 85–86, 91,
    92, 96–98
Albanian mafia, 92–93
Albanian nationalism, 21, 51, 55, 57,
    62, 66, 68–70, 85–90, 95–97,
    100–104, 106, 252
Algeria, 75, 82n, 148, 150, 210
Al-Binaa, 144
Al Jazeera, 125, 127, 129
Al Nusra Front, 133
al Qaeda, 15, 19, 144, 152

Albright, Madeleine, 22, 90, 115–116,
    127
Allende, Salvador, 179
Alternative for Germany (AfD), 253,
    255
Amamuddin, Amal, 36
Amanpour, Christiane, 59, 83
Amazon, 42
American Israel Public Affairs
    Committee (AIPAC), 138, 148
Amnesty International, 70
anarchism, 26
Antifa, 25–29, 253, 255
Antifa: the Antifascist Handbook, 26
anticommunism, 11, 12, 239, 242,
    244
antisemitism, 147, 150–151, 154–156
Anzorov, Abdullakh, 153
Arab countries, 15, 17, 32, 75, 126,
    145, 147–150
Arab nationalism, 32, 132–133,
    147–151
Arab Spring, 126
Arbomavitchous, Aïvaras, 275
Arbour, Louise, 22
Archduke Francis Ferdinand, 52
Arfi, Yonathan, 155
artificial intelligence (AI), 39, 42, 44
Assad, Bashar al, 30–34, 130,
    133–134, 152
Assad, Hafez al, 33
Assange, Julian, 35–37, 234
Auschwitz, 56, 130, 141, 147, 150
Attila the Hun, 145
Australia, 35
Austria, 56, 67

Austro-Hungarian Empire, 51–52, 59,
    62, 67, 85, 239, 259, 267
automation, 39

B
Babbitt, Ashli, 179–180
Baerbock, Annalena, 238, 250
Baghdad, 144
Bahrain, 126
Bakunin, Mikhail, 27
Balkan Action Council, 83
Balkan Odyssey, 111, 122n
Balkans, 49–51, 55, 62–63, 67n, 75,
    83–84, 94, 106–107, 120–121,
    223, 236, 241
Baltic Sea, 246, 249, 267
Baltic States, 204, 223, 230, 245–247,
    273
Bandera, Stepan, 239
Baratta, Mira, 240
Bataclan theater, 153
Bavaria, 59, 240
BBC (British Broadcasting
    Corporation), 107
bear baiting, 257–261
Beijing, 230, 232, 249
Belarus, 252, 263
Belgrade, 49, 52, 54, 57, 66, 67, 84,
    101
Belgrade Times, 66n
Beloff, Nora, 57n-58n
Benghazi, 21, 125–126, 129
Berger, Jens, 246
Berghezan, Georges, 58
Berggruen, Nicolas, 170–171, 177
Berggruen Institute, 171
Berkeley, 25–26
Bernard, Dominique, 153
Bérubé, Michael, 125, 127
Biden, Hunter, 275
Biden, Joe, 40, 171–181, 237, 245,
    261, 275
Bildt, Carl, 218
bin Laden, Osama, 15–17
Binder, David, 96, 103, 104

Black Bloc, 25, 27
Black Lives Matter, 175
Black Sea, 83, 222, 249
Blair, Tony, 218
Bloc of Anti-Bolshevik Nations, 239
Blum-Byrnes agreement, 264
Blum, Léon, 264
Bolshevik Revolution, 5, 9, 12, 32–33
Bolsheviks, 3, 5, 8, 55, 270
Bolshevism, 6, 9, 27, 142, 239
Bonn, 59, 236
Bornholm, 246–247
BosniaHerzegovina, 50–54, 57–59,
    67, 72–77, 81–82, 105–106,
    109–122, 151, 210, 240–241
  war in (1992–1995), 57–59, 72–73,
    105–106, 109–122
Bosnian Muslims, 52–53, 57–59,
    73–77, 81, 105–106, 110–111,
    115–121, 151
Bosnian Serbs, 54n, 111–119, 121,
    122n
Bossi, Umberto, 62
Bouchuiguir, Slimane, 127
bourgeoisie, 3, 5, 195
Bray, Mark, 26–27
Brexit, 202–205
Brezhnev, Leonid, 200
Bricmont, Jean, 8
Britain. *See* United Kingdom
British Foreign Office, 57n
Brittan, Leon, 204
Bronstein, Leon. *See* Trotsky
Brooks, Rosa, 171
Brookings Institution, 44, 53n,
    139–140, 170
Bratunac, 111, 113
Brauman, Rony, 128–130
British Empire, 230, 265
Brzezinski, Zbigniew, 32, 87, 151,
    223, 227, 278
Bücker, Heinrich, 252
Budapest, 197, 200
Bulgaria, 75, 223, 225, 273
Bundestag, 56

Bundesnachrichtendienst (BND),
    55n, 269
Bundeswehr, 103, 268
Burkhalter, Didier, 227
Burns, John, 58
Bush, George H.W., 88
Bush, George, W., 14–20, 88, 221
Byrnes, James, 264

C
California, 175
Cambodia, 10
Camp Bondsteel, 91–92, 95, 104
Canada, 239, 240, 259
Canard Enchainé, 190
capitalism. 4, 6, 61, 138–139, 164,
    202. *See also* finance capitalism
Carter, Jimmy, 151
Caspian oil pipeline routes, 83, 91
Caspian Sea, 91
Castro, Fidel, 19
Catholic Church, 4, 51, 58n, 80n, 82,
    147, 151, 220, 239
Caucasus region, 75
Central America, 61, 140
Central Asia, 151, 265
Central Europe, 71, 199
Central European University, 200
Charlie Hebdo, 153
Charlottesville, 25–26
Chechnya, 99, 153
Cheney, Dick, 221
Chetniks, 52–53
Chile, 179
    1973 coup in, 179
China, 11, 83, 126, 131, 163, 167,
    204, 229–234, 249
Chirac, Jacques, 152
Christianity, 5, 51, 75–76, 79, 82,
    89, 102, 135, 140, 146–147,
    152, 197. *See also* Evangelical
    Christianity; Orthodox
    Christianity
Christie, Agatha, 248

Churchill, Winston, 52, 203, 218,
    265–268
CIA (Central Intelligence Agency),
    55n, 104, 160, 218, 239, 267,
    269
Clark, Richard, 140–141
Clark, Wesley, 88
climate change, 38, 121
Clinton, Bill, 86, 88, 172, 236, 259
Clinton Foundation, 166
Clinton, Hillary, 140, 159–166, 218,
    221
Clooney, George, 36
CNN, 59, 73, 167, 197, 200
Cohen, Roger, 95–98, 101
Cold War, 163, 222–224, 227–228,
    233, 236, 239, 258, 267,
    271–273
Colombia, 99
Cominform, 267n
Common Market, 202, 204
communism, 3–4, 6–7, 9–10, 52, 193,
    197, 207, 210, 223, 242–244,
    259, 266, 267, 269, 271–272
Communist International, 26, 267
Communist Party USA, 5
Conference on Security and
    Cooperation in Europe, 11
Continental Blockade, 202
Consortium News, 30n, 38n, 137n,
    146n, 159n, 170n, 178n, 202n,
    206n, 229n, 235n, 245n, 249n,
    257n, 262n, 270n
conspiracy theories, 14–20, 140,
    160–161, 253
Copenhagen, 57n
Correa, Rafael, 36
Council on Foreign Relations, 170
CounterPunch, 14n, 21n, 25n, 88n,
    95n, 105n, 109n, 125n, 132n,
    185n, 189n, 217, 225n
counter-insurgency, 99
counter-revolution, 3–13, 77, 81, 97,
    99
Covert Action Quarterly, 49n, 72n

Covid-19, 38
Covid-19: The Great Reset, 38–48
Credit Suisse First Boston, 107
Crimea, 218, 222, 225–226, 231, 242,
    275–276
Croatia, 50n, 51–59, 62–63, 65, 67,
    72, 85, 101, 116–117, 120, 121,
    240–241
cross-thinkers (*Querdenker*), 253, 255
Crusaders, 84
Cuba, 64
Czechoslovakia, 200, 222

D
D-Day landings, 262–269
Davos, 39, 41–43
De Gaulle, Charles, 148–149, 264
Daech, 144–145
Darmanin, Gérard, 155
Dayton Accords, 105–106, 116, 122
Debs, Eugene, 5
Decker, Markus, 255
Deep and Comprehensive Free Trade
    Agreement
(DCFTA), 219
deep state, 196, 200, 261
Delimustafic, Alija, 74n
democracy, 10n, 11–12, 33, 41,
    60–62, 65, 71, 72n, 86, 87, 125,
    129, 134–135, 138, 139, 165,
    167, 170, 176–177, 179–180,
    188, 197–198, 201, 205, 213,
    221, 230, 255, 259, 268, 271,
    272, 276
Democratic National Committee
    (DNC), 160, 166
Democratic Party, 88, 160, 166,
    172–178, 190
Democratic Party of Serbia, 101
Denmark, 57n, 203, 246–247
Der Spiegel, 55n
dictatorship of the proletariat, 8, 222
DioGuardi, Joe, 55n
Doctors Without Borders, 84, 128
Donbass, 214, 239, 252, 276–277

Donetsk, 259–260, 275, 277
Dole, Robert, 55n, 240
Dragash, 103
Draskovic, Vuk, 100
Dresden, 130
Dujisin, Zoltan, 242–243
Dumas, Roland, 23
Dyncorp, 104

E
East Asia, 9
East Timor, 106–107
Eastern Europe, 135, 223, 239, 242,
    244, 266, 271
economic sanctions, 54n, 105, 152,
    200, 231, 238, 241, 247, 250,
    258, 261
Ecuador, 36
Eisenhower, Dwight, 264
Electoral College, 175, 177
En Marche, 190, 207
England. *See* United Kingdom
Enlightenment, 82n, 151
Erdemovic, Drazen, 117–119
Esper, Mark, 231–233
ethnic cleansing, 73, 83, 89, 93, 94,
    97, 101, 102, 122, 133
Euro (*common currency of the EU*),
    185, 187, 190, 193–194, 204
Eurostat, 187
European Community, 55, 105
European Economic Community,
    185, 203
European Parliament, 50, 59, 122,
    186, 199, 222, 240, 242, 243,
    274
European Union (EU), 58, 104, 135,
    186–188, 191, 193, 197–199,
    202, 204–208, 212, 219–223,
    231, 236–238, 242–244, 275
Evangelical Christianity, 140
Exxon, 163

F
Fabius, Laurent, 132–133
fascism, 6–7, 26–27, 29, 52, 53, 111,
    156, 181, 191, 193, 195–196,
    200, 206–207, 209, 221, 226,
    228, 239, 240, 253
  role of violence in, 6
Faeser, Nancy, 256
Fatah, 151
Federal Office for the Protection of
    the Constitution (BfV), 251
Fellini, Federico, 25
finance capitalism, 12
Fillon, François, 190
Finland, 90, 246
First Czech Russian Bank (FCRB),
    213
Fischer, Joschka, 56
Flaiano, Ennio, 25
Floyd, George, 175
Fourth Industrial Revolution (4IR),
    39–40, 177
fracking, 219, 223
France, 7, 9, 10, 23, 27, 30, 51,
    59, 72–73, 99, 110, 113, 125,
    127–128, 132–136, 146–156,
    170, 185, 189–196, 199,
    202–214, 222–224, 228, 231,
    237, 240, 247, 251, 260,
    262–266, 276
  2005 referendum on the EU draft
    Constitution, 207–208
  2017 election, 189–196
  2022 election, 206–216
France Insoumise, La, 27, 154, 194,
    208
Franco, Francisco, 4, 26
Frankfurter Allgemeine Zeitung
    (FAZ), 55, 59
Free French armed forces, 263–264
French Communist Party (PCF),
    149–150, 154, 207, 209, 213,
    220, 266, 271
French Guyana, 211

French Socialist Party, 148, 150,
    189–191, 193, 196
French Resistance, 149, 264
French Revolution, 4, 51
Friedman, George, 249–250
Frum, David, 172

G
Gaddafi, Moammer, 21–24, 126,
    128–129, 134, 152, 166
Gaddafi, Seif al-Islam, 21
Galicia (in Eastern Europe), 239, 267
Galileo (Galileo di Vincenzo Bonaiuti
    de' Galilei), 35–36
Gasi, Chamijl, 68n
Gasset, Ortega y, 6, 82n
Gaullism, 152, 190, 195, 206, 212,
    214
Gayssot law, 150–151
Gaza, 146, 151–156
Gehlen, Reinhard, 269, 271
Georgia, 236–237
gender studies, 201
General Confederation of Labor
    (CGT), 211
Geneva, 97
Geneva Convention, 112, 117
genocide, 27, 52, 73, 88–89, 98, 102,
    116–122, 126, 243, 277
Genscher, Hans-Dietrich, 59
German Communist Party, 269
German revanchism, 11, 235,
    238–239
Germany,
  Basic Law, 251, 254
  Federal Republic of, 251
Gilman, Nils, 171, 175
Glagovac, 68n
Glazyev, Sergei, 219
globalization, 34, 60, 65n, 71, 122,
    170, 187, 189, 191, 193, 195,
    203, 213–214, 222, 234
  as imperialism, 164, 234
Golan Heights, 32
Goldman Sachs, 187, 189, 232

Gorani, 102–104
Gore, Al, 176
Goulard, Sylvie, 193
Gracanica monastery, 102
The Grand Chessboard, 223
Great Britain. *See* United Kingdom
Great Patriotic War, 244, 270
Great Reset, 38–45, 177
Greece, 51, 104, 135, 185–188, 204, 266
    debt crisis and austerity measures, 185–188
Green Party of France, 208, 213
Green Party of Germany, 56, 237, 238, 250
Grybauskaite, Dalia, 218
Guadeloupe, 211
Guaidó, Juan, 179
Guantanamo Bay base, 168
Guardian, The, 26
gulags, 242
Gulf War (1991), 119
Gutman, Roy, 58
Gypsies. *See* Roma

H
Habeck, Robert, 237
Habsburg, Otto von, 59, 240
Habsburg monarchy, 51, 67, 85, 239, 240, 259, 267
Hague, The, 21–22, 98, 107, 113, 117–118
    ICTY tribunal at, 21–22, 98, 107, 113, 117–118
Hague, William, 226
Haliti, Xhavit, 103
Hamas, 146, 152–156
    Oct 7, 2022 attack on Israel by, 154–156
Hanoi, 10
Haradinaj, Ramush, 103
Harari, Yuval, 43
Harris, Kamala, 174
Hartmann, Ralph, 67n

Harvard Kennedy School's Center for Public Leadership, 170
Hangzhou, 43
Hegel, Georg Wilhelm Friedrich, 137
Helsinki Accords (Final Act, 1975), 11, 54n
Helsinki Watch, 11. *See also* Human Rights Watch
Helsinki Summit, 165–167
Henin-Beaumont, 209
Hidalgo, Anne, 207
Hiroshima, 130
Hitler, Adolf, 7, 26, 41, 50, 55, 105, 107, 116, 121, 217, 222, 225–226, 229, 235, 244, 260, 262, 268, 275
Ho Chi Minh, 9
Holbrooke, Richard, 105–108, 110
Holkeri, Harri, 90
Hollande, François, 190, 193
Hollywood films, 224, 264–265, 267
Holocaust (Shoah), 20, 26, 83–84, 116, 141, 146–150, 156, 209, 239, 242–243, 251, 268
Holocaust Museum, 83–84
Holodomor, 8
Honduras, 161, 165, 179
Hooper, James, 83
Hoti, Beci, 96
Howe, Marvine, 96
Hoxha, Enver, 85
Huawei, 231–232
Huxley, Aldous
human rights, 9, 11–12, 56, 61, 64–65, 70, 90–91, 93–94, 101, 106, 130, 135, 138, 151, 168, 185, 186, 188, 195, 198, 201, 230, 242, 277
    as a pretext for Western intervention, 11–12, 56, 277
Human Rights Watch, 11, 66–67, 69–71, 126
humanitarian intervention, 109, 116, 127–128, 130–131

Hungary, 51, 135, 197–201, 273
Hussein, Saddam, 117, 152

I
Iaresko, Natalia, 275
Ibar River, 93, 100
identity politics, 84, 86, 162, 164,
    166, 208, 209, 255
Ignatieff, Michael, 200
IMF (International Monetary Fund),
    49, 53, 61, 92, 186, 188, 221
immigration, 28, 42, 73n, 135,
    150–151, 195, 198–199, 201,
    209–210, 253
Imperialism, 10n, 29–32, 34, 64, 71,
    84, 106, 125, 137n, 138–141,
    143, 188, 230, 236, 272
In These Times, 49
India, 265
Indonesia, 75, 106
industrialization, 4, 6
Intellectuals, 3, 8–10, 51, 73, 149,
    163–164, 255–257, 267
International Brigades, 26
International Committee of the Red
    Cross, 115
"international community," 50, 55,
    66, 69n, 71, 89, 92–94, 119, 121,
    200, 231
International Criminal Court (ICC),
    21–24, 62
International Criminal Tribunal for
    Yugoslavia (ICTY)/
International Criminal Tribunal for
    Former Yugoslavia, 22, 61, 66,
    113, 118
International Crisis Group (ICG),
    68n, 69n
International Helsinki Federation for
    Human Rights, 69
International Herald Tribune, 68,
    69n, 95
International Socialist Review, 30
Intifada, First, 152

Iran, 31, 32, 132, 144–145, 163, 168
    Islamic Revolution in, 76–77, 144,
        151, 152
Iraq-Iran war, 144
Iraq, 10n, 31, 88, 90, 99, 104, 116,
    117, 120, 122, 126, 133–134,
    144, 148, 152, 153, 167, 168,
    252
Ireland, 99, 188, 203
Iron Curtain, 217–224, 267, 271
Islamic Brotherhood, 151
Islamic State of Iraq and Syria (ISIS),
    32, 133–135, 153
Islamic extremism, 31–32, 152, 210,
    251
Ismay, Hastings Lionel "Pug," 249,
    268
Israel, 10, 12, 17, 19, 20, 29, 32, 43,
    132–134, 137–156, 159, 163,
    165, 168, 211, 268
Israel lobby, 137–143, 168
Italy, 52, 62, 135, 188, 203, 204, 223,
    264, 266
Izetbegovic, Alija, 72–82, 105,
    110–112, 115, 121
    Islamic Declaration (1970), 74–77,
        81, 82n
    Islam Between East and West
        (1984), 74, 77–81, 82n

J
Jadot, Yannick, 208–214
January 6, 2021 Capitol riot, 178–181
Jasenovac death camp, 53
Jerusalem Post, 140
Joint Statement on the U.S.-Ukraine
    Strategic Partnership, 276
Jopp, Mathias, 193
Jordan, 134
"Judeo-Bolshevism," 142
"Judeo-Christian," 146, 152
"Judeo-Masonic," 142

K

Kagan, Robert, 221
Kardelj, Edvard, 62
Krajina, 116
"Kanun," 85
Karadzic, Radovan, 111–112, 118
Kennedy, John F.,
    assasination of, 19
Kerry, John, 88, 218
Keynesian economic policies, 187.
    See also Military Keynesianism
KFOR (Kosovo Force), 89–90
Khan, Jemima, 36
Khmer Rouge, 10
Kibbutz, 148
Kinkel, Klaus, 55n
Kissinger, Henry, 167, 249
Klarsfeld, Serge, 155
Klinz, Wolf, 186
Klitschko, Vitaly, 221
Koran, 76, 79
Korea, 272
Kosova, 95
Kosovo, 21–22, 52–53, 55n, 57,
    83–104, 106
    organized crime in, 91–93
Kosovo Liberation Army (UCK,
    KLA), 68n, 86, 91
Kosovo Polje, 96, 97
"Kosovo Spring" report, 68n, 69n
Kosovo War, 21–22, 83, 88, 102, 106,
    116, 273, 277
Kostunica, Vojislav, 100, 101
Kouchner, Bernard, 110, 128
Kraljevo, 100
Kremlin, 257
Kristol, William, 172
Krstic, Radislav, 117, 119
Khrushchev, Nikita, 218, 259, 275

L

Labour Party (UK), 266
Lafontaine, Oskar, 255
laïcité, 150–151. *See also* secularism
Lavrov, Sergei, 97, 233

Le Drian, Jean-Yves, 193
Le Monde, 84, 128
Le Pen, Jean Marie, 150–151,
    209–210
Le Pen, Marine, 154, 155, 189, 191,
    193–196, 206–214
Le Pen, Marion Maréchal, 195
Lebanon, 134
Left Party (*Die Linke*), 253, 255
Lehman Brothers, 107
Lenin, Vladimir, 3, 137
Leningrad, 274. *See also* Saint
    Petersburg
Lettmayer, Martin, 58
LGBTQI, 208
libertarianism, 61
liberation struggles, 7, 9, 10, 33, 51,
    61, 75, 95, 148, 154, 266
Liberazione, 119
Libya, 21–24, 32, 125–131, 133–134,
    152, 168, 210, 277
Libyan League for Human Rights,
    127
Likud Party, 10n
Lisbon Treaty, 208
Lithuania, 218, 220, 237, 259, 263,
    275
Little, Allan, 74n, 82n
Lockheed Martin, 232
London, 36, 219, 261, 263
London Observer, 57
Lugansk, 259

M

Macedonia, 62, 67n, 69n, 86, 91, 97
MacMillan, Harold, 202
Macron, Emmanuel, 156, 170,
    189–196, 205–207, 211–214,
    231, 234
Maidan Square massacre, 228
Malinowski, Tom, 126
Malleret, Thierry, 38–45
"Manifesto for Peace," 251, 254
Manning, Chelsea, 234
Marshall Plan, 264, 267n

Marshall, Will, 88
Martinique, 211
Marx, Karl, 27
Marxism, 9, 151, 272
Matlock, Jack, 272
Mauriac, François, 147
May 1968 movement (France), 10,
    149
McCain, John, 200
McKenna, Tony, 32–33
McKinsey & Company, 214
Mélenchon, Jean-Luc, 27, 154–155,
    193–194, 207–208, 211–213
Memory Institutes, 242–244
Merah, Mohammed, 152–153
Merkel, Angela, 135, 187, 192, 198,
    204, 221
Merlino, Jacques, 57
Metz, 99
Meyssan, Thierry, 18
Middle Ages, 84
Middle East, 12, 31–32, 91, 133–134,
    139–142, 145, 152, 159, 162,
    166, 168, 188, 204, 234
Military Industrial Complex (MIC),
    40, 83, 131, 139, 168, 177, 228
Military Keynesianism, 271
militarism, 12, 140, 251
Mill, John Stuart, 51
Milosevic, Slobodan, 22, 96, 99,
    106–107, 111, 116–117, 120, 241
Minsk, 263
Minsk accords (*Minsk Agreement*),
    214, 259–260
Missouri, 266
Mitrovica, 93, 100
Mitterrand, François, 110, 150, 204,
    209, 210
Moldova, 236
Mollet, Guy, 148
Molotov-Ribbentrop Pact, 243–244
Monti, Mario, 218
Morillon, Philippe, 113
Morocco, 75
Mossad, 19

Moscow, 5, 11, 31, 53, 160, 197,
    230–231, 244, 259, 260, 263,
    266, 271, 272, 274
MoveOn, 175
Movement Against Racism and for
    Friendship among
    Peoples (MRAP)
Mubarak, Hosni, 126
Mujahidin, 151
Mujamma, 151–152
Munich, 229, 231, 233, 269
Munich Agreement, 271
Munich Security Conference (MSC),
    229–234, 273
Mussolini, Benito, 6, 26, 52

N
NachDenkSeiten, 246
Nagasaki, 130
natural gas, 219, 223, 232, 233, 245,
    248, 261
Navalny, Alexei, 213
Napoleon Bonaparte, 150, 202
NATO (North Atlantic Treaty
    Alliance), 21–24, 32, 55–56,
    65–71, 83–90, 92, 95–104, 106,
    110, 116, 120–122, 126–130,
    133–136, 138, 142, 144, 152,
    159, 166, 194, 196, 203, 208,
    210, 212, 217, 221–223,
    225–226, 229–231, 233,
    236–237, 241, 244–250, 252,
    254, 257–261, 268, 271–278
    expansion of, 63, 229–230, 233,
    236, 252, 259, 275
National Endowment for Democracy
    (NED), 168, 200, 238
National Front (France, *Front
    Nationale*), 150, 195–196, 209
National Rifle Association (NRA),
    138–139
National Security State, 171
nation states, 61, 188
National Transition Council, 129

Nazi Germany, 52, 224, 225, 244, 265, 274
   1941 invasion of USSR, 263
Nazism (National Socialism)
NBC, 26
neoconservatism, 10n, 132, 159, 172
Neoliberalism, 28, 32–34, 93, 168, 190, 202, 204, 206–209, 212
Netanyahu, Benjamin, 139, 142, 146, 168
Netherlands, 112, 168, 188
Netherlands Institute for War Documentation, 112
New Deal, 40
New York Times, 26, 58, 74n, 96–97, 103
Newsday, 58
Nice, 153
Nixon, Richard, 11, 249
Nitze, Paul, 267
nongovernmental organizations (NGOs), 61, 64–71, 92, 211
Nordstream pipelines, 247, 250, 254, 261
Normandy, 153
   1944 Allied landings in, 203, 224, 262–265, 268, 272, 274
Normandy agreement, 260
Northern Ireland, 99
Norway, 230, 247
Novi Pazar, 100
Novi Sad, 118
NSC-68, 267
Nuland, Victoria, 221–222, 228, 275
Nuremberg Tribunal, 130, 242, 268
NYU Commission on Global Citizenship, 170

O
Obama, Barack, 133, 139, 160–161, 221–224
Ocampo, Luis Moreno, 21–23
Odessa, 225–226
Operation Bagration, 263
Operation Barbarossa, 277

Operation Overlord, 262–263, 265
Operation Unthinkable, 266
Ophuls, Marcel, 149
Orban, Viktor, 197–200
Oregon, 175
Organization for Security and Cooperation in Europe (OSCE), 60n, 66, 227, 260
Oric, Naser, 111–113
Otpor, 179
Orthodox (Christians), 51, 75, 82, 89, 96, 113
Ottoman Empire, 51, 57n, 62, 75, 85, 102
Owen, David (Lord), 111, 122n

P
Pakistan, 76, 134
Palestine Liberation Organization (PLO), 152
Palestinians, 10n, 20, 32, 132, 142, 146, 148–149, 152–156, 168
Palme, Olof, 36
Palmer raids, 5
Papandreou, George, 185
Paris, 80n, 132, 147, 148, 150, 153–156, 170, 195, 202, 207, 211, 264
PASOK, 185
Partisans (Yugoslavia), 52
Party of Democratic Action (SDA), 72, 74n
Petraeus, David, 218
patriarchy, 27, 85, 117
Paty, Samuel, 153
Pearl Harbor, 15, 263
Pécresse, Valérie, 207, 213
Pelosi, Nancy, 231
Pentagon, 14, 15, 18–19, 91, 104, 145, 152, 162–163, 168, 171, 232, 257–258, 271
Peres, Shimon, 218
permanent revolution, 7, 10–11, 30, 34
Perseus LLC, 107

Petersen, Soeren Jessen, 104
Peyrefitte, Alain, 263
Philippot, Florian, 196
Philippe, Edouard, 191
Philippines, 99, 140
Pilice, 118
Platform of European Memory and
    Conscience, 243
Podesta, John, 172
Pohrt, Wolfgang, 55n
Pol Pot, 19
Poland, 191, 204, 220, 222, 223, 229,
    230, 235, 239, 244, 246–248,
    259, 263, 273
Pompeo, Mike, 229
Popular Front for the Liberation of
    Palestine (PFLP), 151
Popovic, Alexandre, 81n
Portugal, 188, 204, 213
Pristina, 97, 99–102
Pristina University, 85–86
privatization, 53, 69n, 91, 192, 207,
    214
Progressive Policy Institute, 88
Project for a New American Century
    (PNAC), 14
Prophet Mohammed, 76, 153
proletariat, 3, 8, 198, 222
Proyect, Louis, 34
Pulitzer Prize, 58
Putin, Vladimir, 160–162, 165, 168,
    173, 197, 199–200, 207, 213,
    217–219, 221, 223–229, 242,
    244, 248, 253–255, 260, 262,
    268, 273–274, 277–278

Q
Qatar, 125–127, 233
Queen Elizabeth I, 257

R
Radical Party, 100
Radio Free Europe, 239
RAND corporation, 257–258
rape, 57n-58, 96

Rassemblement National, 155, 209
Raytheon, 232
Reagan National Airport, 18
"Red-brown," 27, 253
Red Army, 7, 224, 229, 235, 263–266,
    270, 274
Red Scare, 5
refugees, 58, 67, 86, 91, 93, 101, 111,
    114, 117, 133–135, 198, 204
regime change, 11, 127, 132–133,
    163, 174–175, 178, 200, 225,
    275
Republican Party (France), 190, 191,
    207
Republican Party (US), 41, 88, 140,
    172, 179, 200
Representative Council of Jewish
    Institutions in
France (CRIF), 148
Republika Srpska Army, 112
'Responsibility to Protect' (R2P)
    doctrine, 12, 131, 277
RIA Novosti, 227
Rice, Susan, 134
Rieff, David, 73n
Rhodes, Aaron, 68
Robots, 39, 42–43
Roma, 52, 67n, 89, 104, 277
Romania (Rumania), 191, 199, 263,
    273
Roosevelt, Franklin Delano, 266
Rothschild Bank, 191
Roussel, Fabien, 207
Rubin, James, 83, 90
Ruder Finn, 57–58, 111
Rufin, Jean-Christophe, 84
Rugova, Ibrahim, 101
Russia, 3–13, 31–33, 95, 97–98, 104,
    131, 135, 141–142, 147, 151,
    153, 159–169, 171, 180, 190,
    193, 196, 197, 201, 203–204,
    210, 212–214, 217–278
    alleged interference in 2016 U.S.
    election, 165–169
Russian Duma, 260

Russian Revolution, 3–13, 32
Russophobia, 160, 193, 204,
    213–214, 238, 242, 267

S
Saban, Haim, 140
Saban Center for Middle East Studies,
    140
Sachs, Jeffrey, 254
Sacirbey, Mohamed, 72
Saint Petersburg, 245, 274. *See also*
    Leningrad
Salazar, António de Oliveira, 4
Sandawi, Sammi, 103
Sanders, Bernie, 161, 166
Sarajevo, 58, 67, 72–73, 81, 110, 112
Sarkozy, Nicolas, 23, 128, 134, 210
Saudi Arabia, 16, 32, 77, 92, 126,
    144, 159, 233
SBU (Security Service of Ukraine),
    227
Scharf, Michael, 117
Scholz, Olaf, 213, 236–237, 250, 251
Scholz, Rupert, 240, 241n
Scheffer, David, 21–23
Schröder, Gerhard, 218
Schultz, Debbie Wasserman, 166
Schwab, Klaus, 38–45, 177
Schook, Steve, 104
Sebastopol, 222, 259, 275
Second Amendment of the
    Constitution of the United
States, 138–140
Secret Service, 176
secularism, 75, 150–151
Senussi, Abdullah, 21
Serbia, 51–58, 62–70, 81–88, 91–106,
    111, 116–120, 128, 133, 151,
    165, 179, 223, 231, 240–241,
    252, 276
  minorities in, 67, 116
  press freedom in, 66–67
Serbian Academy of Sciences and
    Arts, 81

Serbian Socialist Party, 54n
Serbo-Croatian, 66
Serbs, 50–58, 67, 69n, 73, 74n, 81,
    85–105, 110–120, 122, 133, 240
Seselj, Vojislav, 100
Sicily, 93
Shi'ite Muslims, 76n, 145
Shoah. *See* Holocaust
Sibenik, 85
Silajdzic, Haris, 72
Silber, Laura, 74n, 82n
Silicon Valley, 40, 41
Sikorsky, Radek, 248
Six Days War, 148
Skugor, Davo, 85
Skype, 41
Slavs, 51, 75, 97, 270, 277
Slovakia, 104, 273
Slovenia, 50n
social democracy, 11–12, 187–188,
    272
Sons and Daughters of Deported Jews
    of France, 155
Soleimani, Qassem, 144–145
Sorbonne, 211
Soros Foundation, 67n
Soros, George, 170, 171
South Stream pipeline, 223
South Sudan, 134
soviets, 3
Soviet Union (USSR), 4–5, 6, 9–12,
    33, 60, 83, 135, 148, 155,
    197, 201, 220–221, 235–236,
    239, 249, 252, 254, 269, 263,
    265–275
SPD (Social Democratic Party of
    Germany), 236, 256
Spain, 4–5, 26, 135, 140, 141, 142,
    188, 204, 213
Spanish Civil War, 4–5, 26, 141, 142
Spengler, Oswald, 6, 233
Srebrenica,
    1995 massacre, 109–122
Sri Lanka, 99

SS, 52, 53, 266
St Lô, 263
Stalin, Josef, 7, 30, 32, 33, 105, 107, 218, 266, 267, 271
Stalinism, 10, 32, 242
Statue of Liberty, 16, 101
Steele, Michael, 172
Steinmeier, Frank-Walter, 230–231
Stettin, 267
Strauss-Kahn, Dominique, 218
Stubbs, Paul, 65n
Sufism, 75, 76n
Sudan, 23, 134
Suharto, 106
Summers, Lawrence, 218
Sunni Muslims, 76n
Surroi, Veton, 89
Sweden, 35–36, 246
Switzerland, 39, 227
Syria, 30–34, 126, 132–136, 145, 148, 152, 153, 162, 166, 168, 204
Szamuely, George, 104

T
Tel Aviv, 43, 148
teleconferences, 41
terrorism, 12, 136, 146, 149, 152–153, 155
Tetova, 86
Thaci, Hashim, 90, 103
Thailand, 99
Thatcher, Margaret, 204
Third International, 5, 7
Third Reich, 235, 240, 268
Third World, 7, 9–10, 33, 84, 188
Teil, Julien, 127
Tillerson, Rex W., 163
Tito, Josip Broz, 49, 52, 53, 55n, 62, 266
totalitarianism, 7, 79, 97, 242–244
Tolimir, Zdravko, 112
trade unions, 28, 226, 267
Transition Integrity Project (TIP), 171–174

transphobia, 27
Trieste, 267
Tripoli, 21, 23–24, 129
Trotsky, Leon, 7, 30, 33
Trotskyism, 7–10, 30–34, 198
Truman, Harry, 266
Trump, Donald, 159–169, 172, 174, 176, 178, 229
Tudjman, Franjo, 55n, 81
Turkey, 75–76, 83, 92, 203
Twin Towers, 14–19

U
Ukraine, 162, 165, 210, 212–214, 217–228, 236, 238–239, 244–246, 249–250, 252–262, 267, 270, 275–278
   2014 revolution in, 179, 217, 228, 254
   fascism in, 239
Ukrainian diaspora, 259
U.N. Human Rights Commission, 127
U.N. Mission in Kosovo (UNMIK), 90, 92, 104
UNRWA (United Nations Relief and Works Agency for Palestine Refugees in the Near East), 156
U.N. Security Council Resolution 1244, 90–91
U.N. Special Rapporteur on Torture, 234
UNICEF, 69n
Union of Russian Workers, 5
UNESCO, 61
United Kingdom, 23, 34, 36, 57n, 65n, 125, 133, 136, 202–205, 239, 257, 262–266, 274, 276–277
United Nations (U.N.), 63, 84, 104, 116
   Security Council, 91, 116

United States (U.S.), 5–20, 23, 28–40,
    49, 55, 57–64, 72–74, 77, 82, 84,
    86–87, 89–91, 95–106, 115–117,
    121– 126, 128, 131–147,
    151–152, 159–184, 203, 214,
    217–224, 228, 230–235,
    239–251, 257–259, 262–278
  Department of Defense, 232
  Marines, 246
  State Department, 106, 221, 228,
    267, 275
U.S. Center for Democracy, 72n
UNPROFOR (United Nations
    Protection Force), 112–113
"Uprising for Peace", 250–252, 254
USS *Kearsarge,* 246–247
Ustasha (Ustashe), 52–53, 55n, 62,
    240

V
vaccination, 69n, 181
Valéry, Paul, 6
Vatican, 54, 67n
Venezuela, 179
Vergès, Jacques, 23
Verhofstadt, Guy, 198–201
Vietnam, 7, 9–11, 30, 106–107, 116,
    119, 272
Vietnam War, 9–10, 30, 106–107,
    116, 119, 164, 249, 252, 272,
    278
Vietnamese boat people, 10
Voivodina, 53, 62
von Braun, Wernher, 271
von der Leyen, Ursula Gertrud, 170,
    238

W
Wagenknecht, Sahra, 251
Wahhabism, 31
Wall Street, 28, 41, 177, 271
Wang Yi, 232
Washington DC, 28, 30, 36, 43, 55,
    57n, 83, 111, 131, 138, 139, 144,
    151, 160, 161, 163, 164, 171,

    192, 200, 203–204, 221–223,
    227, 237, 240–241, 245, 261,
    268, 271, 275
Washington (state), 175
Washington Post, 26
Weapons of Mas Destruction
    (WMD's), 88
Wehrmacht, 251, 254–255
Weimar Republic, 253
West, Rebecca, 52
Western Civilization, 6, 82n, 155
Wiebes, Cees, 112
Wiesel, Eliezer, 147
Wikileaks, 35
Williams, Ian, 127
Wilson, Woodrow, 5, 10n
World Bank, 65n, 92, 218
World Economic Forum, 38–39, 170,
    177
World Health Organization (WHO),
    69
World Socialist Web Site (WSWS)
World Trade Center, 15, 16, 115, 152
World Trade Organization (WTO), 61
World War I, 4–5, 52, 56, 67, 73, 199
World War II, 11, 40, 52, 62–63, 68,
    85, 89, 93, 97, 120, 130, 147,
    151, 209, 220, 224, 229–230,
    235–244, 251, 262, 264, 268,
    270
World War III, 44, 235–244, 270–274,
    278
working class, 4, 5, 8, 12, 138, 162,
    187, 194–195, 208, 210, 212,
    253

Y
Yalta, 218–219, 221, 266
  1945 meeting of Allied leaders in,
    266, 271
  2013 conference on Ukraine's
    future in, 218–219, 221
Yanukovych, Victor, 218–221, 228,
    259, 275
Yassin, Sheikh Ahmad, 151–152

Yellow Vests, 207, 234
Yeltsin, Boris, 160, 272–273
Yemen, 134
Yinon, Oded, 145
Yugoslav Assembly House of
    Citizens, 68n
Yugoslavia, 49–72, 74, 76–77, 81–83,
    91, 92, 96–98, 103, 107, 113,
    116, 120–122, 240–241, 266,
    273, 276–277
    1941 German invasion of, 52, 56,
    120, 240
    1999 NATO bombing of, 22, 83,
    241, 252, 276–277
    debt crisis in, 53, 240

Z
Zagreb, 55n, 57, 58, 65n
Zelensky, Vladimir (Volodymyr), 262,
    268, 278
Zemmour, Eric, 154, 155, 210–212
Zepa, 110, 117
Zimmermann, Warren, 105–106
Zionism, 15, 141–142, 148, 211
Zoellick, Robert, 218
Zoom, 41
Zubin Potok, 99–101